THE
MASS MEDIA
AND
MODERN SOCIETY

HOLT, RINEHART AND WINSTON, INC.

THE
MASS MEDIA
AND
MODERN SOCIETY

Theodore Peterson

Jay W. Jensen

University of Illinois

William L. Rivers

Stanford University

NEW YORK · CHICAGO · SAN FRANCISCO · TORONTO · LONDON

To Fred Siebert
teacher, colleague, and friend

Preface

We have written *The Mass Media and Modern Society* to show the student not only how the media of communication operate in American society but also to show why they operate as they do. We cheerfully admit to a bias which even the casual reader will soon detect—a conviction that one can understand the media only if he puts them into a broad context. They neither grew up in a vacuum nor perform in one. They emerged, grew, changed, and in some cases even died as a result of geographical, technological, economic, cultural, and other forces. To understand the media, then, one must look at them in their historical, intellectual, economic, political, and social contexts. What may otherwise seem the result of perversity, stupidity, chance, or caprice becomes understandable when one looks at the development in such a perspective.

Some will perhaps say that this is a critical book. In a sense, we hope it is. Surely we have not tried to gloss over the shortcomings of the media as we see them. It would be presumptuous indeed to think that the mass media require any defense from us. But it was not criticism in the sense of fault-finding that was uppermost in our minds as we wrote. Rather, we have tried conscientiously to make this book critical in the sense that it is an analysis of both the strengths and weaknesses of the media as they play their roles in society.

Some may find the book slightly repetitious. The repetitions which the reader will note in some chapters are not, we assure him, the results of professorial absent-mindedness. They occur because we think that certain points and certain themes are so important that they are worth repeating in different contexts.

In writing this volume, we have benefited from the ideas of a number of friends and academic colleagues at the University of Illinois and elsewhere, although we alone, of course, take full responsibility for whatever uses we have made of those ideas. It is impractical to name all of the persons to whom we are indebted, but a few deserve special recognition. As students and co-workers of Wilbur Schramm, we have profited enormously from his perceptive insights, from his rare and broad perspective, and above all from his unmatched ability to synthesize findings relevant to communications from a half-dozen or more disciplines. Fred Siebert taught us a great deal about both the history and the philosophy of mass media in the political order. The ways in which each has helped us, directly and indirectly, are beyond measure. We also give public thanks to Dr. Eleanor Blum, librarian in the College of Journalism and Communications at the University of Illinois, who helped us to track down many sources and elusive facts.

T. P.

J. W. J.

W. L. R.

Urbana, Illinois
Stanford, California
March 1965

Contents

THE
MASS MEDIA
AND
MODERN SOCIETY

1

Journalism

or Communications?

Not One but Both

In the fading years of the nineteenth century, there was a handsome, dashing newspaperman named Richard Harding Davis who took the world for his beat. In clothes of the most fashionable English cut he covered his assignments and found news where other reporters did not. He disguised himself as a burglar and hung out in shady dives to expose a robber band and get the full story of its operations for his paper. He penned stories for the best magazines, and the best magazines bid for his manuscripts. He posed for Charles Dana Gibson's illustrations for the leading magazines of his day. At parties he traded conversation with such celebrities as Oscar Wilde, Mark Twain, Sarah Bernhardt, and Ellen Terry, and in the quiet elegance of Delmonico's, where dining was a ritual, he ordered dinners and wines with the discrimination of a continental gourmet. From time to time, leaving such comforts, Davis dashed off to cover the little wars which broke the tedium of the later Victorian age. When love came to him, he met the young lady's rebuffs with a characteristic flourish, handing to the messenger at his club in London a note for Miss Cecil Clark, Prairie Avenue, Chicago. The imperturbable Jaggers carried the message across the Atlantic and in time, in the best story-book tradition, Miss Clark became Mrs. Richard Harding Davis.

In the years when Denver was growing from a raw mining

town into the metropolis of the Rockies, its daily *Post* was owned by two life-loving publishers, Harry Tammen, a former peripatetic bartender, and Frederick Bonfils, a one-time lottery operator. A story's sales value, not its significance, was their guide in judging news, and no cause was too minor for their newspaper to champion. When two children complained that a vendor had sold them a nickel's worth of rancid peanuts, Bonfils turned loose three reporters to expose "the peanut situation." The publishers got their readers into the proper spirit for Christmas by having a National Guard plane fly over the community with a huge neon-tube cross affixed to its underside. Tammen once hired a sports writer named Otto Floto because he had "the most beautiful name in the world"; and when Bonfils and Tammen became owners of a circus, they worked in the writer's name—Sells-Floto Circus—even though he owned no part of it. After themselves they named an elephant, Tambon. When it died, Tammen sorrowfully had it stuffed and mounted in a large glass case outside his office.

For almost a quarter-century before a day in 1918 when his own newspaper carried a headline saying that he was wanted for murder, Charles Chapin drove the staff of the New York *World* in his fanatic worship of "that inky-nosed, nine-eyed, clay-footed god called News." More heartless than any city editor in fiction, he fired reporters who missed getting a story by as little as a minute or two. "That," he once told the assembled city-room staff, "is the hundred and eighth man I've fired." One reporter, whom Chapin had warned not to return without his story, plunged into the icy East River to get an interview with a woman ambulance driver at Bellevue. After he was dragged from the river unconscious and taken to the hospital, someone thoughtfully telephoned Chapin to let him know that the reporter would survive. "Tell him that he's fired," Chapin replied. And then one night Chapin quietly murdered his wife, hung a "Do Not Disturb" sign on the door of the hotel suite in which the body lay, wandered through the city for hours, and finally gave himself up. His life thereafter was spent cultivating beautiful gardens on the prison grounds at Sing Sing, where he served out his sentence until his death in 1930.

Those men and scores of others just as colorful really lived. They live on today in such plays as *The Front Page* by Ben Hecht and Charles MacArthur; in books of reminiscences; in novels, movies, and comic strips depicting newspaper work; and in television dramas in which the reporter exposes corruption in city hall, solves a mysterious murder, and wins the pretty girl, all between the first and concluding commercials. They are so interesting, so colorful, these newspapermen of the past, that it is rather unfortunate they bear little relationship to reality today.

The New Journalism

Journalism is still exciting, but the days of wild unrestraint have, by and large, gone. Several developments helped speed their departure. One surely was the technological-industrial revolution, which increased the size, speed, and efficiency of newspapers and changed them from small personal or party organs into vast, expensive, mass-produced, and generally impersonal social institutions. Newspapers became fewer. And they become large enterprises, too costly to be jeopardized by irresponsible individualism. The success of a paper came to rest less upon the single performances of virtuosos than upon the aggregate performance of a whole staff of specialists. In short, the newspaper became institutionalized, not unlike other American businesses and industries.

Another development certainly was a growing sense of responsibility. As journalism attracted an increasing number of men interested in raising the level of their papers and of the press as a whole; as it became good business for newspapers to consider the wishes of their audiences; and as local publishing monopolies raised the possibility of outside restraint, publishers began avowing a duty to the public as well as to their cash boxes. It was not always so. Freedom of the press, as originally interpreted, gave publishers the right to lie, to distort, and to pander to the lowest appetites, and some so used their freedom. Journalism seems to have shared in the increasing awareness of social responsibility which has characterized American business generally since the start of the twentieth century. And over all blew the sharp wind of criticism. Articulate segments of the public were loud in calling attention to what they regarded as shortcomings in press performance.

Still another development was a change in the sort of person drawn to journalism. College-educated reporters and editors became more and more common, especially after the advent of the schools of journalism in the early years of this century. The American Newspaper Guild was founded in the 1930s in the hope of improving the professional status of newspaper workers. Even if it has been more concerned with the material conditions of life than with professionalism, as its critics have charged, it certainly has contributed to stability among newspaper personnel.

stability of staff

This much is certain: newspaper publishers, editors, and reporters have become more stable, sober, and responsible. Gone is the tramp newspaperman who, hearing of a job in Tulsa, would catch the next train without even bothering to pull the copy paper from his typewriter. The typical newspaperman today is a craftsman, often a highly specialized one, who does his own small part in turning out a mass-produced product. He ordinarily stays in one locality, raises a family, tries to pay off the mortgage on his house, and goes for long spells without covering a murder, let alone solving one.

The executive of a typical Midwestern daily with a circulation of between 20,000 and 30,000 has told how he chooses his staff members: "We pick people who won't be just reporters out on a story. They are representatives of the *Daily*. They come from average middle-class families. They are Midwesterners. They have imagination. They meet people well. We expect them to stay quite a while." A publisher in a small Southern city says that he tries to pay his staff members good salaries because he wants them to associate on an equal footing with the business and professional men of the community. And at least one Midwestern newspaper chain subjects all candidates for jobs to a battery of psychological tests, a procedure which would have appalled hard-bitten editors like Charles Chapin.

A similar change has come over the printers who set news into type. Once they were as colorful a breed as the reporters who wrote the copy they set. "In the days before typesetting machines and time studies, when steam beer went at a nickel a pint and railroads had not found all of the valleys," Paul Fisher has written in *Journalism Quarterly*, "in these days the American tramp printer had his time in the sun." In the bright years between Appomattox and Ottmar Mergenthaler's Linotype, tramp printers drifted across the land, their beds clean sheets of newsprint on the composing room floors. Some had taken to the road because of seasonal fluctuations in the industry, some because of financial or marital mistakes, some because of old age or alcohol. They would stay at a newspaper sometimes for a week, sometimes for a month, gratuitously sharing with editors their superior knowledge of fact and grammar and, with all who would listen, their contempt for reporters. When the Linotype invaded the composing rooms in the mid-1890s, nomadic typesetters such as "Old Slugs" Biggsby and "Muskogee Red" were driven into oblivion, their departure hastened no doubt by unionization of the graphic arts trades and the mass death of small weekly newspapers as urbanization made cities trading centers for ever-larger areas.

Why Communications?

The passing of footloose eccentrics from newspaper staffs is just part of the much larger story of the impact of technological and social change upon America's means of communication, a major theme of this book. Within the past dozen years, that change has given a new meaning to an old term—mass communication.

At one time *journalism* was an adequate term to describe the media of communication. That perennial authority, *Webster's New International Dictionary*, defines journalism: "The business of managing, editing, or writing for, journals or newspapers; also, journals or newspapers collectively." Journalism, then, was a good word for describing the media in the days when most communications were carried on by magazines and newspapers.

printed journalism

And those years spanned a long period. The first mechanical device by which man could share his thoughts with others on an extended scale was the printing press, the invention of which almost at once broadened the outlook of the whole Western world. No longer did the reader have to decipher the cramped handwriting of manuscripts; instead, his eyes and mind could race along the printed page. With printing came a revival of classical learning, an end to the monopoly of knowledge by the exclusive few, the standardization of languages, and the growth of national literature. With it too came the birth of journalism.

This is not to suggest that journalism sprang full-blown soon after William Caxton set up the first press at Westminster in 1476. Actually, about a century and a half elapsed between the introduction of printing to England and the emergence of a regular periodical devoted to the dissemination of news, although the newspaper did have forerunners in broadsides and pamphlets. There were perhaps good reasons for the delay. Primitive means of communication made it difficult to gather and distribute news. Literacy was not yet diffused throughout the population, and not everyone could afford the products of the press. Printing itself was a sometimes dangerous trade, bound by restrictions.

The rise of journalism paralleled the rise of printing, which in turn grew up alongside capitalism and industrialization, in the broad meanings of those terms. Indeed, printing itself represents an early form of industrialization, bringing workers together under one roof, substituting the machine for a task once done by hand, and inexpensively reproducing hundreds of identical items by mechanical means.

The printed word was so important that it is doubtful that the modern nation-state could have emerged without it. For centuries, it was in large measure through printed material in one form or another that common ideals, aspirations, traditions, and political allegiances were maintained over wide areas. The printed media alone performed the functions which today society expects all the media of communication to share. The printed media informed and enlightened the public, interpreted events and issues, challenged capricious authority, entertained the populace, and even, to a limited degree, brought together the buyers and sellers of goods and services.

the widening field

Then the communications revolution of the nineteenth and twentieth centuries brought the motion picture, radio, and television, which joined the printed media in spreading information, ideas, and entertainment. Both because of their electronic nature and because of the variety of ways in which they have carried out their functions, they have made *journalism* an obsolescent term for denoting all media.

Moreover, the communications revolution brought with it types of persuasive communication which scarcely fall within the traditional meaning of journalism. Advertising became an important adjunct of the marketing system; its persuasive function is not clearly covered by the word *journalism*. Nurtured by the utility companies, which believed that their monopolistic position could best be maintained by public satisfaction, public relations grew from a tiny infant in the late nineteenth century into a strong half-brother of advertising in the mid-twentieth. At its enlightened best, public relations brings the policies of institutions into harmony with the public interest and then extolls them. In doing so, it uses the media of communication—from which it has recruited many of its practitioners—but its manipulative intent puts it, too, beyond the meaning of journalism. An offshoot of both advertising and public relations, the company-sponsored newspaper or magazine, the house organ, proliferated after World War II. One can argue plausibly that it also is not best described as journalism.

mass communication

Today one can more correctly speak of "mass communication" or "the mass media" than of "journalism" when referring to media other than newspapers and magazines. In a sense, of course, every communication uses some medium, is committed to some channel for transmission. The letterhead or sheet of notepaper in correspondence, the sound waves utilized in conversation—these are channels or media. But in mass communication, a whole institution becomes the message carrier—a newspaper, a magazine, a broadcasting station—and is capable of carrying its messages to thousands or millions of persons almost simultaneously. It is also affected by the problems which beset it as a social institution: control, government restriction, economic support, and the like. The various media, therefore, characterize various branches of mass communication.

The term *mass communication* has sometimes been defined in two ways: communication by the media and communication for the masses

Mass communication, however, does not mean communication for every-one. Actually, mass communication is selective because the media are selective. The media tend to select their audiences; audiences likewise select among and within the media. In short, then, mass communication involves a selection by the media themselves as well as by various groups within the masses on the basis of the media and their content.

characteristics of mass communication

Mass communication has several distinguishing characteristics. First, it is mostly one-way. Usually there is no quick or easy way for the reader, viewer, or listener to talk back, to ask questions, or to get clarification if he needs it. Second, it involves a good deal of selection. The medium, for instance, chooses the audience it wishes to reach. The *New Yorker* is aimed at a sophisticated, urban readership. *Successful Farming* is aimed at farmers in the richly agricultural Midwest. *The New York Times* and New York *Daily News* seek different types of readers in New York. Those on the receiving end, on the other hand, select among the media. They decide whether they will switch on the television set or pick up a book or newspaper. They choose what they want from the available content. They may listen to a television news program but switch to another channel when a quiz program comes on. They choose the times that they will use the media.

Third, because the media are capable of reaching vast, widespread audiences, there is actually a need for fewer media than there used to be. To transmit a message throughout the entire United States by the human voice alone, one needs the assistance of many, many speakers. But a single broadcasting network can reach millions of people at the same time. This has its parallel in the whole economic and social system. Under the American system of mass production, for instance, a relatively few manu-facturers can turn out an astronomically large number of standardized products.

Fourth, to attract as large an audience as possible, the media are addressed to some mythical center point, to some common denominator. City editors used to tell their cub reporters to write for "the guy who moves his lips when he reads." That man was the lowest common de-nominator of the newspaper audience. If he could understand the news-paper's stories, so could the better educated. According to readability studies, three-fourths of the American people—those with average educa-tion—can be expected to understand writing at the level of that in the slick-paper and digest magazines. Obviously, the lowest common denomi-nator thought necessary for attracting an enormous following might well be below the educational average of the audience. Because the media are addressed to a mythical reader, listener, or viewer, they lose the intimacy of communications addressed to a single individual. A newspaper account of an event is vastly more impersonal than a letter from a friend telling about it.

Fifth, in mass communication, the communicating is done by a social institution which is responsive to the environment in which it operates. As this book will show, there is an interaction between the media and society. The media not only influence the social, economic, and political order in which they perform; they are influenced by it. To understand the media properly, therefore, one must understand the society in which they exist. And to understand society, one must examine its setting, its major assumptions, its basic beliefs. All of which is to say that a knowledge of history, sociology, economics, and philosophy is necessary for a true understanding of the media. And that is the sort of understanding which the best schools of journalism attempt to impart to their students.

Education for Communications

As the media of communication expanded, some schools and departments of journalism sought names more clearly descriptive of their functions. A few have been redesignated departments, schools, or colleges of communications, of communications arts, or journalism and communications. They wear the badge of communications somewhat self-consciously, however, for they remember their beginnings.

In their early years, schools of journalism concentrated largely on supplying the demand for newspaper staff members. And a grudging demand it was; city editors regarded the new graduates as incompetent theorists, and educators of traditional bent decried what they saw as unhealthy trade-school training at the college or university level. Today, by and large, the schools of journalism have proved themselves. The best of them pride themselves on providing a professional education, not mere technical training.

Moreover, some of them have broadened their offerings to include more than preparation for newspaper work. Today their graduates go, for example, into public relations and public information work. Others take positions with broadcasting stations as scriptwriters, announcers, newscasters, directors, or producers. Still others find work on magazines—general, trade, technical, professional, company-sponsored—as writers, editorial assistants, or editors. Some graduates, combining journalism with a specialty, have gone into such fields as agricultural journalism, home economics journalism, and medical journalism. Some go into positions in many phases of advertising: with agencies as copywriters, layout specialists, research workers; with retail stores and mail-order firms; with newspapers; broadcasting stations; and magazines, both general and specialized. Schools of journalism, in short, have come to serve all media.

In the past dozen years, graduate as well as undergraduate instruction has, in some schools of journalism, reflected a broadening of outlook and a change from concentration on journalism to a concern with all media. Few schools of journalism offered academic instruction beyond the master's level before World War II. The University of Missouri awarded its first doctorate in journalism in 1934, to be sure, and a few other institutions offered a journalism minor in combination with a doctorate in some other field, such as political science. Speaking to his fellow educators in journalism in 1937, Grant Hyde of the University of Wisconsin said, "We have our own M.A.—our double minor for the Ph.D. Should we push on toward our own Ph.D.? Yes. When we have decided what it is all about—and why."

Since the war, several schools have decided to their own satisfaction what it is all about. Stanford University, the University of Wisconsin, and the University of Minnesota have established doctoral programs in communications. In general, those programs have attempted to apply the methods and disciplines of the various social sciences to the basic problems of communications. They cover such areas as the communications process, the philosophy of communications, policies and structures of communications systems, public opinion and attitude formation, and so on. At Illinois, where the program is administered by an interdepartmental committee, students have the option of concentrating in either the individual communications process, which embraces such disciplines as psychology and linguistics, or social communications, which embraces the mass media.

Likewise, communications research has flourished in the past twenty years. Before World War II, there was comparatively little research in schools of journalism, and only a small handful of men associated with those schools had earned national stature as scholars. For the most part, research in the mass media was left to workers in other academic disciplines—political science, sociology, and psychology, for example—who became interested in communications problems as an outgrowth of their other studies, dealt with them, then passed on to something else. To borrow an expression from Wilbur Schramm, communications was a crossroad which many passed but where few tarried. Today some schools of journalism that are unable to afford elaborate research departments have at least one staff member whose primary assignment is research. And a few schools or colleges of journalism support research centers, among them Stanford University, Michigan State University, the University of Wisconsin, and the University of Illinois. The Institute of Communications Research at the University of Illinois is dedicated to an interdisciplinary approach to the problems of both interpersonal and mass communications, and its staff members represent such academic specialties as anthropology, economics, linguistics, psychology, and sociology. They, like those elsewhere, have a professional commitment to communications research, to which they bring the knowledge and methods of their various academic specialties.

vocational opportunities

For the young person in search of a career, mass communication has become a broad term embracing a multitude of opportunities. Despite a persistent stereotype to the contrary, the communications industries are not hopelessly overcrowded or hopelessly unrewarding financially.

Finding new staff members is a perennial topic of discussion at conventions and meetings of industry organizations representing such fields as newspapers, advertising, farm magazines, business publications, and broadcasting. Some employers aggressively seek out talented young persons. One Midwestern daily sends its personnel representative as far as five hundred miles away to look for promising staff members. At least two Eastern magazine publishers have representatives tour Midwest colleges each year in search of editorial and business talent.

other rewards

Nor has excitement entirely departed from what one might rather impersonally call the communications industries. A newspaper reporter may still risk his life or at least his well-being to land an important story. A magazine writer may still courageously outrage the complacent with a significant exposé. An advertising agency man may be privy to secret details when a new product is launched and may have a voice in its advertising strategy.

The New Orleans *States* recently broke a fact-crammed, five-installment series documenting gambling activities in Jefferson Parish, Louisiana. Writer of the series was Edwin Strickland, a thirty-nine-year-old reporter for the Birmingham *News,* who had earlier exposed the rackets in Birmingham, then had been six months digging out the story of crime and corruption in Phenix City, Alabama. The *States* imported him because its own reporters were too well-known; gamblers had foresightedly collected photographs of every newsman in New Orleans. Flashing a hefty roll of bills, carrying a well-thumbed racing form, Strickland made the rounds of barrooms and bookie joints, won the confidence of their proprietors and habitués over drinks, then worked his way into the gambling houses for a first-hand look. What he saw gave him the basis for his series.

Louis Clifford, city editor of the Cleveland *Press,* wanted to give his readers thorough, well-documented answers to some important questions about the city's police department. What sort of men was police work attracting? What training did they get, what discipline were they under? How did they treat the public? He assigned a new reporter, Hank Gordon, to the story. For six months Gordon lived the life of a policeman. None of the police and only a few of the newspaper staff knew that he was a reporter after a story, not just another police rookie. In his six months, Gordon attended the police academy, worked on zone car duty, served on the night detail in the "jungle," even joined the Fraternal Order of Police. He gathered six hundred single-spaced pages of notes which were the basis for an impressive series, almost sociological in tone, for the *Press*.

In gathering material for his crime articles for such magazines as the *Saturday Evening Post*, John Bartlow Martin has occasionally spent an evening in a strange city driving around with an ex-convict in his car, the meeting unknown to anyone but the informant's friends, and once he was warned to drop a story and get out of town. Herbert Matthews scored a news beat for *The New York Times* in 1957 by making his way to the mountain hideout of Fidel Castro for an exclusive interview.

But the excitement is rarely of that sort. Much more often it lies in being on the inside when big events are happening, in learning—firsthand—of the most recent discoveries and advances in many spheres of activity; in dealing with the men and women who make news; in mingling with leaders and celebrities; in being part of the glamor and tensions and pressures which seem to surround every newspaper, radio station, magazine, and advertising agency. There is a thrill in getting a good news story from a recalcitrant source, in creating a smooth television program from the chaos which precedes and surrounds the performance, in finding the right words to sell a pair of seersucker trousers or a bedroom suite. One woman graduate of Medill School of Journalism once told her professors that she was finding romance—*romance* was the word she chose—in covering the chemical fertilizer industry for a business newspaper.

For those willing to seek them, the old glamor and excitement are still there.

References

BARNOUW, ERIK, *Mass Communications* (New York: Holt, Rinehart and Winston, Inc., 1956).

BLUM, ELEANOR, *Reference Books in the Mass Media: An Annotated Selected Booklist* (Urbana: University of Illinois Press, 1962).

CLARK, WESLEY CLARKE, ed., *Journalism Tomorrow* (Syracuse, N.Y.: Syracuse University Press, 1958).

EMERY, EDWIN, PHILLIP H. AULT, AND WARREN K. AGEE, *Introduction to Mass Communications* (New York: Dodd, Mead & Co., 1960).

KEARL, BRYANT, "Journalism—What Is It? A Re-definition," *Journalism Quarterly*, 20 (March 1943) 41–44.

O'HARA, ROBERT C., *Media for the Millions: The Process of Mass Communications* (New York: Random House, Inc., 1961).

PORTER, WILLIAM E., RICHARD F. CARTER, JAY W. JENSEN, AND THEODORE PETERSON, "Journalism, Communications and the Future of the Discipline, a Symposium," *Journalism Quarterly* 40 (Autumn 1963) 580–93.

SCHRAMM, WILBUR, *The Mass Media and National Development* (Stanford, Calif.: Stanford University Press, 1964).

2

The

Mass Media and

Society

Americans today more or less take their mass media for granted. As a matter of course, they expect their daily newspapers to be plopped at their doors by carriers or handed to them by news dealers. Without a second thought, they expect commentators, comedians, singers, and actors to perform in their living rooms at the click of a switch. They accept without question the brightly covered magazines which decorate their newsstands and living-room tables.

Indeed, Americans take their mass media so much for granted that it is hard for most people to imagine a world without them—a world without *Time* to reveal just what the visiting dignitary whispered to the President when his plane set down at the Washington airport; without the *Reader's Digest* and its "unforgettable characters," medical marvels, homely philosophy, and shining deeds; without Drew Pearson, Louella Parsons, Mike Hammer, Matt Dillon, Elizabeth Taylor, and the Beatles—all creatures of the mass media.

Because Americans take their media so much for granted, most people overlook how important the media really are. Most people do not consider the influence of the media on their ways of thinking and acting or on the functioning of society. From time to time, of course, some citizens do show concern over the ways in which the media affect their interests, likes, and dislikes. If broadcasting fare seems overladen with the trivial or if a rash of books or magazines exploiting violence and sex seems likely to impair the morals of the young, a few outraged citizens may speak out in protest. And sometimes a few will applaud a newspaper for its exposé of delinquency or of graft in city hall, or will praise a television station for its timely documentaries.

But most persons are concerned at best about the immediate, almost ephemeral, effects of the media on their day-to-day lives. They rarely consider how important the existence of a mass-communication system is to modern industrial society. They seldom think about the unseen ways in which media help to shape and sustain political, social, economic, and cultural life.

This chapter will try to show how the communication system is related in the most fundamental way to man and society, to show how it is related to the very nature of man as a human being and to the world of politics, industry, art, religion that man creates and lives in.

At the outset, the terms *communication* and *communications* need clarification. They are not just the singular and plural forms of the same word. Put simply, their difference is this: Communication is the process of communicating; communications is the technical means used to carry out the process. Communication, then, is a central fact of human existence and social process. It is all the ways by which a person influences another and is influenced by him. The ways may be direct, as when a teacher talks to a student, or indirect, as when a tom-tom or television station carries the message. Communication is the carrier of social process; it makes interaction within humankind possible and enables men to become and remain social beings.

On the other hand, communications—with the final *s*—has a much narrower meaning. It embraces all the technical means of indirect or "mediated" communication, from tribal drums, smoke signals, and stone tablets to telegraphy, printing, broadcasting, and film. The mass media, then, comprise a technical system—communications—by which a single person may communicate rapidly and simultaneously with a multitude of others.

The mass media, like the spoken word and the raised eyebrow, are just an aspect of human communication in general. They are technical extensions of speech and gesture, much as the shovel and pile driver are technical extensions of the human arm. But such an obvious point is often overlooked. In their thinking about the mass media, people do not always recognize this fundamental relationship of the media to human nature and human society. Because they do not, they often misread the role of the mass media in their lives. Many intellectuals, for instance, see the mass media as a kind of accidental by-product of technology that has been taken over by hucksters, propagandists, and manipulators for selfish purposes. That view may have some truth in it, but what it ignores are the objective relationships between the mass media and society which seem to exist quite apart from the motives and interests of owners, managers, editors, writers, and so on.

Man as Symbol Maker

Traditionally, philosophers have set man apart from other animals because of his powers of reason. But man has another faculty which also distinguishes him from other animals—his ability to communicate by symbols. He is the one creature that reacts not only to his real physical environment but also to a symbolic environment of his own making. A hungry dog reacts to food by eating it. A man might, too, but just what he eats often depends on symbolic considerations. He may avoid some foods for fear of offending the deity; he may eat others for their reputed curative powers; he may even eat some, such as caviar, for status.

What all of this means is that man has an environment far different from that of other creatures. Most creatures live in just their physical environments. They receive stimuli, and they respond to them. They have no sense of past, no sense of future; as Kenneth Boulding reminds us, a dog has no idea that there were dogs on earth before he arrived and will be here after he has gone. But man, by creating a symbolic world, has given reality a dimension known only to the human species. Between the mere stimulus and response of other creatures, he has erected a symbolic system that transforms the whole of human life and sets it apart from the life of all other animals. This distinctive mark of human life is not necessarily related to man's rationality (or to his irrationality, for that matter). It is a remarkable achievement that has taken man out of a merely physical universe and put him into a symbolic universe of language, art, and myth.

Man does not confront reality first-hand. Instead of always dealing with things themselves, as other animals do, he develops *ideas* about things. He so envelops himself in linguistic forms, in artistic images, in mythical symbols, or in religious rites that he cannot see or know anything except through his symbolic system. As Epictetus said, "What disturbs and alarms man are not the things, but his opinions and fancies about the things."

Reality of course contains all the things which are given to man by his senses; but the framework and structure of reality are not something which man can touch or directly see. They are something intellectual, something he can perceive only indirectly through symbols. Animals react to outside stimuli either directly or not at all. Men, on the other hand, respond largely in a cerebral, invisible way. They produce images, notions, figments of all sorts, as symbols for ideas about things. A cat may cower under a porch during a thunderstorm; only a man would interpret the storm as a sign of a god's wrath. For man the symbol-maker, then, the world is mainly a pseudo-world, a web of symbols, of his own making.

Yet his pseudo-world is not sheer fantasy. Even the mythologies of man, like mathematics, language, and the formula $E = mc^2$, are his rational and practical efforts to deal with experience. They are attempts to organize his sensations and to build up around them symbolic systems that give meaning to his existence.

As a result, man's world is different from that of other animals, for it is both more and other than the physical stimuli which surround him. More important, it is precisely this symbol-making function that makes human communication and the social process possible.

Communication as the Basis for Human Society

Man, of course, is not the only social animal. Bees and ants, for instance, have a complex organization of activity, including even division of labor. But man's sociability, like the world he lives in, differs from that of other animals. As other creatures do, man lives in a society of action. However, he also lives in a sphere of thought and symbolic communication, one made up of language, art, myth, religion, philosophy and science. His higher form of society makes his sociability unique. He may submit to society's rules like other animals. But because he can create symbols, he has powers that other animals do not—the power to communicate intentions, meanings, and desire, and, therefore, the power to change the forms of social life.

Communication is thus the carrier of the social process. It is the means man has for organizing, stabilizing, and modifying his social life and passing on its forms and meaning from generation to generation. The social process depends upon the accumulation, exchange, and transmission of knowledge. Knowledge in turn depends upon communication. Without it, man could achieve only the most primitive knowledge and hence only the most primitive society. Without it, human society would remain static, grounded in instinctive behavior, not much different from the societies of other animals.

No wonder, then, John Dewey once remarked that communication is "of all affairs the most wonderful." In Dewey's view, society not only continues to exist by communication; in a sense, it originated in communication. For obviously communication was necessary before people could band together into society—necessary for all of the adjustments and understandings that society demands of its members and for reaching the agreements without which society would disintegrate. By communication, man maintains his social institutions, each with its values and ways of behaving, not just from day to day but from generation to generation.

Processes of Communication

Edward Sapir, too, makes an important distinction between communication and communications with the final *s*. For him, the singular form covers what he calls the primary processes—conscious and unconscious behavior that communicates. The four processes that he mentions are language, gesture in the widest sense of the term, imitation of the overt behavior of others, and a large group that might be vaguely called social suggestion. He uses the plural communications to cover what he calls secondary techniques—the instruments and systems which help to carry out communication. Among them he lists Morse code, wigwagging, bugle calls, the telephone, and radio, but he could have added thousands more: the stylus, brush, reed pen, papyrus, parchment, paper, the printing press, celluloid film, and the television transmitter.

The distinction between the two words has real historical and socio- logical importance, Sapir thinks, for all mankind is blessed with the primary processes of language, gesture, imitation of behavior, and social suggestion, but only relatively advanced civilizations have developed the secondary techniques into systems of communication.

All secondary techniques have two things in common. First, even though they are physically different, their main task is to extend com- munication by language to situations in which face-to-face contact is impossible. Some of the techniques extend communication by gesture, or movement, as well: painting, sculpture, still photography, motion pictures, and television. Second, all the secondary techniques provide the indirect means by which the primary processes of imitation and social suggestion are carried out. Indirect they are; the telegraph and radio, for example, do not communicate by themselves; they can do so only when someone uses them to convey his symbols.

It is hard to overemphasize the importance to civilization of man's devising these indirect ways of communicating. By creating, improving, and multiplying these technical means, man has virtually freed the com- munication process from the limitations of time and space. Some of the means enable man to communicate not only with his contemporaries but with unborn generations. Some enable him to get in touch quickly with others in far-flung areas. Modern communications has so greatly ex- panded the communication process that, as Sapir says, the whole civilized world is potentially the psychological equivalent of a primitive tribe.

Moreover, the communications system has made it possible for remote parts of the world to be more like each other in social behavior than they may be to adjoining regions. Geographical contiguity has lost much of its importance. Today the "scientific community," which has no clear-cut location on the map, shares common values, attitudes, and beliefs. In general, so do the "democratic world," the "Christian world," the "totalitarian world," and so on.

Later chapters will have more to say about the social effects of technical advances in communication. Here is a good place, however, for some general observations about the relationship of communications and society.

Mass Media and Society

Every society, from the most primitive to the most complex, has some system of technical, indirect communication to help it conduct its affairs. In any society, the communication system performs three broad tasks. Harold Lasswell has defined them as: surveillance of the environment, correlation of the components of society in responding to the environment, and transmission of the social heritage. Wilbur Schramm has used the simpler terms of watcher, forum, and teacher.

Every society has its watchers who provide other members with information and interpretation of events. They survey the environment, so to speak, and report on the threats and dangers as well as on the good omens and opportunities. They may vary from the elder in the tribe who complains that the younger generation is showing less and less respect for ritual to the foreign correspondent who reports political tension in the Middle East.

In deciding what to do about the threats and opportunities, society uses its communication system as a forum. Because its ways are always changing, society needs some way of reaching agreement on what those changes shall be. Without agreement, there may be a breakdown of social organization. Through the discussion carried on via its communication system, society settles upon the direction of change so that individuals and groups act together as a community. Simple societies may reach their consensus from face-to-face discussion; complex industrial ones may rely largely on the mass media.

Society also uses its communication system as a teacher to pass the social heritage from one generation to the next. As the system can be compared to the tribal council or the New England town meeting in its function of correlating responses to the environment, so it can be compared to the institutions of home, church, and school in its task as teacher.

communications as a means of social interaction

Communication systems have a dual role: providing for social control and providing for harmonious social change. On the one hand, they make for stability, since they always tend to purvey the values and beliefs of the society in which they operate. Media content in the United States, for example, is colored by the values which Americans cherish and by the assumptions they have made about the good life. On the other hand, communication systems also bring about change, since they are one means by which the existing order is challenged. Thus on the one hand they tend to maintain the status quo and on the other to disrupt it.

Moreover, a communication system itself is an institution. As such it affects and is affected by other institutions—politics and industry, for instance. Politics and industry are both important in deciding the kind of communication system a society has and the tasks it performs. Just how important politics and industry are will become evident in later chapters, which show in some detail how the rise of democracy and the industrial revolution helped to shape the mass media in the United States. However, politics and industry in turn are influenced—sometimes decisively— by the communication system. The growth of the mass media in the United States greatly affected the development of American political institutions and the American form of mass production. Probably no modern form of political organization could ever have developed without the conquest of time and space by the mass media.

communications as an adjunct of other institutions

As an institution, a communication system has a good deal of power in its own right. It also is a means by which other institutions make their power felt. Its ability to spread messages to multitudes of people over large territories makes the system a source of power, no matter what information and ideas it carries. By influencing what the system sends out, other institutions can use it for their own ends, or attempt to do so.

Traditionally, communications have been an adjunct of other institutions in their exercise of power. Especially have they been used by the political, religious and economic orders. For centuries in England the Crown controlled the infant press and used it to promote the interests of the state, and the church long held a monopoly of communications to maintain its supremacy.

Only in very recent years, since the rise of mass media, has it been possible to think of communications as a form of power with interests and a will of its own. But even now, despite the formidable power of the mass media, many observers would argue that communications is still largely the adjunct of other institutions. For instance, in the United

States, the communication system is closely harnessed to industry, with the sale of goods as a major task, and in Soviet Russia it is fundamentally linked to the political order.

When joined to other organizations, communications has been used for social control. In every society, either the rulers or the most powerful groups have used communications to stabilize the social order and to consolidate power. The early Romans, for instance, tried to hold their large territory under control by developing a body of central doctrine, by building roads, and then by using those roads to spread their doctrines to people in the outposts of the empire. Centuries later, when printing first came to England, the Crown saw it as a serious threat to the divine right of kings and to the status quo. Its immediate response was control. By forbidding anything that threatened its security, the Crown made the press an adjunct of the state. For the same reason, the Soviet state has harnessed communications to promote and support its system of socialism.

In revolutionary times, the rebelling as well as the ruling orders will generally use communications for their own purposes. What usually comes about after the turmoil of revolution is simply a shift in the center of power. And the new ruling order, like the old, looks to communications to impose its will on society. For example, after the Puritans took power in England, they controlled the press as tightly in their own interests as did the earlier monarchs. After the American Revolution, the controlling groups of the new society—represented in politics by the Federalists—tried to make the press an organ for perpetuating their interests and beliefs. The Communists in their seizures of power around the world have made the communication systems tools of the new political order.

communications as a key to cultural change

However, communication systems are more than just a means of social control reflecting the values and interests of the ruling groups and major institutions of a society. They also are a force for bringing about cultural change.

Communication media, according to the Canadian historian H. A. Innis, have profoundly influenced the development of Western civilization, and many of the influences over the centuries have been determined by changes in the character and capabilities of media.

Some media, such as papyrus and parchment, are not suited to wide distribution. They are suited to keeping knowledge the property of the few and to perpetuating traditional ideas and opinions. Other media, such as cheap printed matter and radio, are suited for disseminating knowledge of all kinds over vast expanses of territory. Thus, as new technologies were developed, communication systems became more suited to disseminating knowledge and less suited to restricting it.

Christianity exploited the advantages of parchment for maintaining the old order. The durability of parchment gave the church a means for preserving a nucleus of ideas over many centuries; the scarcity of parchment limited the guardianship of those ideas to a few people and for a long time left the church relatively free from the challenge of dissent. The succeeding secular state, on the other hand, used cheap paper for disseminating knowledge widely, thus challenging the traditional order and extending control over large areas.

So the church, faced with barbarian invasions and the ambitions of kings and princes, tried to maintain a monopoly of knowledge stressing stability and continuity through dependence on a limited body of scriptural writings in Latin. And so, too, its control of ideas and opinion, aided by the durability and scarcity of parchment, helped the church to defend itself against ideological challenge.

However, the church's monopoly over knowledge was gradually destroyed in the competition for men's minds that followed the increased use of paper and the renaissance of classical learning, especially Greek science and philosophy. The invention of printing and increasing supplies of cheap paper supported the Reformation and the growth of vernacular literature, both of which became important in determining the character of the new nation-state.

The industrial revolution and the application of steam power to the paper and printing industries were similarly important. They profoundly influenced the rise to power of the middle class and the emergence of liberal democracies in western Europe and America. Indeed, contemporary forms of society, democratic or totalitarian, probably would not have been possible without high-speed presses and electronic media for rapid communication with large numbers of people over vast areas.

Increasing Importance of the Media Today

Serious students disagree sharply over the influence of the mass media on the minds of men and hence on man's values and beliefs, on his ways of behaving, and on the new forms of society he is creating. Some observers are alarmed by the high potential the media have for manipulating audiences. Others, making light of the alarmists, insist that the manipulative powers of the media are exaggerated, that communications simply mirror passively the existing values and beliefs of society.

Yet whether the media are manipulative or merely passive, their effects on the social process seem to be generally the same. And certainly as highly technical and efficient means of indirect, symbolic communication, the media play an increasingly important part, dangerous or not, in modern society.

mass media as watcher, forum, and teacher

Until about two centuries ago, oral communication was largely sufficient to carry out the three main tasks of communications—surveying the
environment, correlating response to the environment, and transmitting
the social heritage. But oral communication became inadequate as a
speedily rising birth rate crowded the world with people; as private
actions took on public consequences; and as the industrial and technological revolutions drew the world together and made even nations
depend upon one another in ways unknown before. In time the mass
media were relied upon more and more to perform those three functions.
Today most persons know little of the world at first hand. A great deal
of what they do know comes, often in highly generalized or stereotyped
form, from the mass media.

People depend upon the mass media to report on the environment for
them. In an earlier day, man could explore his narrow little world first-
hand or with little help. Travelers and letters may have brought him
accounts of the great world outside of his neighborhood, but the events
taking place there often had little or no immediate effect on his life. He
himself could see and test the things that really mattered. By merely
looking, he could learn crop conditions; by observation, he could tell if
the mill was busy or idle, if the haul of fish was heavy or lean. But today
how can a man learn, except from the mass media, of an uprising in Asia
which may touch off World War III or of a rise in the price of steel which
may boost his cost of living? The great majority of Americans are governed by persons whom they have seen only in the mirror of the mass
media. They learn the issues of their times largely through the media.
And if they do not know what values they should cherish, what beliefs
they should hold, they have only to look to the mass media. The media,
in words and sounds and pictures, make it all clear to them.

And what of thought, of the individual's thinking out issues for himself? More and more such intellectual tasks become unnecessary, for the
issues are largely resolved for him by the mass media. All one needs to do
is watch and listen. In an earlier age, men carried on their discussion,
like observation, first-hand. In tavern and town meeting, over coffee and
port, one could compare his first-hand observations with those of other
men and talk over the consequences. From experience, he could detect
the truth tellers and the chronic falsifiers among his acquaintances.

But today Americans have become spectators in discussion just as they
have become spectators in sports. They may talk over some affairs and
issues with friends, barbers, or barkeepers. But for the most part, they
pay specialists to do the discussing for them in the mass media. Usually
they are content so long as views approximating their own turn up in
the arena of discussion. Much of the discussion today, then, is done by

professionals using the mass media—by columnists, commentators, and editorial writers who speculate on the outcome and significance of political and economic events; by critics who talk over the merits of books, plays, and records; by copywriters and pitchmen, and even comedians and masters of ceremony, who tell about the good life and how to lead it; by newspaper, magazine, and book writers who judge the consequences to society and to the individual of marital infidelity, neuroses, cigarette smoking, and sparing the rod to save the child. The result, of course, is not entirely stultifying. Discussion today is based on a much wider view of the world and a much deeper understanding of it.

mass media as pseudo-environment

The mass media can be looked on as a kind of pseudo-environment between man and the objective "real" world. That view has important implications for the role of the media in society. For one thing, the media have brought speed, ubiquity and pervasiveness to the traditional role of communications as watcher, forum, and teacher. Therefore, the media are sometimes seen as enveloping modern man in a kind of ersatz reality. For another thing, as a means by which the dominant institutions exercise social control, the media are widely regarded as so imbuing the public with the prevailing values and beliefs of their culture that society is in danger of becoming stagnant. The fear is that people will behave toward one another in almost ritualistic fashion because the commonly accepted pattern goes unchallenged. As a result, their lives and institutions will become fossilized.

In his *Public Opinion,* which came out in 1922, Walter Lippmann painted perhaps the earliest and best portrait of the mass media as pseudo-environment. The objective world that man deals with, Lippmann said, is "out of reach, out of sight, out of mind." In his head man gradually makes for himself a more or less trustworthy picture of the world outside. Thus people—alone or together—behave not on direct and certain knowledge of the real world but on pictures which they have made or got from others. What a man does depends on those pictures in his head.

This internal picture-making process inevitably colors the messages that man gets from the world outside. Stored-up images, preconceptions, prejudices, motivations, and interests—they all interpret the messages, fill them out, and in turn direct the play of attention and the vision itself. These interpretations and expansions become patterns or "stereotypes." And these stereotypes, Lippmann thought, determine human action. Originally, a stereotype was the plate made by taking a mold of a printing surface and casting type metal from it. According to Lippmann, the minds of men too are poured into molds—their pictures of the world outside. The minds then reproduce ideas and react to stimuli according to the patterns of the molds.

Lippmann was writing only of the relationship between public opinion and the newspaper press. However, his concept can profitably be extended to all mass media. As a chief source of knowledge, the media provide people with messages from the outside world. People use these messages to form mental pictures of the world of public affairs.

If one regards the media as pseudo-environment, he gets a fresh view of the media as an agency of social control. He can see the communication system as an institution of social control mirroring the beliefs and values of society itself. Or he can see it as an arm of the ruling orders of society. Such an idea is a sharp break with traditional Anglo-American theory. Traditional theory saw the press as freeing men from the tyranny of ignorance and inherited superstition and thus enabling them to govern themselves by right reason and individual conscience. The new theory does not necessarily deny the traditional importance of the press in public enlightenment. But it does give a new angle of vision for looking at the media without regard for what they ought to be and do.

Social control by the mass media is so extensive and effective, some observers believe, that it is their chief characteristic and function. For instance, Joseph Klapper sees the "engineering of consent"—his term for the process of social control—as the most significant feature of the mass media. Attempts to engineer consent are neither new nor limited to those with sinister motives, of course. Indeed, consent is necessary for any stable society, and communications has always sought to engineer it. But never before has there been engineering on such a vast scale, according to some social scientists, and the media work in such unison that there is little counter-engineering.

Because of their importance, the media have brought about a change in the types of social control. Paul Lazarsfeld and Robert K. Merton are among those who see coercion as giving way to subtle persuasion through the mass media. "Increasingly," they say, "the chief power groups, among which organized business occupies the most spectacular place, have come to adopt techniques for manipulating mass publics through propaganda in place of more direct means of control." In short, wielders of political and economic power have reduced their direct exploitation and turned to psychological exploitation through the mass media. Even the ruling powers in totalitarian societies such as Communist Russia and China have made this change, although they continue to use the more direct methods of organized violence and terror as well. American society is perhaps the best example of a social order in which direct coercion is at a minimum. Here those who wish to control opinions and beliefs turn less to physical force than to mass persuasion in the form of news and views and entertainment. They use the advertising campaign and the public-relations program instead of the threat of firing squad or concentration camp.

But even if modern democracies use psychological manipulation instead of totalitarianism's direct and violent forms of social control, the results are not necessarily less effective. Never before have such pervasive and ubiquitous means of communication existed; never before has public opinion been so completely at the mercy of whoever may control the instrument. Possibly the saving factor is that unregenerate element in man's nature which refuses to be homogenized by even the most subtle means.

mass media as an adjunct of the industrial order

The mass media in America are businesses, whether big or little; they are, as George Gerbner has said, "the cultural arm of American industry." That is the primary fact about the mass media in the United States, oriented as they are to marketing. One must understand that fact to grasp the essential meaning of the media and their relationship to the American social order. A similar understanding is necessary for analysis of the Soviet communication system. To grasp the essential meaning of the Soviet mass media and their relationship to Communist society, one must first recognize that the Soviet communication system is an arm of the political order, as it is in any authoritarian society.

In the United States, the industrial order which directly and indirectly controls the mass media is concerned largely with preserving the status quo. It does not wish to encourage revolutionary changes in a social system which provides it with abundant freedom and benefits. It has no more interest in doing so than the ruling political order in an authoritarian society has in furthering dissent. On the contrary, industry tries to keep the social system pretty much as it is. To that end, it seeks to intensify and mold certain existing tendencies of the system, to nurture sanctioned values and beliefs, and to sharpen public attitudes and desires so as to produce particular actions in the market place. The media are an important means of realizing those objectives.

This is not to say that business interests have conspired to control the policy and content of the mass media for their own selfish ends. That point is worth emphasizing. Deliberate, organized, and calculated propaganda in support of the existing system and against social change is, as Klapper says, "statistically insignificant." There is no plot, no cabal, no organized effort to preserve the status quo, but the media serve the industrial order nonetheless.

The strategic policy and the bulk of content of the mass media work toward engineering consent in favor of the existing order. Commercial control of the media and the resulting need to please the largest possible audience virtually assure that they will. The media operator seeks to saturate the market he has cut out for his product in order to hold down his unit costs and, if he accepts advertising, to justify high rates for space or time. To attract a huge following, the media must stick to majority views, reflect prevailing values, and reinforce the primary assumptions of the social order. The more completely their content reasserts the form and character of existing society, the more efficiently the mass media perform as an adjunct of the industrial order. As Klapper says, to depart from the popularly sanctioned path is to invite economic disaster.

mass media as an agency of social control

For at least two reasons, the American mass media are "exquisitely fitted to turn the status quo into social law," to use Klapper's phrase. One reason is that the media operate in a democracy grounded upon public opinion—a public opinion which countless special pleaders of all sorts wish to shape. Another is that the media are directly and indirectly controlled by commercial interests, which have increasingly used persuasion to reach their goals.

Organized business and such lesser interests as the major political parties and church groups have virtually a "psychological monopoly" of the media. News and comment, entertainment, advertising, political rhetoric and religious exhortation alike are far more concerned with channeling existing beliefs than with radically changing them. With few exceptions, the media have not tried to work fundamental changes in American culture. The media seldom give voice to genuinely new ideas, especially profound or radical ones. And the voices they do occasionally carry are unlikely to find a large or interested audience. As Klapper says, "Dangerous capabilities the media most certainly possess—but in America the danger is of dross rather than of revolution."

The danger lies not only in the proved technical ability of the mass media to encompass the American public orally and visually. It lies also in the growing tendency and suspected ability of the media to inflate existing taste and opinion, to reinforce the status quo of values, ideas, and social norms to a point of dull unanimity. What John Stuart Mill feared most—the tyranny of society, of custom, of tradition, of majority opinion, and the stifling of individualism—is close to becoming an accomplished fact, some observers think. For a liberal democratic society, which must depend upon the free communication of a wide range of information, ideas, and opinions, such conformity could mean death by self-strangulation.

But the question is far from settled. Not all observers are convinced that the social control exercised by the mass media is as extensive and decisive as the appraisals of Klapper, Lazarsfeld, Merton and others seem to imply. And these dissenters include many who nevertheless speak of the media in fearful tones.

Louis Wirth, for instance, somewhat uneasily acknowledges the citizen's increasing dependence on the mass media for knowledge and guidance. Yet he says that the high degree of consensus already existing in society lends the media much of their apparent effectiveness. The media, he says, operate in situations already prepared for them in the social process. It is easy to get the "mistaken impression that they or the content and symbols which they disseminate do the trick."

Richard T. LaPiere, in his *Theory of Social Control,* carries the argument further. He sees membership in small, primary groups—the family, church, and intimate circle of friends—as more influential in determining an individual's values, attitudes, and behavior than any influences of the media.

Even so, it seems clear enough that the mass media have been and will continue to be important in transforming contemporary social life. Succeeding chapters will tell how they became "mass" and thus more formidable instruments of communication than man had ever known before, how social and intellectual forces have shaped them, how they have been accommodated to the American system of private enterprise, and what, according to democratic theory, Americans think they ought to be and do.

References

BERELSON, BERNARD, AND MORRIS JANOWITZ, eds., *Reader in Public Opinion and Communication,* enlarged ed. (New York: The Free Press of Glencoe, 1953).

CASSIRER, ERNST, *An Essay on Man* (New Haven, Conn.: Yale University Press, 1962).

INKELES, ALEX, *Public Opinion in Soviet Russia: A Study in Mass Persuasion* (Cambridge, Mass.: Harvard University Press, 1950).

INNIS, HAROLD, *The Bias of Communication* (Toronto: Toronto University Press, 1951).

————, *Empire and Communications* (Oxford: Clarendon Press, 1950).

JENSEN, JAY W., "A Method and a Perspective for Criticism of the Mass Media," *Journalism Quarterly* 37 (Spring 1960) 261–66.

KLAPPER, JOSEPH T., "Mass Media and the Engineering of Consent," *American Scholar* 17 (Autumn 1948) 419–29.

LIPPMANN, WALTER, *Public Opinion* (New York: Harcourt, Brace & World, Inc., 1922).

SCHRAMM, WILBUR, ed., *Mass Communications: A Book of Readings,* 2nd ed. (Urbana: University of Illinois Press, 1960).

————, ed., *The Science of Human Communication* (New York: Basic Books, Inc., Publishers, 1963).

SIEBERT, FREDRICK S., *Freedom of the Press in England, 1476–1776* (Urbana: University of Illinois Press, 1952).

WRIGHT, CHARLES, *Mass Communication: A Sociological Perspective* (New York: Random House, Inc., 1959).

3

The Media

and Their Social

and Economic Environment

One day in 1690, a printer in a Boston printing shop, using a deerskin swab tied to the end of a stick, inked some forms of type, screwed down the wooden platen on a wooden press, and pulled off a copy of Benjamin Harris' *Publick Occurrences*. That was the first newspaper attempted in the American colonies. A two-column affair of four pages, one of them blank, it was dedicated to recording "Memorable Occurrences of Divine Providence."

Anticlimactically, *Publick Occurrences* died with its first issue. But even its quick death resulted from ideas then current about the press. The paper offended authorities, presumably with a story about brutalities committed by Indian allies of the Colonial military forces. The authorities responded by forbidding publishers to bring out printed materials without first getting permission from the government. Such censorship rested on the right of colonial governors to control the press on instructions from the British crown. It was consistent with a firmly established idea about the press: It should be controlled to serve the interests of the government in power. A later chapter will explore in some detail the ways in which the intellectual environment has shaped the press since *Publick Occurrences* was born.

Social and economic forces also were in part responsible

for the birth of *Publick Occurrences* and of the more enduring news-papers which followed some fourteen years later. Indeed, their social and economic environments have shaped all later mass media: the magazine, which appeared in 1741 but underwent a drastic change in the late years of the nineteenth century; the movies, which also were born in the late nineteenth century and moved into marble palaces of their own in the early twentieth; radio, which came squawking into the world in the 1920s; and television, which grew as rapidly after World War II as radio had after World War I. All were conditioned by the rise of democracy, industrialization, and urbanization.

Colonial Environment

Before we consider the ways in which those things have shaped our communication system, let us look briefly at how its setting affected the Colonial press, which provides a good case study in the interaction between media and environment.

For good reason, Colonial newspapers first sprang up in seaports. Sea-ports were communication centers, places where news was available from ship, stage, and post, from sailors, travelers, and people coming to mar-ket. As trading centers, the ports were the places most likely to provide sources of advertising. As population centers, they had the greatest poten-tial audiences to support newspapers; more than that, because the ports were social and cultural centers, the audiences were likely to welcome newspapers. Moreover, the seaports were political centers, where the governor lived and the council convened. They were not only good news sources; they were also places where the publisher might augment his income by doing public printing or might find financial support by align-ing with one of the political factions.

For good reason, too, the early publishers were often postmasters. From the government's viewpoint, postmasters made good publishers. Their views were likely to be those of the ruling group and, as political ap-pointees, they could be held in line. From his own viewpoint, the post-master had several qualifications as news purveyor. He was in a good position to gather news, as he had access to incoming papers and was visited by travelers. His franking privilege enabled him to hold down the cost of distributing his paper.

The times, as well, encouraged the birth of the newspaper. As the eighteenth century opened, the colonies were firmly established. With the frontier won, people had time to read, and the school systems were pro-viding an audience for the press. Trade had developed sufficiently to justify newspapers as economic enterprises.

Similarly, a number of forces shaped the press which arose in America after Colonial times. As we will see in a later chapter, the libertarian philosophy of the Enlightenment gave Americans their ideas of what the press should be and do. In this chapter we will examine three major forces which have molded the American communication system and tremendously affected American social, economic, and political institutions. These forces are the rise of democracy, the industrial and technological revolution, and urbanization. Especially after the Civil War, although their foundations were laid before then, these forces wrought a powerful revolution which affected virtually every aspect of American life. Let us look at these forces, and then see how they have influenced the media. For convenience, we will treat them separately, although in fact, of course, they were closely interrelated.

Rise of Democracy

The rise of democracy had a profound influence on our communication system as well as on American life and culture in general. It helped to create the great democratic middle class; that class has largely dominated American culture, as Ralph D. Casey has observed, and its tastes, interests, and demands have shaped our communication channels.

In America, government by the élite gave way in the nineteenth century to government by the masses. For the first time in modern history, an entire adult population achieved effective power to choose its own rulers and to steer itself toward its own destiny. Awakened to his political power by the Revolution, the common man began to concern himself with public issues which previously had been settled for him by others. Gradually, restrictions on voting broke down so that suffrage was extended to the entire adult population.

universal suffrage

Even after the Revolution the older states denied the vote to a substantial part of the population. Most of them limited the vote to adult property-owners or taxpayers and set high requirements of property ownership for eligibility to hold public office.

But several conditions worked to give the common man the ballot. People in the new agricultural states admitted to the union between 1789 and 1840 were more alike in wealth and social status than those in the original colonies. No wealthy ruling class dominated those states, as it did the older ones, and their constitutions were more liberal. They generally granted adult white males not only the right to vote with few or no restrictions but also the right to hold public office. The new states sent a growing number of representatives to Congress, and they became increasingly influential in determining Presidential elections. Politicians from along the seaboard in time had little choice but to yield to the rising democratic spirit.

At the same time, class differences were breaking down in the eastern states. Political equality there was fostered by a growing political consciousness among the farmers; by the labor parties and trade unions springing up in the industrial cities; and by the tide of immigrants who were acquiring citizenship.

Gradually, the states along the seaboard altered their constitutions to drop or lower the property requirement for voting. By mid-century, adult white males generally could vote without holding property. After the Civil War, women renewed their agitation for suffrage. They won local gains in some states and then eventual victory in 1920, when the Nineteenth Amendment assured their right to vote. Meanwhile, the franchise had been extended to the Negro.

Popular rule was strengthened by another development taking place while voting was becoming a universal right. The spread of democracy broke down the restrictions which had limited the right to hold public office to men of wealth or to men with certain religious qualifications.

free universal education

As the democratic movement surged forward, so did a cause closely tied to it, that of free universal education. Although popular education was a cause to chagrin the taxpayer, it also was one which could unite the liberal and the conservative. Liberals saw free universal education a concomitant of universal suffrage, for only an educated populace could be counted on to govern itself wisely and to supply candidates worthy of public office. Conservatives saw it as a means of making the great mass of people less prone to embrace the radical ideas of demagogues. Little by little the movement made headway. By 1860 the principle of free public education was well established in most of the northern states and in a few of the southern ones.

The big gains in popular education came after the Civil War, when the high school became an American institution. The mere 100 high schools of 1860 had grown to 6,000 by 1900 and to more than 10,000 by 1910. An ever larger share of children found their way into the classrooms; between 1870 and 1890, the proportion of children attending school increased from 57 to 72 percent. In that same period the number of illiterates dropped from about one person in five to slightly more than one in ten. By 1910 only 7.7 percent of persons age ten or older were illiterate, and the figure for the white population was but 4.9 percent.

After the Civil War, colleges too entered a period of growth. Federal subsidies stimulated growth of the state universities, and wealthy benefactors such as Leland Stanford and John D. Rockefeller helped to establish or support private colleges. Higher education, like the ballot, became available to women as well as men. The state universities opened their classrooms to both sexes, and the strong current of women's suffrage helped to create such colleges as Radcliffe and Bryn Mawr.

Industrial and Technological Revolution

From the late eighteenth century onward, inventors and experimenters were busy devising machinery which would lighten man's burden. Eli Whitney in 1794 patented his cotton gin, which could clean fifty pounds of lint a day and was in such demand that he could not fill orders for it fast enough. When wearying fights with infringers caused him to look for another business, he set up a firearms factory, in which he anticipated mass production by introducing division of labor and standardized parts. In 1802 Oliver Evans finished work on a high-pressure steam engine which worked with greater efficiency than the one James Watt had designed. Five years later Robert Fulton, a portrait painter turned engineer, began runs between Albany and New York with his steamboat, the *Clermont,* and so successfully demonstrated the benefits of steam-powered transportation that a grateful government gave him a navigation monopoly.

Inventor after inventor gave the world new discoveries, new devices, new mechanical processes: Cyrus McCormick contributed the automatic reaper; Elias Howe, Jr., the sewing machine; Samuel Morse, the telegraph; Sir Henry Bessemer, the process of steel-making; Thomas A. Edison, dynamos, electric motors, and lamps. Man's ingenuity excited the imaginations of manufacturers, investors, and ordinary citizens. Some of the miracles seemed beyond belief. When Joseph Jefferson received his first telegram in Cumberland, Maryland, he hurried to the office to make sure he was really hearing from his partner in Baltimore. The miracle had happened to others as well, and, as he recalled later, "People were rushing to and fro with little messages in their hands, and stopping one another in the street to talk and wonder over the new event."

Slowly, then more rapidly, machines began taking over the work of man. Water power gave way to steam, which turned factory wheels and propelled boats and trains. By the time the nineteenth century ended, electricity had appeared as a new servant to run man's motors and light his cities, and the internal-combustion engine was on the threshold of helping man to conquer distance on land and in the skies.

growth of industry

Industrialization and mechanization hit America with the force of revolution between the end of the Civil War and the opening of the new century. In those years the nation shifted from an agrarian to an industrial economy. The impact was so great that a man of George Washington's time probably would have been more at home in the Holy Land in the days of Jesus Christ than in America in 1900. By the concluding years of the nineteenth century, steel bands of railroad tracks were binding the nation together. In 1869 the Union Pacific, pushing west from the Missouri River, met with the Central Pacific, building from San Francisco. For the first time one could cross the continent by rail. Within twenty years three other lines spanned the continent, and locomotives chugged over a network of still other lines linking scattered towns and cities. The number of miles of track jumped from 3,000 in 1860 to more than 193,000 in 1900, and as the century turned crews were laying down about 5,000 miles of new track a year.

Those tracks tied together a land rich in natural resources—coal, oil, ore, lumber—and rich in farm lands only partly tilled. Adventurous men saw the fortunes to be made in converting that raw bounty of nature into salable goods, and a swelling number of persons existed to develop those resources. Between 1870 and 1900, the population of the nation approximately doubled. It was fed by a swift stream of immigrants who poured into the country from all over the world. More than 11,500,000 of those foreign born flocked to America between 1870 and the end of the century, some 5 million of them in the decade 1881–1890 alone.

What happened is reflected in a few statistics. The number of industries of all types shot up from 140,000 in 1860 to more than 500,000 in 1900. In the sixty years from 1850 to 1910, the average manufacturing plant increased its capital more than thirty-nine times, its number of wage earners nearly seven times, and the value of its output more than nineteen times. Partly to feed the furnaces which made that expansion possible, miners dug out ten times as much coal in 1900 as they had in 1865. Between those same years, the estimated national wealth increased fourfold.

mass production

Behind those figures lay a system of production geared increasingly to standardized mass consumption. Eli Whitney had based his factory on that idea in 1798, when he used division of labor to turn out firearms with interchangeable parts. Samuel Colt, in the mid-nineteenth century, pushed that idea further than any manufacturer before him. When the government gave him an order for a thousand revolvers during the Mexican War of 1846–1848, he took over Whitney's plant to fill it. Then,

moving into a factory of his own, he perfected his system of interchangeable parts and his system of the production line to such an extent that
soon his mechanized factory with some 400 machines was making more
than 24,000 revolvers a year. Colt's factory grew into the largest private
arsenal in the world, his fortune to one of the largest of its time.

Henry Ford, too, built his fortune by refining the principles of mass
production. "Manufacturing is not buying low and selling high," he once
said. "It is the process of buying materials fairly and, with the smallest
possible addition of cost, transforming those materials into a consumable
product and giving it to the consumer." The assembly line kept automobiles which were in the process of manufacture flowing continuously
through Ford factories, dividing the work so that each employee made
his small contribution to the finished product.

Mass production is possible, Ford once wrote, only if the public is able
to absorb vast quantities of a product. It consists, then, of seeing a need—
one of which the public may be unaware—and of satisfying that need with
a product which in price and quality matches the wants of the greatest
possible number of consumers. By constantly lowering the price as consumption goes up, one can increase the number of consumers.

results of mass production

Mass production meant a greater use of products than ever before. Few
persons could afford an automobile if it had to be built entirely by hand
according to their personal specifications. But Henry Ford, by turning out
thousands of Model T Fords, all shiny black, all very much alike, put the
automobile within reach of the average wage earner. When industry after
industry adopted mass production techniques, the assembly lines of
America spewed forth a profusion of all sorts of products for the consumer. In time some economists warned the consumer that it was his
duty to consume in order to maintain the level of the economy. For
production was geared to mass consumption; if the consumer faltered in
his consumption, the wheels of industry slowed down.

Mass production also inevitably meant a standardization of product.
Aiming at a mass market, the manufacturer could not afford to take into
account the wishes of a small minority. The individualist who wanted
an automobile painted in a checkered pattern of heliotrope and orange
with leopard-skin upholstery could not count on the automobile makers
of Detroit to supply it. A bachelor once complained that food processors
never packaged food in the proper quantity for a single person. If anyone departed in any way from the tastes and wants of his fellow consumers, he could search in vain in the bazaars of the market place.

Mass production, furthermore, necessitated changes in the system of
marketing. Before the industrial and technological revolution hit with

full force, in the days before railroads had spun their web over the land, the manufacturer produced for local consumption. His market was a local area—his own community or region. The system of retailing made brand names relatively unimportant. Grocers weighed out sacks of flour for their customers from a large barrel, and druggists poured perfume from a big jug on their shelves. Mass production and its need for mass distribution helped to change all this.

The conception of markets changed from areas to people—to consumers living anywhere in this vast land. The manufacturer detected a need common to a large number of people and set about filling it. Advertising could make people aware of the product; the burgeoning transportation system could convey it to retailers anywhere in the nation, and they could get it into the hands of the consumer. In the late nineteenth century, manufacturers and retailers began to see the advantages which packaged goods had over those sold in bulk. As packaged goods replaced bulk goods, the brand name and the trademark became important assets, identifying the product in the mind of the consumer and giving the manufacturer control over a share of the market. The manufacturer of Evergreen Soap, for instance, had a fairly firm hold on the patronage of every consumer who swore by his product and would accept no other.

Inevitably advertising became the handmaiden of mass production and mass marketing. When production was little above the subsistence level, manufacturers had no great need to sell potential buyers on the benefits of their goods. Nor were elaborate advertising campaigns necessary when distribution was chiefly local or regional. The small newspaper notice, the handbill, the shop sign generally sufficed. But as manufacturers turned from local markets to national ones, they needed some inexpensive form of salesmanship. They needed, too, some way of impressing a particular brand name on the consumer's mind. Advertising was well suited to those tasks and its development, as we will see, had manifold effects on the media.

concentration of power

With industrialization came concentrations of economic power in almost every field. As profits flowed back to them, the industrial leaders had to reinvest their money if they were to earn a return on it. Sometimes they plowed it back into their own companies to enlarge them; if a company grew large enough, it often could gain control of its market by driving out competitors. Sometimes the industrial leaders invested in other industries and took control of them. Thus Andrew Carnegie, who had made a fortune in manufacturing iron, branched out into railroads, Great Lakes shipping, mining, and steel. Competition itself, paradoxically, often seemed to encourage concentration of control. A manufacturer who found that the high cost of raw materials put him at a competitive disadvantage, for instance, might buy control of their sources. Or a manufacturer whose competitive position was shaky might combine with others in his industry to dominate the market.

For a time, people quietly accepted unrestrained exploitation of natural resources and a supra-government run by financial and industrial barons who put private gain high above common good. The blessings of industrialization were so rich and so many that for a while they discouraged public interference with the magic system which had brought them. Eventually, however, Americans cried out in protest against the greed and arbitrary power of what seemed a new feudal order. The Interstate Commerce Act of 1887; the Sherman Anti-Trust Act of 1890; the Populist movement of the early nineties; the crusades conducted for the workingman by the metropolitan newspapers of the late nineteenth and early twentieth centuries; the muckraking movement among magazines for the decade after 1902—all were manifestations of popular indignation at the excesses of big business.

Urbanization

The rise of the city followed rapidly in the wake of the industrial and technological revolution. When the nineteenth century opened, America was still a rural nation. Only five towns had populations of more than 8,000 in 1790—Boston, New York, Philadelphia, Baltimore, and Charleston—and their combined population of under 135,000 accounted for only about 3 percent of the nation's total. Even thirty years later, only thirteen towns had populations of 8,000 or more.

But as the century wore on, as factories attracted uprooted farm laborers and as steamboats carried more and more immigrants to American shores, an increasing number of persons settled down to life in the city. When Lincoln became President, New York and its environs already comprised a metropolis of more than a million inhabitants.

The most rapid growth in urbanization came in the last two decades of the nineteenth century. In those years, the number of towns and cities with populations of 8,000 or more doubled. So did their populations, which jumped from 11 million to 25 million. By 1890 about one-third of the population was living in communities of 4,000 or more.

Redistribution of Income

The rise of democracy, industrialization, and urbanization were all forces apparent before the twentieth century opened. In the new century, a fourth development also made some impact on the media. It was a redistribution of income which narrowed the extremes in purchasing power and, in doing so, heightened the role played by the mass market in the American economy. Just as the rise of democracy brought a redistribution of political power, so this change brought a redistribution of wealth. Even today, of course, some Americans live in bleak poverty, many, many more in want; but gone is the great chasm which separated rich and poor when the new century opened.

In the single year 1900, when the dollar bought considerably more than it does today, Andrew Carnegie had a personal income of $23 million—all of it free of income tax. Life could hold baronial splendors for the happy few with such great wealth. In the 1870s, at his mansion near Hartford, Samuel Colt could afford to hire thirty men just to cut, trim, and roll his lawn each day. J. P. Morgan, as the century turned, could afford to build a temporary ballroom near his big brownstone house in New York to accommodate the 2,400 guests at his daughter's wedding.

But the slums were not far away, and in them, amidst squalor and misery, thousands of people tried to fight off starvation with pennies. Not far from J. P. Morgan's town house at 291 Madison Avenue, garment workers in 1900 were cutting cloth for men's hats for as little as two and a half cents an hour, finishing men's trousers for as little as thirty cents a day.

The great majority of Americans had low incomes in 1900. The average working man took home somewhere between $400 and $500 a year. If he could find work—and odds were that he would be idle several months a year—the unskilled laborerer could hope for the standard $1.50 for a ten-hour working day. His annual income was less than $460 in the North, less than $300 in the South. Thus, as Frederick Lewis Allen has pointed out, Andrew Carnegie's annual income was at least 20,000 times greater than that of the average working man.

Such disparities had largely disappeared by the mid-twentieth century. The graduated income tax; the coming to power of the labor unions; a changed attitude of business toward its public responsibilities; laws establishing minimum wages and fair employment practices; rising productivity; and full employment born of the war—all contributed to the emergence of a large, moneyed middle class.

Effects on the Media

The media, like other American institutions, changed under the impact of the rise of democracy, the industrial and technological revolutions, and the rise of the cities.

When common men got the ballot, they became self-governing individuals with a strong stake in government and, with varying degrees of intensity, took an interest in public affairs. The press became an important means of keeping the political system in operation. It also became a source of education, new cultural values, and entertainment for the working man and immigrant. The influx of foreign-born and the spread of free education both helped to enlarge the audience of the media.

The technological revolution changed communications from craft to industry. As in other fields, the machine took over many of the tasks once performed by man. Clattering Linotypes replaced the printers who had once set all type by hand from the California job case. Automatic presses replaced the crews who had once fed paper onto inked forms a sheet at a time. Photoengraving meant an end to the tedious process of reproducing drawings by painstakingly engraving them on wooden blocks, and color presses liberated the hundreds of women who had once tinted magazine illustrations with brushes.

As the technological revolution increased the size and efficiency of the printed media, it brought into being the new media: motion pictures, radio, and television. Electricity, harnessed for power in factories and transportation, was the foundation of radio and television from the start and of the motion picture after its first groping years. The electric trolley car and the radio set, then, descended from a common ancestor.

Urbanization brought together the huddled multitudes which made possible the large circulations of newspapers and magazines and, in later years, the huge audiences of local broadcasting stations. As cities grew in size and number, more and more of them could support daily newspapers, which reached their numerical peak of 2,600 in 1909. Then economic forces helped to reduce that number. Improved communications enabled the big dailies to expand their coverage and to win over readers once served by smaller papers. The big became bigger—the more so as high fixed costs brought about suspensions and mergers.

The redistribution of income raised the number of persons able to afford the media; when television came along after World War II, aerials sprouted from the rooftops of homes on both sides of the tracks. The expanding mass market intensified use of the media by advertisers as they competed for their share of the money in the consumer's fattened purse.

Working in combination, the political, social, economic, and technological changes we have talked about transformed the audiences of the media and altered the way in which the media derived their financial support. These same changes also contributed to division of labor within the media, standardization of policies and content, and concentration of ownership.

References

BEARD, CHARLES A., AND MARY R. BEARD, *The Rise of American Civilization* 2 vols. (New York: The Macmillan Company, 1931).

CASEY, RALPH D., "Communication Channels" in Bruce Lannes Smith,

Harold D. Lasswell, and Ralph D. Casey, *Propaganda, Communication, and Public Opinion* (Princeton, N.J.: Princeton University Press, 1946).

FISH, CARL R., *The Rise of the Common Man* (New York: The Macmillan Company, 1927).

NOSSITER, BERNARD, *The Mythmakers* (Boston: Houghton Mifflin Company, 1964).

SCHLESINGER, ARTHUR M., *The Rise of the City, 1878–1898* (New York: The Macmillan Company, 1933, 1940).

SINCLAIR, UPTON, *The Cry for Justice* (New York: Lyle Stuart, Inc., 1964).

STEFFENS, LINCOLN, *The Autobiography of Lincoln Steffens* (New York: Harcourt, Brace & World, Inc., 1931).

TARBELL, IDA M., *The Nationalizing of Business, 1878–1898* (New York: The Macmillan Company, 1936).

4

How

the Environment

Affected the Media

Lincoln Steffens, that keen analyst of American institutions, took a long look at newspaper journalism across the United States in 1897 and shared with the readers of *Scribner's* just what he had found. Talking shop the previous spring, the executive heads of some two score great newspapers had spoken of their properties as factories, he reported, and had likened the management of their editorial departments to that of department stores. "Journalism today is a business," he wrote with a little of the awe of discovery.

And by that time indeed it was. By then Joseph Pulitzer and William Randolph Hearst had clearly emerged as industrial capitalists of the press. They were demonstrating, even as Steffens wrote his article, that the newspaper could not only market news, it could manufacture it as well, as Hearst's reporters were doing, for instance, by tracking down criminals and building circulation as a result. Journalism had become a business in no small measure as a result of the forces discussed in the previous chapter, forces which brought a new approach to the content of the media, changed the way in which they earned their keep, increased their efficiency, standardized their products and made those products available to an ever increasing number of Americans.

Democratization of Content

One important effect was what might be called democratization of content. Newspapers, magazines, and books once addressed themselves to a small circle of educated, well-to-do readers. But in time, just as political power, education, and economic well-being spread from the élite to the population at large, so did use of the media. The printed media geared their contents to the common man's tastes, their prices to his purse. Movies, radio, and television, arriving after the democratic movement had achieved victory, appealed to a mass audience from the start. The tastes and interests of the great majority of that audience came to determine the fare that the media served and the ways in which they served it.

newspapers

In the early nineteenth century the newspaper turned from a small upper-class audience to a mass, popular audience. After the American Revolution, the majority of newspapers were mercantile or political publications for well-to-do businessmen and politicians. But as education came to the small shopkeeper, mechanic, artisan, and farmer, and as immigrants swelled the populations of the growing American cities, publishers saw a new market for their newspapers. They aimed at that new and expanding audience, and their newspapers accordingly were changed in content.

Newspapers with both content and price calculated to win a mass audience were officially born in September, 1833, when a young printer named Ben Day turned out the first issue of his New York *Sun* on a hand press. Day sold his paper for a penny, a price in sharp contrast with the six cents which publishers typically charged. He counted on a mass demand to bring him his financial return, despite a low profit margin, and he cannily concentrated on the street sales made possible by urbanization.

While the six-penny papers served their readers prolix stories of heavily political cast, Day wooed his audience with short, bright items about police-court doings, executions, suicides, wonders and marvels of the world, and local trivia. By 1835, when steam-driven presses were helping him turn out enough copies to meet the demand, Day was boasting that his *Sun* had a circulation of 19,360: "the largest of any daily newspaper in the world." After Day had shown that it could be done, other publishers levelled their newspapers at the audience he had tapped. The so-called penny press which thus emerged in the 1830s brought about some highly important changes in newspaper content.

Street sales, made possible by the growth of the cities, were important from the time of the penny press onward. Competition for the coins of the newspaper-buying public led at times, then and later, to sensation and to speed rather than to completeness in coverage of the news. Newspapers increased their emphasis on local news, human interest copy, crime reports. From about the time of the penny press, no doubt as a result of the agitation for women's rights, editorial copy slanted toward women's interests bulked large in newspaper fare. James Gordon Bennett, who in his New York *Herald* gave the inexpensive newspaper a wider appeal than other penny papers did, created the idea that the newspaper is primarily a purveyor of news, not of editorial opinion.

In 1883 Joseph Pulitzer bought the New York *World* and introduced a new journalism which served readers generous helpings of human interest, gossip, sensation, and scandal. What Pulitzer did was to revive the sensation of the penny press and present it with greater skill and better technical execution. His reporters, masquerading as inmates, wrote sensational exposés of conditions in jails, hospitals, and asylums; they were ever alert to witness incidents which, by bright writing and piquant headlines, could enliven the paper. But, in addition, Pulitzer gave his readers complete coverage of the news of the day and a liberal editorial policy which championed the cause of the workingman against the aristocracy of wealth and social position. His *World* crusaded, for instance, against graft and for a better reception of immigrants at Ellis Island, and it provided the poor with free Christmas dinners, summer excursions, and medical aid. Human interest and sensation were simply the bait necessary to lure readers, Pulitzer said, so that they could be exposed to the significant news and editorials.

Pulitzer's formula was well suited to winning him a large following. Technological advances by then had made mammoth circulations feasible, and urbanization had created the potential audience. New York's population increased 50 percent in the decade of the 1880s, and many of the newcomers were the immigrants who streamed to America in unprecedented numbers in that decade. Transported to a strange world, lonely and helpless, the immigrants turned first to their foreign-language newspapers for reassurance, comfort, aid, and escape. In Europe they had not read newspapers, which were priced beyond their means; village gossip had told them all they had needed to know. But in this unfamiliar land the immigrant papers, by keeping them in touch with the old country and helping them to adjust to the new, converted them to newspaper reading. From the foreign-language papers, they sometimes moved on to the English-language dailies. Their sons and daughters, scorning a foreign tongue, were quick to accept the American dailies.

Pulitzer knew his audience well. He had worked for a German-language newspaper in St. Louis and perhaps, as Oscar Handlin has sug gested, his skill in making the *World* attractive to a second generation of German-Americans contributed to its success. Dailies of the new journalism to which the *World* gave birth took on some of the characteristics of the immigrant press in their emphasis on entertainment, their willingness to help and advise their readers, and their identification with the welfare and emotions of immigrant groups.

At its extremes the democratization of the newspaper led to sensationalism. Ben Day's *Sun* is still remembered for one of the greatest newspaper hoaxes of all time, a series of stories by Richard Adams Locke which described life on the moon in straight-faced but thrilling detail. Pulitzer's new journalism was based on sensation, which was justified—or rationalized—as a means of gaining readers for worthier material. But in the circulation wars of the 1890s, sensation became an end in itself. In 1895 William Randolph Hearst, confident that he had mastered the techniques of mass journalism on the West Coast, bought the New York *Journal* and challenged Pulitzer's *World*. The unprincipled race for circulation which followed gave America its era of yellow journalism, marked by extravagant use of pictures; campaigns which championed the underdog with perhaps more cynicism than altruism; screaming headlines in oversize type, sometimes in bright color; manufactured and fraudulent news; and lurid Sunday supplements. The jingoism which permeated the content of the *Journal* and *World*, according to even so sober a historian of the press as Frank Luther Mott, was probably responsible for touching off the Spanish-American War.

Another debasement of the newspaper's democratization led to the gaudy era of tabloid journalism in the 1920s when, as someone once remarked, "sin sold for two cents a day." The tempo of life in America went into high gear after World War I. The postwar period was a time of speeding automobiles, faster trains, distance-eradicating airplanes; a time of frenetic dancing to the jazz which had come up the Mississippi from New Orleans; a time in which many Americans frantically sought to enjoy their new prosperity and to forget their disillusionment about politics.

Into that setting came the tabloid. Its smaller size, its generous use of pictures, its emphasis on brevity and brightness all made it well adapted to the person who read on the run. It completely identified itself with the masses from the start, and its formula was compounded of such elemental ingredients as birth, death, sex, and violence. Its photographs were often faked, retouched, and in appallingly bad taste; its stories were often ghost-written accounts in the first person; its headlines were cynically written to fetch coins: "He Beat Me—I Love Him," "I Am a Merry Gold Digger But I Don't Take Pay," and "Valentino Poisoned," with a smaller line of qualification, "Broadway Hears Doctors Deny." The tabloids demonstrated that the newspaper could compete with other amusements, which had expanded to include movies, radio, phonograph records, dance bands, and marathons.

the modern magazine emerges

The change from a class audience to a popular audience came to magazines about a half century later than it did to newspapers. The modern magazine of low price, popular appeal and large, national circulation emerged in the last decades of the nineteenth century. By then such fruits of democracy as popular education had resulted in a potentially large reading audience which magazines could serve. Machines had freed man from many irksome tasks and had given him the leisure time in which to read. The technological revolution had brought about the high-speed presses and other equipment which publishers needed to reach large audiences; a network of railroads had begun to permit distribution over a vast territory. But more than that, large-scale advertising was emerging as manufacturers sought to sell their mass-produced products across the entire land, and the magazine became a national medium for reaching the growing body of consumers with whom producers wished to get in touch.

Magazines had existed in America long before they turned to their popular audience, of course. Andrew Bradford began the first magazine in America in 1741, a few days before Benjamin Franklin launched the second. But even as late as the Civil War, magazines were short on advertising, short on circulation, and short in life span, and few of them ventured any great distance from their places of publication.

Even in 1890 the magazines leading in prestige and circulation—magazines such as *Harper's, Century,* and *Scribner's*—were edited for only a minority of the population, the well-bred society of culture and means. They were edited, as the late Frederick Lewis Allen once put it, for "the educated man, the philosopher, who is at home not merely in his own land and his own age, but in all lands and ages; from whose point of perspective the Babylonian seal-workers are as interesting as the Pittsburgh steelworkers; who lives not merely in the world of food and drink and shelter and business and politics and everyday commonplace, but in the timeless world of ideas." Their content was remote from the lives and interests of the great bulk of the population. Flipping through the pages of *Atlantic* and *Harper's,* readers of the early 1890s encountered such articles as "The Social Side of Yachting," "Along the Frontier of Proteus's Realm," and "A Successful Highwayman in the Middle Ages."

In the 1890s, S. S. McClure, Frank Munsey, Cyrus Curtis and a handful of other publishers revolutionized magazine publishing. They saw that an audience numbering in hundreds of thousands wished inexpensive reading matter. They also saw the important role that advertising was beginning to play in the American economy. They brought the content of their magazines into harmony with the tastes and interests of the great and growing middle class. Gone were articles of esoteric appeal. Instead, *Munsey's* and *McClure's* ran articles about athletics at Harvard, "the horseless age," the modern war correspondent, the writers of popular songs, cattle brands of the West, a man who supplied zoos with wild animals, and personages in the public eye. Edward W. Bok made Curtis' *Ladies' Home Journal* one of the first magazines to achieve a circulation of a million by giving his women readers practical advice on the business of running a home and rearing a family, by trying to elevate their standards in art and architecture, and by crusading against public drinking cups and patent medicines.

Publishers cut the prices of their magazines to what the average American could afford—prices that meant selling their publications for less than the cost of production. Frank Munsey put *Munsey's* on sale in 1893 for ten cents, a price so low that the major magazine distributors refused to handle it and he had to deal directly with retailers. Later Curtis sold his *Saturday Evening Post* for five cents, which did not even pay for the paper on which it was printed.

But the popular content and the low prices attracted readers by the tens of thousands. Advertisers paid handsomely to reach them. What the publisher lost from the sale of copies, he got back in revenues from the advertising which his large circulation attracted. As the redistribution of income narrowed the extremes in purchasing power, the great middle class became the market for mass-produced goods, and this was the readership toward which magazines generally were aimed. Publishers sought not just large numbers of readers; they also sought homogeneous groups of readers—groups tied together by common interests or by a common trade or profession. Thus, through magazines the advertiser could reach the particular consumer group most likely to be interested in his product.

books

Today the book remains the least democratic of the mass media, reaching, according to some estimates, perhaps 35 percent of the adult population. Americans simply are not book readers, as foreigners are fond of observing. And there is some truth in their generalization that while Europeans are readers of books, Americans typically are readers of periodicals. It is perhaps significant that fewer than a dozen of the 1,760 daily newspapers in the United States carry regular book-review supplements.

Hellmut Lehmann-Haupt, a historian of book publishing, has pointed out that in America books are somewhat dependent on the more powerful periodical press; in contrast, this dependence does not exist in Europe, where books have their own traditions, older and more substantial than those of periodicals. He has found a clue to the different attitudes Europeans and Americans take toward books in the different purposes for which printing was originally used on the two continents. In Europe, he says, printing was started in long-established communities as a cheap and easy way of duplicating the literary heritage of the classical and medieval world from the accumulated wealth of manuscripts. In America, on the other hand, printing almost at once became an important force in the colonization and westward expansion of the nation. He adds: "The European press primarily nourished thought; the American, action. In Europe printing from the very beginning meant 'books,' in America almost from the start, 'newspapers.' "

Even so, the book in its own way turned from a restricted class audience to a wider popular one, much as the newspaper and magazine did. In England the book-reading public shifted from the upper class to the middle class in the eighteenth century. By the middle of the century, the intellectuals and wits were no longer writing for their own little coteries. Instead, middle-class novelists such as Richardson and Fielding were writing for a middle-class audience, many members of which liked to think that they were improving themselves while they were being entertained. By the latter half of the century, literacy—and book-reading—had penetrated to the working class. The new reading public was still small compared to the mass reading public of today but large compared with that of previous periods. With that change in audience seems to have come a tendency to read more exclusively for pleasure and relaxation than in the past, a tendency which contributed to the development of the novel and to the craze for novel-reading which swept England toward the end of the eighteenth century.

Much of what Americans read until late in the nineteenth century came from England—that is, the words did, although the books did not. Books published in England were not protected by copyright in this country, and American publishers found it more profitable to reprint English books without paying royalties to the authors than to take a chance on American writers. One result was that cheap books for the masses in this country exceeded those in England. Even after the middle of the nineteenth century, when cheap reprints became common in England, American publishers could bring out those same books in New York as new offerings at twenty-five or fifty cents.

The audience for books in the American colonies was restricted by limitations of various sorts: the comparative lack of printing facilities, the high costs of books, the exigencies of establishing a way of life in a new land, the lack of widespread education. While the colonists evidently regarded books highly, they were hard to come by for the average man. The books that the colonists favored were, for the most part, serious or utilitarian works; there was little demand for books designed chiefly for entertainment or amusement.

Although the audience grew after the Revolution and the popularity of the novel in England was reflected in this country, it is doubtful that the average American could afford any sort of library until the 1840s. Up until then, well-printed books in cloth bindings were expensive and, with few exceptions, sold only in small editions. Cheap paper and faster presses helped to bring about a revolution in book publishing in the 1840s. Publishers not only brought out inexpensive periodicals laden with the most popular English novels but also published frequent "extras" or "supplements" which enabled the masses to buy this form of book from newsboys on the streets for twenty-five cents or less.

Thereafter, although there was a market for high-priced books, the inexpensive book was a part of the American publishing scene. Dime novels, cheap library sets, reprints, paperbacks all helped to satisfy the demand for inexpensive reading.

The first of two recent revolutions in the dissemination of inexpensive books came in 1939 when three publishers formed Pocket Books, Inc., to bring out twenty-five-cent paperbound reprints. Their success led other publishers to try paperback publishing, and the firms tapped thousands of retail outlets never before used for books—newsstands, drugstores, cigar counters, supermarkets, train stations, bus depots, airline terminals, post exchanges. In its first twenty-five years, Pocket Books, Inc. alone published nearly three thousand titles with total sales of a billion copies.

The second came in the early 1950s with the introduction of the so-called quality paperbacks. They were higher-priced than the early paperbacks, but their major difference was their appeal to highly educated readers, readers with sometimes amazingly esoteric tastes. Between 1956 and 1961, sales of these quality paperbacks increased from $3,712,000 to $15,738,000; from 7,700,000 copies to 25,900,000. In 1962, for the first time, there were more quality paperback titles on the market than mass appeal titles.

Paperbacks of all kinds accounted for less than 1 percent of book titles on the market in 1939; they accounted for nearly 33 percent in 1962, when their sales amounted to about $106,500,000, and in 1963 sales were $154,980,000.

In both England and America, then, books changed from a medium for the cultured few to one for the great middle class. Some authors continue to address themselves to a small audience of intellectuals, and their books remain an exceedingly important medium for the introduction of new ideas and for transmitting the cultural heritage. But many more writers gear their output to more popular tastes, thus making books also a medium of mass entertainment.

the electronic media

The electronic media—movies, radio, television—have histories differing sharply in some respects from those of the printed media. They themselves were the products of the industrial and technological revolution. They first appeared when the democratic movement was full-blown and when urbanization had brought together multitudes whom they could address simultaneously.

For those reasons, the electronic media were democratized from their very start, appealing to popular rather than to class audiences. Unlike the printed media, they require that their viewers or listeners attend to them in a single body; indeed, one characteristic of either radio or television is instantaneous transmission. This evening one can pick up a copy of Plato which has lain undisturbed on a library shelf for the past ten years and read it in utter solitude. But if one switches on his television set too late, his favorite program is gone forever and the millions who viewed it have become occupied with something else.

Technology, the nature of the electronic media, and the hard facts of economic support almost from the start dictated a mass audience for movies, radio, and television. Even a short, unpretentious movie or radio program is expensive to produce, requiring the services of many specialists: writers, producers, directors, performers, engineers, and technicians of many types. To spread its cost over a large base, its producer inevitably must address a mass audience.

The movies were plebeian from their inception. Originally they were little more than peepshows in penny arcades. In New York gay blades of 1894 could step up, one at a time, to squint into a battery of machines which amazed them with snatches of vaudeville acts, boxers in brief fistic encounters, dance bits, and short slapstick routines. When those jerky peepshow shorts were joined with the magic lantern, whole audiences could view a movie at the same time.

Almost at once, the movie became a popular addition to the bills of variety shows in vaudeville houses. Traveling carnivals and amusement parks pitched black tents where the curious could watch movies. In 1903 Edwin S. Porter filmed *The Great Train Robbery*, the first movie with a story, although its plot was rudimentary. Two years later the film was a hit at a small theater which had been opened in Pittsburgh with movies as its only attraction. In quick imitation, other small nickelodeons sprang up—five thousand within a year.

The forces of democracy, urbanization, and industrialization all were important to their growth. Most of the nickelodeons were established in large cities where there was a high concentration of foreign-born—a concentration fed by the immigration movement then at high tide—for the film was a form of amusement that recent arrivals to this country could afford and comprehend. The early silent movies were heavy on pantomime. Even if an immigrant could not translate the elementary subtitles, he could follow the plot, which transported him momentarily from his humdrum job and from the difficulties of adjusting to this strange land. It did so at a price he could afford; admission was a standard five cents, a small price for such entertainment.

An air of disrepute hung over the movies in those nickelodeon days. In an advertisement in the St. Louis *Republic* in 1910, one exhibitor commented on "the general known prejudice against the motion-picture theater," and in 1914 respectable people were a little surprised that a poet—Vachel Lindsay—should take the movies seriously enough to write a book about their art. The development of the motion picture was retarded in part by restrictions on its length. David Wark Griffith, developing the art of story-telling with film, was impatient to spread his techniques over more than a single reel. His backers grudgingly allowed him to go to two reels—about twenty minutes' showing time—but no more on the grounds that longer films would bore and fatigue audiences. An independent operator named Adolph Zukor was under no such restraint. He imported a four-reel French film play, *Queen Elizabeth,* starring the famous Sarah Bernhardt in the title role. Playing at the Lyceum Theater in New York in 1912, *Queen Elizabeth* attracted and impressed a fashionable upper-income audience which would never have patronized the nickelodeons. Zukor was convinced that the motion picture was capable, like the legitimate stage, of offering audiences a full evening's entertainment, and he went on to produce longer films of his own under the slogan, "Famous Players in Famous Plays." Griffith also gave impetus to the development of the feature film, breaking with his employers and striking off independently to film the epic, *The Birth of a Nation.* It opened at the Liberty Theater in New York in March, 1915, at a two-dollar admission.

Meanwhile, as the audience for the motion picture expanded, theaters moved from laboring-class districts into middle-class neighborhoods. Their accommodations became more comfortable, their decor more fashionable, their names more appealing or exotic, their prices of admission higher.

For a time the novelty of the movie itself brought many persons into the theaters. Each big production converted more of them to the movie-going habit. Paul Rotha, film producer and critic, has said: "During this period, therefore, from about 1912 until 1920, the very marvelling of the

general public, watching every new film with mouths agape, was sufficient for the studios to become established on a practical basis, capable
of mass production." By the time the novelty had begun to wear thin,
movie makers had begun to feature individual actors and actresses, and
the star system became entrenched. Charlie Chaplin, Mary Pickford,
Douglas Fairbanks, Francis X. Bushman, Beverly Bayne—their names
alone were enough to fill theaters across the nation.

As the motion picture grew up, the costs of film production mounted.
The new stars, who were valuable properties, commanded high salaries.
As studios chose locations other than rooftops and city streets for shooting scenes; as artificial lighting replaced the sun; as scripts took the
place of directors' and cameramen's improvisations; and as equipment
and techniques underwent refinements, more and more dollars were
needed to complete a feature film. To get the greatest return on their
outlay, movie-makers tried to turn out films which would appeal to the
widest possible public.

Similarly, commercial broadcasting from its inception aimed at a mass
audience. For a time, curiosity alone held listeners' ears fast to the
crackling headphones of the early receivers and brought the family together around the spluttering loudspeakers. But eventually curiosity
was not enough. Then advertising moved in to sponsor the various programs and made mass appeal inevitable. A person could listen to only
one program at a time; each advertiser wanted potential customers to
listen to *his* program, and he wanted them in multitudes. By 1929 radio
had begun to develop its star system, as the movies had earlier, and
famous entertainers from vaudeville and Hollywood headed for the
microphones of radio. To keep listeners clustered around their sets,
producers of the 1930s filled the air with variety hours, comedy shows,
and dramatic programs. Shows became more elaborate; an advertiser
who once had wooed listeners on a budget of $25,000 a year now some-
times spent ten times that on one star-studded variety show alone,
employing a staff of hundreds. Americans made the star performers their
darlings, and in everyday conversation echoed the taglines of their
favorite comedians. Listening to Edgar Bergen and Charlie McCarthy
became a Sunday evening ritual in millions of homes, and in some circles
a person who was not abreast of the latest doings of Amos and Andy was
a social oddity.

Increased Utilization of the Media

Predictably, as the media focused on the great mass of Americans,
the public responded by making greater use of the media than ever
before. The growth of population and the spread of free education

expanded the market for what the media had to offer, and technological improvements enabled the media to satisfy the demands of that market.

A few figures will show what was happening in the newspaper field. Within six months after Ben Day brought out the first issue of his New York *Sun* in 1833, the paper had reached a circulation of about 8,000, nearly double that of its nearest competitor, and by mid-1835 it boasted that its circulation of 15,000 far surpassed that of any other U.S. daily and, with one or two exceptions, that of any paper in the world. Sales had mounted to 30,000 by 1836, the year before Day sold his interest. The circulation of Joseph Pulitzer's New York *World* rocketed from 22,000 for its first edition in 1883 to almost double that four months later and to 100,000 at the end of about sixteen months. By the end of the 1880s, the *World's* Sunday edition was selling 250,000 copies.

Magazines entered their period of glorious expansion in the last years of the nineteenth century. Just before the Civil War, no magazine had as many as a half-million readers, a fairly modest circulation today, and publishers claiming circulations of even a quarter-million were considered hopeless braggarts.

Circulation figures of the nineteenth century are notoriously undependable, but they are reliable enough to show that magazine sales soared rapidly after publishers such as McClure and Munsey discovered the potentialities of the great middle-class market. *Harper's,* one of the leaders in prestige and circulation, was selling only about 100,000 copies a month in 1891. Two years later Frank Munsey brought out his ten-cent *Munsey's* with a popular audience as his target. His sales jumped from 40,000 for that first ten-cent issue to 275,000 at the end of the first year. Nineteen months after his start he had a circulation of 500,000. Nor was his experience unique. John Brisben Walker took over a languishing *Cosmopolitan* in 1889 and ran its circulation up from 16,000 to 400,000 in five years. *Hampton's* circulation soared from 13,000 in 1907 to 444,000 four years later. By 1904, when the *Ladies' Home Journal* achieved sales of a million copies, the magazine of mammoth circulation had come to stay.

Both the modern newspaper and the national magazine of large circulation and low price were made possible only through technological advances in printing and graphic arts. Large circulations had to await the development of high-speed presses which could turn out thousands of copies in a relatively short time. The first issue of Ben Day's *Sun* was produced on a hand press capable of turning out only 200 copies an hour. When Munsey brought out his first issue priced at ten cents, he had to stop production before the demand was satisfied so that he could get the next issue on the presses. Improved rotary presses increased the number of copies which could be printed in an hour; color presses made possible brighter editorial and advertising pages. Books, too, were able to expand their audience, limited as that expansion may have been, only as the result of speedier, more efficient composition and printing.

In the twentieth century, the new electronic media expanded their audiences just as the printed media had in the nineteenth but at a much more rapid pace.

Change in Support

Since publishing newspapers or magazines and broadcasting via radio or television is expensive, someone must put up the money if the communication system is to exist. Over the years, three major sources have been tapped singly or in combination. One has been subsidy by government, political party, religious denomination, labor, industry, philanthropic foundation, or some special interest group. Another has been the customer, who pays not only the cost of production but enough in addition to give the owner a profit. The third has been advertising, the sale of space or time.

With industrialization, the advertiser emerged as the man who indirectly pays the bills of the most substantial part of our communication system. Mass production and mass distribution required mass selling to bring together the buyers and sellers of goods and services on a nation-wide basis. Urbanization confronted retailers with the necessity of reaching a widening local consuming public. The redistribution of income enlarged the market, fattened the consumer's pocketbook, and helped to convert one-time luxuries into necessities. Advertising came to be the economic foundation undergirding the newspaper, magazine, and broadcasting industries.

Some of the media do get their money from other sources, of course. The customer ordinarily pays the bill for movies and books. Subsidy provides the support for the entire house-organ press. And while advertising is the chief source of revenue for periodicals and broadcasting, there are numerous exceptions. A number of radio and television stations are subsidized by colleges, for instance, and philanthropic friends often help to make up the deficit of such magazines of opinion and comment as the *New Republic* and *Nation*. In the recent past, there has been one fairly protracted experiment with a metropolitan daily which accepted no advertising, *P M*, which Marshall Field published in New York from 1940 to 1948.

Advertising, however, became the lifeblood without which most periodicals and broadcasting operations could not exist, and its development profoundly altered the role of the publisher. In an earlier day, the publisher of a newspaper or magazine was essentially the manufacturer of a product. He produced it as inexpensively as he could, and he took his profits from the difference between cost and selling price. True, some newspaper publishers also sold their editorial services to a party or faction, but once partisan journalism had declined, the publisher's big job was manufacturing a product for the reader. Advertising changed everything. The publisher became a dealer in both a product and a service. His product, as always, was a newspaper or magazine; his service was giving advertisers the opportunity to reach a large or carefully screened body of consumers with their sales messages. Thus advertising converted the newspaper and magazine—and later broadcasting—into adjuncts of the marketing system.

support in the past

In their earlier years newspapers and magazines counted little on advertising for revenue, and in its infancy radio did not lean heavily on the advertiser.

Colonial newspapers seem to have depended primarily on their readers for revenue, although the income from notices inserted by merchants and traders was by no means negligible by the mid-eighteenth century. In the political warfare after the Revolution, the subsidized newspaper came to be almost typical. Especially in the bitter political struggle between the Federalists and anti-Federalists in the early nineteenth century, newspapers drew some of their support from political factions and were frankly biased organs of views rather than news. From the time of the penny press onward, however, advertising became increasingly counted on to replace a newspaper's other sources of revenue, and by the early 1900s some critics were complaining that commercialism dominated the entire news and editorial operations of the American newspaper.

Although advertising was of growing importance to magazines after the Civil War, it did not really begin to alter the nature of the industry until the 1890s, when the national magazine of popular appeal, low price, and large circulation emerged. Well into the second half of the nineteenth century, many publishers refused or limited advertising because they thought it detracted from the dignity of their publications. They ran advertisements where they would be most unobtrusive, and they treated advertising people with little more than contempt. George P. Rowell, a young advertising agent, once approached the publishers of *Harper's Weekly*, a magazine in which he had been placing advertisements for his clients, to learn its circulation. The publishers were so shocked by such impertinence that they turned down his next batch of advertisements. Fletcher Harper refused $18,000 which a sewing machine manufacturer had offered for the back page of *Harper's* for a year. Harper thought the advertisements unworthy of his magazine, and he wanted the space to promote his own books.

Few of the magazines which accepted advertising actively sought it. One that did was *Century,* a magazine of prestige which circulated among well-to-do, well-educated readers. Its aggressive attention to advertising in the 1870s and 1880s has been credited with helping to break down the resistance of other leading magazines to carrying advertisements. In the 1890s Frank Munsey, as mentioned earlier, hit upon what has since become standard publishing practice. He sold his magazines for less than cost to win readers and took his profits from the advertising which a large circulation attracted. As Munsey and his followers demonstrated the money to be made from this practice, publishers joined the scramble for circulation and advertising.

Pioneer broadcasters regarded radio mainly as an instrument for the widespread dissemination of culture. Owners of receiving sets could support radio by paying an annual license fee, some thought, and manufacturers would profit handsomely from the sale of sets and other equipment. Advertising support was not ignored; rather, it was positively denounced. Even the advertising and broadcasting trade press carried articles warning of the harm that advertising could work. *Printers' Ink,* the advertising trade weekly, in April, 1922, declared that radio advertising would offend a great number of persons. "The family circle is not a public place," it observed, "and advertising has no business intruding there unless it is invited." That same year *Radio Broadcasting* magazine complained about the advertising, some of it indirect, which already had begun to invade the ether:

> Concerts are seasoned here and there with a dash of advertising paprika. You can't miss it; every little classic number has a slogan all its own, if it is only the mention of the name—and the shrill address, and the phone number—of the music house which arranged the program. More of this sort of thing may be expected. And once the avalanche gets a good start, nothing short of an Act of Congress or a repetition of Noah's excitement will suffice to stop it.

Not everyone was critical. When his son tuned in a theater orchestra on a homemade crystal set, William H. Rankin, head of a New York advertising agency, was at once impressed by the potentialities of radio as an advertising medium. Before recommending it to his clients, Rankin tested its effectiveness by buying time on WEAF in December, 1922, to give a fifteen-minute talk on advertising. The response to his talk included a $500,000 contract to handle the advertising of a new client, whose product Rankin immediately began promoting in a thirteen-week series of talks. Within weeks, Rankin was using radio as a means of extolling the products of other clients. His agency has been credited with being the first to use sponsored radio programs as advertising. Other agencies and their clients also recognized the possibilities of radio; broadcasters quickly saw the great commercial potential which lay in abandoning their dreams of cultural enrichment and dedicating themselves to building up audiences for the advertiser's sales pitch. In a few years the listening public had largely ceased questioning the desirability of using the air waves to sell products. By the time television came along, commercial sponsorship of broadcasting had become so ingrained in the system that any other means of support seemed beyond consideration.

Specialization of Function

Caught in the wind of industrialization and technological change, the communications industries in the nineteenth century began to use the division of labor techniques which were making possible mass production in other industries. Specialization was a concomitant of the growing size and increased efficiency which came to characterize the media in the twentieth century. It helped to bring about a standardized product, as it did in the manufacture of automobiles and soap and refrigerators.

the media

The one-man newspaper gave way to the newspaper manned by scores of specialists, each of whom made his particular contribution to its production. In 1835, when James Gordon Bennett started his New York *Herald,* he tramped the sidewalks for news, penned many of the stories which gave his paper its bright personality, managed the paper's business affairs, and even waited on customers at a desk consisting of a plank laid over two barrels. Most newspapers of that time depended little on regular reporters. The editor covered what local news he could and filled the rest of the paper with telegraphed news, items from his correspondents and clippings from exchanges. By the 1870s, the big metropolitan papers had cadres of what their staffs are today. By the 1890s the staffs, in number and in specialization of duties, were similar to what they are now. Specific persons were charged with supervising the reporters, handling telegraph news, covering sports and women's interests, writing literary and dramatic criticism, and so forth.

So it was with the other media. In his autobiography, *King of Comedy,* Mack Sennett tells of the first movie he made on his arrival in Hollywood in 1912. Thirty minutes after getting off the train, he and his co-workers saw a Shriners' parade on Main Street, too impressive a free spectacle to pass up. He sent one of his workers to a department store to buy a doll which could pass as his star actress' baby and a shawl for a head-dress

With just those props—and the parade—he improvised a script, cast it, and filmed it on the spot. He needed only a few additional scenes and closeups shot in his small studio to tie the film together. Thus Sennett performed many of the tasks which were later to become the province of specialists. He was script writer, property man, producer, director, and assistant cameraman.

Specialization invaded broadcasting as well. A program became not the creation of one man but the result of complex interactions among packagers of talent, producers, directors, script writers, performers, announcers, musicians. Network news commentators no longer prepared their own scripts. Instead, they read the work of their writers, who in turn depended on the network's own news-gathering facilities and other sources.

advertising

The advertising agency, which serves all media, also underwent a series of mutations which enlarged and specialized its functions. When Volney Palmer created the first advertising agency in the early 1840s, he and his followers were little more than space brokers. Those early agencies simply bought large blocks of space in newspapers and magazines and sold it in smaller units to advertisers. Neither the cost nor the selling price of space was standardized, and the agencies performed no services for advertisers beyond making space available.

After 1900 advertising agencies underwent what C. H. Sandage has called a period of consolidation. Advertising and agency rates became standardized, and agencies began to take on new functions on behalf of the advertiser such as copy writing and layout, media selection, and pioneer market research. Conducting research for their clients in which the techniques and findings of the social sciences were applied became an ever more important task of agencies in the twentieth century.

Today the advertising agency occupies an important and specialized position between advertiser and media. On the one hand, the media recognize the unique position of the advertising agency by allowing it to deduct a 15 percent commission from the standard or "card" rate on the advertising it places. This commission forms the basic income of an agency, although it also charges advertisers fees for collateral services. An advertiser who wishes to work directly with a medium pays the full card rate; he saves nothing by circumventing the agency. On the other hand, the advertiser recognizes the unique position of the advertising agency by assigning it responsibility for planning an advertising program, creating the ads, and placing the ads in the media most effective for the purpose. The advertiser may go far beyond that in making the agency his ally in his entire sales and marketing program. He may have the agency handle research involving his product, market, and individual advertisements; he may even call on the agency for help in developing a new product, creating its trademark, designing its package, and advising on its distribution.

Increased Efficiency

When President Abraham Lincoln delivered his Gettysburg address on a November day in 1863, he had the attention of about 15,000 persons at most. When President Franklin D. Roosevelt spoke to the nation over the radio shortly after the Japanese attack on Pearl Harbor in December, 1941, he was heard by some 62 million adults out of a possible 90 million. Thus did the new electronic media which came with America's industrialization enlarge a speaker's audience. They enabled man not only to communicate directly with multitudes but to do so instantaneously.

So, too, did the industrial and technological revolution increase the efficiency and speed of the older printed media. Before technology had borne such fruit as high-speed presses, Linotypes, telegraph, and railroads, newspapers were low in news volume, low in circulation, and costly to the reader. The screw-type press of Gutenberg, modelled on the wine press, gave way in the early nineteenth century to the iron Columbian press, which was operated by a system of levers but which still was capable of a severely limited hourly output. In 1825 American newspapers began to install steam-driven cylinder presses which could print 2,000 copies an hour, and a few years later some were using double-cylinder presses which could turn out twice that many copies. The steam-driven press eventually gave way to the electrically powered rotary press capable of spewing out 20,000 or more impressions an hour.

No longer was a newspaper restricted in size because of the slowness of its printing operations. Presses could quickly print newspapers for large audiences, and their speed meant timeliness in news coverage. The large audiences, coupled with speedy presses, meant large circulations, a factor in reducing costs through the principles of mass production.

Transmission of news and pictures to newspapers was hastened by the steamship, telegraph, camera, and photoengraving process. In the early nineteenth century, England was still thirty-six days away from America, as far as news was concerned, but the regular steamship runs after 1838 shortened the time to less than three weeks, then to two. After the Civil War, the trans-Atlantic cable put America in almost instant touch with Europe.

Even domestic news was slow in reaching print. In the War of 1812, news that New Orleans had successfully resisted the British reached New

York a month after Jackson's defense had taken place. Five days after New Yorkers learned that New Orleans had withstood attack, they heard that a peace treaty had been signed in London—signed two weeks before the battle at New Orleans.

Editors used a number of ingenious methods for speeding the gathering of news. Some sent reporters by fast boat to incoming ships to gather news from abroad and speed back with it. Some had swift pony express service between key cities. Daniel Craig earned a good living by meeting the incoming ships off Boston, summarizing whatever news from abroad he could collect, and hastening it to his clients by carrier pigeon. His system soon spread to Philadelphia and New York, where James Gordon Bennett offered Craig $500 for every hour that his *Herald* received the news ahead of its competitors.

None of those methods could compare with the telegraph, however. In its issue of May 25, 1844, the Baltimore *Patriot* ran a short telegraphic dispatch about an action by Congress, the first wire story to appear in an American paper. Two years later a column of telegraphic news briefs was a staple in all New York dailies. The amount of wire copy increased, and so did the number of papers carrying it, as soon as the first really co-operative news-gathering agency was formed in 1848. In time the press agencies expanded the coverage of individual newspapers. The telegraph made it possible for press agencies to flash news to papers within moments after an event had happened. The newspaper became able to take the entire world for its beat and to cover it immediately.

One spur to the adoption of more efficient methods of news-gathering and newspaper production was the Civil War. Public interest was intense; readers wanted to know what happened yesterday, not two or three weeks ago. Out of sheer competition, newspapers were forced to send corps of reporters and artists into the field. To issue the news promptly despite the exigencies of war, papers substituted machines for men wherever they could. The war forced *The New York Times* into buying additional presses, for instance, and into adopting the process of stereotyping—casting whole pages from papier-mâché matrices.

The spread of photoengraving in the latter part of the nineteenth century made the reproduction of artwork in newspapers and magazines swifter and less expensive than it had been by such earlier means as woodcuts, zincographs, and steel plates. In the days when woodcuts were still an important means of reproducing art, some nineteenth-century magazines, in their fight to speed production, assigned several artists to one illustration, each artist engraving one small portion of the whole. When all pieces were engraved, they were assembled into a single illustration. Photoengraving, of course, was a far less laborious, far less costly process, and it brought artwork to publications which previously had not carried it. Pictorial journalism gained in immediacy with the development of the portable camera, the flashbulb, the camera which could take photographs in natural light. Wirephoto, first used regularly in 1935, made possible the transmission of photographs from one distant point to another in a matter of minutes.

The efficiency of trains, planes, and trucks enabled publishers to put copies of their publications into the hands of readers soon after they had rolled from the presses.

Standardization of Product

If one compares the large metropolitan dailies on any given day, he is struck more by their similarities than by their differences. They are, by and large, alike in size, format, and general appearance. They use similar systems of headlining their stories, and many stories are written to a common pattern—summary lead atop an inverted pyramid structure which presents the facts in order of decreasing importance. The papers are even much alike in the national and international news they carry and in the relative play they give it.

Magazines too have become standardized. The circulation leaders play the same general themes, developed in basically the same way. A current issue of a given magazine is very much like the last issue; the editor has struck upon an editorial formula, a balance of content, which he repeats issue after issue. So it is with radio and television, in which the programming of one station is much like that of every other.

Such standardization of product was perhaps an almost inevitable consequence of the impact on the media of industrialization, mechanization, urbanization, and the redistribution of income. The media changed from crafts to industries—to industries utilizing such techniques of mass production as division of labor and heavy use of machinery. Efficiency required some standardized method of writing the script, the news story, the magazine article. Competition for a mass market required the media to aim at some low common denominator of interest and ability to absorb their messages. The media could no more afford to accommodate the tastes of the individualist than could the automobile makers of Detroit. The necessity of pleasing the majority contributed to a conservatism in the realm of ideas which seemed to characterize the mass media generally in the twentieth century.

newspapers

When newspapers became caught up in the industrial and financial expansion after the Civil War, they underwent a transition from personal ventures to corporate enterprise. The great editors whose papers were personal organs and whose names were familiar to their readers became a vanishing breed. On large papers and even on many of the small, the editor became a hired hand, aided by a paid staff, and the newspaper itself became an impersonal institution which objectively reported the news and anonymously editorialized about it.

There were good reasons for the shift from personal to corporate journalism. The growth of cities made possible large circulations, which required huge outlays in equipment and high operating costs. The demands of readers for efficient and expanded services added to the cost. The corporation could raise the money with greater ease and run the risks with less jeopardy than the entrepreneur. Corporate journalism, however, encouraged a mass-produced, standardized product.

So did the newspaper chain. There were the seeds of newspaper chains as early as Colonial times, when Benjamin Franklin was a partner in at least a half-dozen papers as a result of helping his former printers set up businesses for themselves as editors and publishers. However, chains really flowered in the late nineteenth century when consolidation and trusts were commonplace in virtually every field. William Randolph Hearst piled holding upon holding, and Frank Munsey recklessly bought, merged, and killed newspapers in an unsuccessful attempt to realize his dream of a great national chain of papers run from a common headquarters. Between 1878 and 1917, E. W. Scripps and Milton McRae started twenty-seven newspapers and bought another five as links in their chain. Although there were exceptions, chain newspapers tended to be standardized in editorial policies, in appearance, or both.

While the press associations such as Associated Press and United Press enlarged the coverage of individual newspapers; while syndicates offered papers a variety of features they otherwise could not have afforded, both also added to standardization. The dailies subscribing to the wire services gave their readers essentially the same account of events. And those accounts were written to a standard formula of summary lead and inverted pyramid which discouraged the individualist.

magazines

When magazines fervently embraced advertising in the late nineteenth century, they became inextricably joined to the marketing system. Content was the bait with which the publisher coaxed an audience to his magazine—an audience of consumers valuable to the advertiser for its sheer size, its homogeneity, or both. After a publisher had struck upon a happy balance of content which attracted the desired readers, he was reluctant to change it. Hence every issue of a given magazine tended to be similar to every other.

Such standardization of content was a natural outgrowth of the quest for a popular market and the mass production necessary if a magazine was to compete successfully for that market. Well into the nineteenth century, when magazines were still generally edited for just the élite few, an editor could remain an aloof arbiter who chose what he liked from among the contributions of aspiring writers. However, the editor of a mass-produced magazine tailored to the interests of a specific popular audience could not count on filling it with stories and articles selected from chance contributions. The types of material he used and the distinctive handling his writers gave it determined the editorial personality of his magazine, and it was that personality which caused readers to buy. Thus an increasingly large proportion of magazine content came to be planned by the staff. Walter Hines Page demonstrated the feasibility of such planning during his tenure as editor of the *Forum* from 1887 to 1895. He astounded his colleagues by jotting down a table of contents months in advance of publication and then scouting out writers qualified to produce the articles he wanted. Today the major magazines have adopted Page's basic idea of editorial planning. On many publications, the staff originates ideas for a high percentage of the features the magazine carries. Some of the ideas are assigned to established free-lance authors who research and write the articles. Others are developed by staff writers. In either instance, the net effect is standardization.

Imitation also contributed to the standardization of magazine fare. When a publisher succeeds with an original publishing idea or with an adaptation of an old one, competitors rush to bring out imitations in order to get a share of the market. In 1922, a young man named DeWitt Wallace brought out the first issue of a modest little magazine which summarized what he considered the best articles from the magazines of the day. He called it the *Reader's Digest,* and readers were soon flocking to it. Other publishers brought out imitations. Eventually, a whole new category of magazines—the digests—had sprung up. Similarly, other new categories arose as imitators aped successful new ventures: the fact detective magazines, the confession magazines, the news magazines, the picture magazines, the men's adventure magazines.

other media

Standardization of content and technique became a characteristic of the other media as well. Movie producers, by capitalizing on what they thought to be peaks of public interest, brought forth cycles of movies of similar theme—gangster films and lavish musicals in the 1930s, for instance, and neorealistic films in the postwar 1940s. Quite often motion pictures simply reiterated the content of the printed media. Gambling millions on a single picture, producers often tried to reduce their risks by filming stories which had already proved their success in magazines or books or on the stage. "I think it's a legitimate attitude considering the economics of the industry," Ernest Lehman, a veteran script-writer, told

Variety. "I can understand the position of the proaucer. He has seen how it played previously and knows what the critics have said. If he has to go with an original, he's not sure what he's getting."

Moreover, the movie script was developed according to a conventional formula. There was small room for the experimentalist, the individualist. "There's no room in motion pictures for writers who want to write for themselves," Lehman said. A writer who wants to express himself had "better go off to some other field where millions of dollars are not riding on his personal aspirations."

On November 1, 1926, the National Broadcasting Company was formed —in time to broadcast the 1927 Rose Bowl Game—and thereafter three or four major networks contributed to the standardization of broadcasting by feeding the same programs to thousands of local stations. Even if the listener had a choice of rival networks, he was likely to get essentially the same sort of fare on each—one soap opera or another in the morning, for instance, or one variety show or another in the prime evening hours.

Television settled comfortably into the rut of standardization which radio had already plowed. It was as imitative as magazines and movies. A successful program of any type bred a rash of others, a point well illustrated by the large number of quiz shows, domestic comedies, and Westerns of the mid-1950s and early 1960s.

Standardization of media fare worried some serious students of the communication system. Standardization encouraged conformity, they warned, and posed a threat to the free flow of information and ideas essential to a democratic society. The danger was sharpened by three characteristics of the media which we will consider in the next chapter: large size, small number, and costliness.

References

BERELSON, BERNARD, AND MORRIS JANOWITZ, eds., *Reader in Public Opinion and Communication*, enlarged ed. (New York: The Free Press of Glencoe, Inc., 1953).

COMMISSION ON FREEDOM OF THE PRESS, "The Communications Revolution," *A Free and Responsible Press* (Chicago: University of Chicago Press, 1947).

EMERY, EDWIN, *The Press and America: An Interpretative History of Journalism*, 2nd ed. (Englewood Cliffs, N.J.: Prentice-Hall, Inc., 1962).

GOODMAN, EZRA, *The Fifty-Year Decline and Fall of Hollywood* (New York: Simon and Schuster, Inc., 1961).

HEAD, SYDNEY W., *Broadcasting in America: A Survey of Television and*

Radio, Chaps. 9 and 10 (Boston: Houghton Mifflin Company, 1956).

KOBRE, SIDNEY, *The Development of the Colonial Newspaper,* Columbia University Ph.D. thesis (Pittsburgh, Pa.: 1944).

LEE, ALFRED McCLUNG, *The Daily Newspaper in America: The Evolution of a Social Instrument* (New York: The Macmillan Company, 1937).

LEHMANN-HAUPT, HELLMUT, in collaboration with Lawrence C. Wroth and Rollo G. Silver, *The Book in America: A History of the Making and Selling of Books in the United States* (New York: R. R. Bowker Co., 1951).

MOTT, FRANK LUTHER, *American Journalism: A History, 1690–1960,* 3rd ed. (New York: The Macmillan Company, 1962).

PETERSON, THEODORE, *Magazines in the Twentieth Century,* 2nd ed. (Urbana: University of Illinois Press, 1964).

RAMSAYE, TERRY, *A Million and One Nights: A History of the Motion Picture* (New York: Simon and Schuster, Inc., 1964).

SCHRAMM, WILBUR, ed., *Mass Communications: A Book of Readings,* 2nd ed. (Urbana: University of Illinois Press, 1960).

——, ed., *The Process and Effects of Mass Communication* (Urbana: University of Illinois Press, 1954).

5

The

Industrial

Structure of the Media

Recovering from a virus infection in 1957 in his rambling ten-room house in Ramsey, New Jersey, J. Fred Muggs, the world's richest and most successful chimpanzee, was keeping his future plans to himself. As *Time* magazine told it, Manhattan's Radio City was abuzz with the news that the chimp was quitting NBC after spending most of his life on Dave Garroway's "Today" show. First reports had it that Muggs was retiring on account of poor health and old age. But his manager soon confirmed what many envious TV colleagues suspected: Muggs had so many offers that he hardly knew where to start raking in the money. And big money it was, too. At NBC, where he started his television career at a handsome $250 a week, Muggs was making an incredible $1,275 when he quit and padding it out with sizable income from manufacturers who used his name. Insiders estimated that the charmer of American TV audiences might earn as much as $1 million before being laid to rest in some animal cemetery for cherished and pampered pets.

About the same time, a former night club comedian revealed that he was making $200,000 yearly as, among other things, a liquid lead pencil, a three-way lamp, a glass of beer, and a cup of instant coffee. The versatile performer was TV mimic Allan Swift, who provided the special sound effects on some 400 commercials and the voices millions of listeners mistakenly believed belonged to tennis champion Pancho Gonzales, golf champion Cary Middlecoff, and bowling champion Don Carter.

Some critics regarded the bonanzas that fell to Messrs. Muggs and Swift as proof of the bizarre and counterfeit character of television, if not the mass media in general. But what is more important is that such windfalls are possible only in an industry that can afford them. In less than a decade, the newest medium became big business, joining the other big businesses of mass communication.

But the dramatic increase in population, the development of immense urban and then national markets, and the increased public utilization of the media did not lead, as one might have expected, to a relative increase in the number of communication units and a diffusion of ownership and control. On the contrary, economic and technological factors resulted generally in a disproportionate number of units to owners. For example, the number of newspapers, instead of increasing with the rise in public utilization, decreased. And as revenues of the newspaper industry soared, there were fewer, rather than more, successful publishers.

Structure of the Newspaper Industry

The creation of mass markets that only large and costly units could efficiently service led inevitably to a contraction of ownership in many cities and towns and thus to the development of newspaper chains. The high point in the number of newspapers published in the United States came in 1909, when there were 2,600 daily publications. Thereafter, consolidation became the dominant theme.

As daily circulation neared 60 million and virtually every literate adult in the United States read at least one newspaper a day, the trend toward elimination of competition continued, especially in cities of fewer than 50,000. In the first half of the twentieth century, more than 2,000 new daily newspapers (including those changing from weekly to daily) were started. But, during the same period, 1,947 suspended publication or became weeklies, 547 disappeared through merger or consolidation, and at least 302 local combinations took place. At the same time, the number of newspaper chains increased from three, publishing 62 newspapers, to seventy, publishing 386, with more than two-fifths of the daily and one-half of the Sunday circulation. In the 1950s there were scarcely more than one hundred cities with competing daily newspapers. In twenty-five years the percentage of one-publisher, or monopoly, cities rose from 57 to 92. In ten states there was not a single city with competing daily newspapers. In twenty-two states not a single city enjoyed competing Sunday papers.

Altogether, 40 percent of daily newspaper circulation was noncompetitive. Today more than 95 percent of American newspapers are monopolies.

Consolidation of newspapers is not, according to Frank Mott, a strictly recent tendency; it can be found in all periods of American journalism. But since World War I, the skyrocketing cost of newspaper publication has been a strong influence in accelerating that tendency. Typesetting machines, high-speed presses, engraving plants, and other expanding mechanical facilities meant not only increased operating costs, but constantly larger investment. Melville E. Stone established the Chicago *Daily News* in 1876 with a few thousand dollars capital, and Adolph S. Ochs was able to acquire *The New York Times* twenty years later for only $100,000. But after the turn of the century, prices of daily newspaper properties rose to million-dollar levels. Stone's *Daily News,* for example, sold for $13 million in 1925. In 1963 two Omaha dailies were sold for $43 million.

Another factor encouraging concentration of the daily newspaper was the standardization of its product. Competition for mass markets discouraged individuality, in newspapers as well as in magazines, broadcasting, and motion picture productions. A newspaper which appealed to only a segment of the market with a distinctive news or editorial policy often found it could not survive in competition with mass-appeal newspapers whose circulation attracted the bulk of the advertising dollar. Moreover, readers of only one newspaper usually chose not the paper which maintained some measure of individuality but the omnibus publication which had given up its individuality and relied on syndicated material and wire service copy.

entry and survival

Then, too, in the typical American town more newspaper publishing ventures were attempted than the economy could support. Some newspapers—for example, those founded solely as voices of political parties or other interest groups—went out of business simply because they could not win general community support. Others were founded by men who went into the business apparently on the assumption that to make money it was only necessary to "buy newsprint white and sell it black." They soon discovered that, aside from the problems of editing a mass medium, such factors as the rigid advertising and circulation rates made newspaper publishing a dubious enterprise at best. For the new entrant today, the problems are even more formidable.

Both in procuring their raw materials and in marketing their products, newspaper publishers exhibit the familiar behavior of monopoly and oligopoly. As buyers, they use the customary pressures for keeping down costs; as sellers, they maintain rigid advertising and circulation rates, discriminate by rate differentials, and practice block selling of space in morning and evening newspapers in combination. The typical newspaper pays out for newsprint roughly one-third of its revenues, which is just about what it receives in circulation revenue. Practically all newsprint is sold in carload lots under long-term contracts, mostly to large publishers. Those who cannot afford carload purchases get their newsprint from jobbers, brokers, and paper merchants at open-market prices, which are sometimes higher by 10 percent or more than the carload rates.

Procurement of syndicated features and wire services is, as Theodore J. Kreps has pointed out, "no less difficult for the new entrant." The syndicated feature business is dominated by four major companies: AP Newsfeatures, King Features, NEA Service, and United Features. Most franchises provide for exclusive territories. Furthermore, package selling enables large publishers to buy up rights to more features than they print. Oligopoly is likewise a chief trait of the wire services. Until recently, Associated Press, United Press, and International News Service dominated the American market. Now there are only two; in 1958, United Press acquired International News Service and became United Press International.

The new as well as the smaller newspaper are confronted in many markets by chain organization. Chains, especially of large newspapers, have certain special advantages. Notably, they make wider use of editorial and feature writers. It is easier for them to obtain new funds from the capital market. They engage in block merchandising of space to national advertisers, in centralized and large-scale research, and in bulk purchases of newsprint, ink, and equipment. They also are better able to make maximum use of specialized technical and managerial services.

In sum, except in some burgeoning suburban markets and publishing situations where a publisher can take advantage of photoreproduction and cold type, the newspaper business is essentially a "closed" industry.

Structure of the Magazine Industry

The modern magazine succeeded as a mass medium mainly because of its original role as an adjunct of the marketing system. Like the newspaper, it was able over the years to appeal to an expanding range of tastes and interests. But, unlike other media, most magazines were designed for homogeneous audiences or special-interest groups. And, in contrast to the newspaper, their circulation was nation-wide. Thus, although many were directed to specialized audiences, magazines in general developed as a mass medium in the sense that they appealed to large numbers in a national market which cut across social, economic, and educational class lines.

Some magazine publishers, notably those of pulps and digests, derived their income from a small unit profit on a high turnover of copies instead of from advertising. Still others relied on trade associations, fraternal organizations, and professional groups to make up any deficit. But with the rise of national advertising, the great majority—both in numbers and circulation—were closely bound to the marketing system. In effect, magazine publishing became fundamentally a matter of the publisher's deciding on a consumer group which advertisers wished to reach, devising an editorial formula to attract and hold that group, and then selling advertisers access to it.

The omnibus newspaper and broadcasting network, like the magazine, are also adjuncts of the marketing system. For they, too, seek to deliver mass audiences to the advertiser. But, in terms of *originating* a market for the advertiser, the relationship of magazines generally to their audiences is quite different from that of other media. Some magazine publishers have first developed a publication and then let both readers and advertisers seek out the magazine. But the typical magazine follows a less risky strategy. It devises an editorial formula that can be counted upon to attract a homogeneous and relatively small special-interest group; then, it assembles advertisers who want to address that particular audience.

entry and survival

Today, a relatively few circulation leaders dominate the consumer magazine industry. But taken together, American magazines reflect virtually every shade of thought and opinion, virtually every interest of their readers. And, despite the fierce competition and the uncertainties, magazine publishing on a small scale is perhaps the communication most accessible to the new investor. What counts most is the idea. If the entrepreneur has a fresh idea for a magazine, there are likely to be persons willing to finance it. If he can sustain his magazine while seeking acceptance by readers and advertisers, there is always some chance that he will achieve a modest success. And there is a remote chance that he will wind up in the company of the giants.

The ease of entry into the magazine industry, in contrast to the formidable obstacles encountered in newspaper publishing, broadcasting, and motion pictures, explains why the industry today is dotted with relatively small units, small staffs, and modest offices with little equipment. The small magazine publisher ordinarily does not invest in presses and equipment, but instead lets out his printing on contract. A publisher who does not wish to compete with the large-circulation leaders can still launch a successful magazine on a few thousand dollars. Survival, however, is a different matter. Factors which make it easy for one publisher to enter the industry make it easy for competitors to enter, also. Successful magazines invariably breed imitators, for the publisher cannot entirely hide the formula for his success, forced as he is by the nature of publishing to exhibit his best ideas in public. Then, too, readers are fickle and it requires a particular genius to anticipate changes in tastes and interests before they are reflected in declining circulation.

cost and concentration of ownership

Although the magazine industry has hundreds of relatively small circulation producers, a few large publishers account for a high percentage of total magazine circulation and of the money advertisers spend on the medium. For example, one year some 4,600 periodicals had a combined per-issue circulation of nearly 400 million. That same year, forty magazines with audiences of at least a million had combined sales of about 90 million copies an issue. Thus, those forty magazines accounted for about 23 percent of the aggregate circulation of more than 4,500 periodicals. The gross advertising revenues of the top five magazines in 1963 were about 40 percent of the total which national advertisers spent in consumer magazines. Of these giants, Time Inc., in the forty years after its inconspicuous founding in 1923, had grown into a business grossing some $357 million. Alone, Time Inc. enterprises in 1963 took in more than one-fifth of total revenues from national advertising in magazines. One of its magazines, *Life,* led all American magazines in gross advertising revenues with $144 million; another, *Time,* was third with $61 million.

In the large-circulation field, costliness is as characteristic of magazine publishing as it is of newspaper publishing, broadcasting, and motion-picture production. Harlan Logan, writing in *Magazine Industry* in 1949, estimated that a new publisher of a mass-circulation magazine needed between $7,500,000 and $15,000,000 to finance a general weekly, with the odds three to one against success. A new general monthly, he calculated, would take from $4 million to $7 million, and the odds would be 10 to 1 against success. By the 1960s, costs were perhaps 50 percent greater than when Logan made his estimates, and the odds against success appreciably higher.

The giants which dominate circulation and advertising in the magazine industry are vast, complex organizations, some of them with extensive foreign operations. Curtis Publishing Company has employed as many as 10,770 persons at one time. It owns forests and paper mills, printing and engraving plants, a subdivision for conducting market surveys and statistical studies, and agencies for soliciting subscriptions and for distributing its own and other magazines. Time Inc. normally employs more than 3,000. Its own news-gathering organization, third largest in the world, ranks just below the Associated Press and United Press International. The company has a special division to operate its activities in foreign countries. In addition to its magazines, Time Inc. owns real estate, radio and television stations, a large export business in magazines, an organization selling technical developments to the printing and allied trades, sizable investments in paper-manufacturing concerns, and a book division.

Cross-media ownership existed in the magazine industry even before the national magazine emerged. In the nineteenth century, several leading magazines were offshoots of book-publishing houses. In this century, magazine publishers have owned book-publishing firms, newspapers, newspaper syndicates, radio and television stations, motion-picture studios, and even book clubs. This tendency is a characteristic of mass media as a whole and is generally considered to be the result of competition for mass markets and for advertising revenue with its demand for large capital expenditure, consolidation of control, and diversification of capital. Over the years, the different media have been interested primarily in their own fields; with few exceptions, even those who owned other communication media regarded them as sidelines. Not many were interested in building communications empires resting on ownership of different kinds of media. And, if anything, magazine publishers were interested in building magazine empires. The two publishers who built up vast communications empires, Frank Munsey and William Randolph Hearst, both hit their stride in publishing at a time when consolidations, trusts, and concentrations of economic power were the outstanding characteristic of American economic life. In comparison with these two empire builders, the cross-media holdings of other publishers in the first half of this century were modest. And the successors to Hearst and Munsey have come generally from the newspaper field and, more recently, from the motion-picture industry.

Structure of the Broadcasting Industry

The rise of radio as a big and costly purveyor of news and entertainment and thus as a full, fearsome competitor, began in 1920 with the broadcasting by station KDKA of the results of the presidential election of that year. Broadcasting was at the time literally a free-for-all. There was no effective regulation of the industry, the powers of government being limited to those of a 1912 act concerned only with radio telegraphy. There was chaos for more than seven years. Government regulation, finally requested by the industry itself, was slow in coming because of official reluctance to interfere. The economic objective of the industry during this period was not revenues from broadcasting, but profits from the sale of receiving sets. Many groups pioneered in broadcasting, but with no clear idea of how they were to cover costs. David Sarnoff of the Radio Corporation of America has been quoted as arguing at the time that radio deserved endowment "similar to that enjoyed by libraries, museums, and educational institutions." He believed, according to Gleason Archer in his *Big Business and Radio,* that "Philanthropists would eventually come to the rescue of a hard-pressed industry."

radio goes commercial

Not until the potentialities of broadcasting in the ever-widening marketing system were recognized did the radio industry begin to flourish. Sponsored programs were first broadcast experimentally in 1922 on station WEAF. Thereafter, they developed rapidly—though not without outcries from the public and government officials. For example, the then Secretary of Commerce Herbert Hoover, at the First Annual Radio Conference in Washington declared, "It is inconceivable that so great a possibility for service . . . be drowned in advertising matter."

Congress finally recognized the confusion resulting from the lack of organization over the use and allocation of wave lengths and passed the Radio Act of 1927. The broadcasting industry then began to develop its four main contemporary characteristics: submitting to legal and administrative control by a system of federal licensing; providing mass entertainment; acting as an adjunct of the marketing system; and concentrating its operational control in network organization.

Three million radio sets were available to listeners who tuned in to the radio coverage of the 1924 presidential election. The newspapers' fear of radio as a competitor for mass markets seemed unjustified, despite radio's spectacular advance as an advertising medium. In 1929 newspapers carried a record $160 million worth of advertising as compared to radio's $40 million. However, with the depression of the thirties and the impact of World War II, radio's percentage of total advertising volume steadily rose from 3.9 percent to a peak 15.7 percent at war's end. Meanwhile, that of newspapers fell from 33.1 percent to 30.9 percent. Magazines, too, suffered heavy losses in percentage of total revenues. With the full development of television in 1949, all other media (including radio) felt the impact of its competition. No other medium had ever grown so spectacularly. Even so, however, the dollar volume of advertising in all media continued to grow.

Radio, unable to get the news from the press associations and under attack for pirating copy from newspapers, undertook to gather news itself. The Press-Radio Bureau, established in Washington in 1934, had

245 subscribers. Five new services jumped in. Finally, in 1935, the United Press and International News Service obtained permission from the American Newspaper Publishers Association to sell full news reports to stations. With the collapse of the newspapers' organized efforts to curtail news broadcasting, radio was entering maturity. The Associated Press, a newspaper-owned cooperative, joined the competition in 1940 and eventually made radio stations eligible for associate membership. Sets in use increased from 13 million in 1930 to 51 million in 1940. The number of stations jumped from 605 in 1935 to 815 in 1940; total advertising revenue nearly doubled. Then the number of stations jumped to 1,025 in 1945, and to more than 2,500 in 1955, and advertising volume climbed to more than $500 million. In 1963 there were more than 5,000 radio stations and more than 600 television stations; broadcasting revenues were at about the 2 billion mark.

Almost from its beginning broadcasting—like newspaper and magazine publishing—found itself characterized by standardization of product, consolidation of capital, bigness, and costliness. As Emery and Smith observe, "Those who complained about a sameness in their newspapers and their mass-circulated magazines fared little better when they turned to radio and television." And standardization of product was not confined to simultaneous broadcasting of programs over a national network of outlets. As in publishing and the Hollywood film, it was manifested in format and story line, and in bandwagon imitation of successful program "innovations" that seldom were more than conventional fare with the names changed, or, in the case of television, with video added.

concentration of ownership

The history of radio (and of television) illustrates both the trend toward concentration in the mass media generally and its persistence despite traditional antitrust sentiment. The Radio Act of 1927 and the Communications Act of 1934 gave the government power to protect against monopoly in broadcasting that it has never had with respect to publishing. The Federal Communications Commission's *Report on Chain Broadcasting,* made public in 1941, revealed in stark detail the extent of the controlling interests and contractual arrangements of the two major networks, National Broadcasting Company and Columbia Broadcasting System. Although the FCC ordered the dissolution of the RCA empire, and although the Blue network was sold (and became the American Broadcasting Company), the major radio networks continued to grow steadily. In 1963, four radio networks had more than 1,350 station affiliates. Behind the national networks lay several regional chains with contractual arrangements for advertising and programming.

network domination

As television stations began to take form after World War II, their owners scrambled to affiliate with the four national networks which dominated the industry. By the summer of 1955, there were 432 television stations, including 13 non-commercial educational stations. More than half of them were served by only three networks—ABC, CBS, and NBC. And, in September of that year, control was further concentrated as the fourth major network, Du Mont, ceased operations. This development moved Frieda B. Hennock, a former FCC commissioner, to state that the major networks maintained a "life and death control over TV." Quoting the president of Crosley Corporation, she warned that networks "seem increasingly inclined to consider individual stations as push-button operations, automatic outlets which cater to programming networks' desires." She called for an "immediate, vigorous network investigation [by Congress] to get at the monopolistic grip" exercised over stations, advertisers, programming, and talent "owing to the monopoly of scarcity created by the networks." The three major networks in 1963 counted more than 600 TV stations among their affiliates.

As the conquest by air of the nation's mass markets brought television programs into most American homes, the costs of broadcasting became enormous. To get even the smallest television station on the air, one needs to invest more than $250,000 in building and equipment. A medium-size station might represent an investment of approximately $1 million. The costs of programming also are impressive. Each of the hour-long Ed Sullivan programs in the early sixties was estimated to cost $232,800 for time, talent, and production. The Ford Motor Company once provided a CBS executive with $12 million for programming, $250,000 a year as salary, and residual interest in the thirty-nine shows he was to produce.

television gobbles up the advertising

Although television required development of new and costly advertising techniques, the growth of the TV advertising dollar has been spectacular from the outset. In 1946, no advertising was carried by the six television stations then existing. But, despite the temporary FCC freeze on the processing of license applications in 1948, by January 1950 the number of stations had reached 98; there were more than 4 million receiving sets in American homes; and the volume of advertising exceeded $170 million. The following year, TV's advertising volume nearly doubled. By 1954 it topped $800 million, or 10 percent of the money spent in all media combined, and in 1955 it passed the $1 billion mark. In 1962 it was about $1.6 billion.

Like the typical mass-circulation magazine and, to a lesser degree, the omnibus newspaper, radio and television are almost entirely dependent on the patronage of advertisers for survival.

Structure of the Movie Industry

The motion-picture industry, on account of its peculiar relationship to the mass markets of an industrial culture, has developed most of the familiar characteristics of publishing and broadcasting. Its techniques and products are standardized, its policies are mass oriented, and it is characterized by bigness, costliness, and concentration of facilities both vertically and horizontally. However, in one important respect the Hollywood film industry is different from its rivals in the contest for the time and money of American consumers. Like book publishing and some notable exceptions in magazine publishing, it is distinguished by its independence from advertising for direct support. Although newspapers, consumer magazines, commercial broadcasting, and the motion-picture industry alike manufacture products designed to appeal to mass markets, the Hollywood film is not, in the way the other media are, an adjunct of the marketing system. Its policies are determined largely by marketing considerations, and the industry makes extensive use of the marketing apparatus to merchandise its products, but the Hollywood film is not a component of the marketing system in the sense that it sells products other than its own to consumers.

The first motion picture exhibited in the United States was shown on April 23, 1896 in New York City. Thomas Edison, after perfecting the earlier peep show, or kinetoscope, abandoned his original plan to exploit the commercial possibilities of movie exhibition because he believed that exhibition on a large screen to many persons simultaneously would too quickly exhaust the market to be profitable. But the success of the first movies changed motion pictures from a novelty to a business, and aggressive entrepreneurs replaced the inventors to seek maximum profits. Almost immediately production, distribution, and exhibition practices were introduced that would characterize the industry half a century later.

size and expense

Today, motion pictures are geared to a mass market; size and expense have become typical of the industry. In the early days, a film could be produced with relatively little capital. In time, however, a single feature-length film came to represent an investment of anywhere from half a million to several million dollars. In 1963 the industry as a whole represented investments of $142,000,000 in studios, $24,000,000 in distribution, and $2,500,000,000 in theaters.

Mack Sennett made 140 movies in his first year in Los Angeles. His Keystone Comedies cost an average of $50,000 each and usually brought him a return of $75,000–$80,000 each. By 1929, with the coming of sound, the cost of the average film had risen to more than $200,000. In the fifties the average cost of feature films produced in Hollywood was about $1,000,000; merchandising and distribution costs added another $500,000 to that amount, and sometimes promotion costs exceeded production costs. To recover production-distribution costs of $1,500,000, a feature film had to attract 7,200,000 paying customers. In contrast, a publishing house could expect to profit from 10,000 copies of a book, and many newspapers and magazines could operate profitably with less than 100,000 circulation. Moreover, unlike radio, television, newspapers, and magazines, motion-picture producers received no revenue from advertising but on the contrary incurred enormous advertising expenses in marketing their films.

Another factor contributing to the size and costliness of the motion-picture industry, and further distinguishing it from broadcasting and publishing generally, is its dependence on foreign markets. Generally, foreign markets account for a substantial proportion of the total receipts of American film companies—52 percent in 1961, when Hollywood production filled about 55 percent of the world's screen time.

entry and survival

For the first dozen years of the motion-picture industry, almost perfect competition prevailed among numerous small companies. Since demand for equipment depended on the popularity of the pictures shown, movie-equipment manufacturers began to produce films to attract large audiences. Exhibitors began to cultivate industrial workers in large cities. Ten-cent tickets fitted wage earners' pocketbooks and visual appeal overcame immigrants' language difficulties. Profits depended on quick turnover of customers which, in turn, relied on short programs with frequent changes in pictures. The demand for films was so increased that the production of movies became the most important branch of the industry. And, as might have been expected, the leading equipment manufacturers —Edison, Biograph, and Vitagraph—joined in an effort to monopolize production through their control of United States patents. But their efforts were unsuccessful. Entry was too easy for new entrepreneurs. Cameras were legally available from abroad and illegally at home. And, as W. F. Hellmuth points out, the prospect of large profits was so alluring that it "overwhelmed the fear of lawsuits over patent rights."

With the eventual lifting of restrictions on equipment, distribution and marketing problems became more important. By 1908, the movies had become a serious competitor of the stage, churches, newspapers, and saloons for the leisure time and money of the public. Demand for better films forced increases in production costs. These in turn required more effective distribution to increase the return on films. This was made possible at first by national organizations of independent distributors, but later the major producers assumed distribution of their own products. Thus, horizontal consolidation of exhibition took place almost immediately after the reorientation of the industry to the mass market. And this was followed in the battle royal for control of the industry before and after World War I by vertical integration of the industry as a whole.

the patents company

In 1909, the ten leading domestic and foreign producers of film and equipment combined in the Motion Picture Patents Company to maximize profits from their pooled patents. The patents trust organized its own nation-wide distribution system, the first vertical integration in the industry, which absorbed or forced out all other distributors except William Fox. But, like the previous efforts of Edison, Biograph, and Vitagraph to monopolize production, the patents trust's attempt to monopolize both production and distribution failed. The independents were far from extirpated, even after several years of bitter competition. To counter the trust's low-cost productions, the independents sought to raise the quality of their films by technical improvements and to enhance their salability by introduction of the star system.

As the independents sought to avoid attacks—both legal and physical— by the Patents Company, the production center shifted from New York to Los Angeles. The independents also countered the Patents Company with production of feature, or long-story, pictures. The first multireel films shown in the United States were foreign importations, but their immediate success led independents to produce feature films while the trust continued to produce one-reelers. The long-story film gave prestige to the independents' movies, appealed to the upper classes, and made higher admissions feasible. By 1914, there was only a minor market for one-reel films. Thereafter, the Patents Company was unimportant, being displaced by an increasing number of independents who reverted to the behavior of those they had overthrown by engaging in a battle for control of exhibition as well as production and distribution.

vertical and horizontal integration

The introduction of the star system and the feature film necessitated large capital investment. To make large investment profitable, production had to be continuous. This meant exhibition facilities had to be increased to consume the products of continuous production. Producers, seeking to acquire distribution and exhibition facilities, started a wave of theater building that continued unabated until the depression of the thirties.

In 1917, Paramount (the leading distributor) and Famous Players-Lasky (the leading major producer) and twelve lesser producers combined under Adolph Zukor to monopolize talent under the star system and to dictate terms to exhibitors. The resultant block booking, not a new trade practice, was ruthlessly used by Zukor to guarantee sales of the combine's less spectacular merchandise. Rivals countered by creating the First National Exhibition Circuit to act as purchasing agent for twenty-six of the largest first-run exhibitors in the country. This not only threatened Zukor's control of the star system, but the combine's domination of production. In retaliation, Zukor went into the theater business and became an exhibitor, producer, and distributor.

The giant rivals, Zukor and First National, were not the only menaces to small independent exhibitors. By 1923, Loew's and Fox also had expanded their holdings considerably; the independently owned first-run theater rapidly became extinct through absorption either by major producer-distributors or by unaffiliated circuits.

the Big Five and Wall Street

By the thirties, the so-called Big Five—Paramount, Loew's, Warner Bros., Twentieth Century-Fox, and Radio-Keith-Orpheum—dominated production, distribution, and exhibition. They remained in oligopical control of the industry until after World War II. Below them in importance were the Little Three—Universal, Columbia, and United Artists, the last a distributing company only. At mid-century, the Big Five and the Little Three were producing 95 percent of American motion pictures. Those same eight companies also distributed about 95 percent of the total films and controlled about 70 percent of the first-run theaters in cities with populations of more than 100,000, and nearly 60 percent of the first-run theaters in cities with populations between 25,000 and 100,000.

During the period of vertical integration by the Big Five, producers were forced to turn to Wall Street for financial backing, a move necessitated by several factors: competition for expensive exhibition palaces, the spiralling costs of the star system, the burdens of publicity and other marketing methods, and the high cost of sound equipment introduced in 1926. All the major companies established alliances with leading banks and investment houses. For example, Loew's tied its fortunes to Liberty National Bank and General Motors; Paramount to Kuhn, Loeb and Co.; and Twentieth Century-Fox to Chase National Bank. By the mid-thirties, the largest financial interests in the country—from Morgan to American Telephone & Telegraph, from Rockefeller to General Electric and RCA—

held powerful positions in the industry. The financiers, to oversee the use of funds and get maximum profits, installed their representatives in important positions throughout the industry. Thus, although the producing facilities were in Hollywood, the nerve center of the industry became New York City.

Entering the field when the production cost of the average feature was approaching the half-million-dollar mark, as against one-fifth of that amount for the same length film a few years before, the financiers quickly established a policy of getting maximum profits from every picture produced. Advertising budgets were increased enormously. The public was encouraged to demand star personalities, mammoth and expensive sets, stories based on famous books or plays, and well-known directors. Producers and directors were instructed to produce pictures to meet these specifications, sacrificing initiative and originality to the demands of the market place. Will Hays, former guardian of the public morals and apologist for the film industry, always maintained that making movies is an art rather than a business. But even artistic commodities require a financial and marketing apparatus when they are produced for mass consumption. The Hollywood end product was exhibited in theaters, but the basic character of the product and its packaging was determined by the chief executives in New York.

Although recent years have seen a resurgence of independent producers (established stars, directors, and producers) acting as their own bankers, and although an old independent such as Cecil B. DeMille was able to survive the motion-picture oligopoly, the major producer-banker combines continue to dominate the industry. A trade association of major producers runs a central casting agency to serve only its members; small producers are sources of low-cost pictures for double-feature programs in exhibition houses owned by the majors; and the United States is carved up into distribution areas serviced by film exchange centers operated by the majors.

anti-trust action

The motion-picture industry was founded six years after passage of the Sherman Anti-Trust Act. But, despite the statute, the major companies uninterruptedly pursued a policy of restraining competition, with monopoly and maximum profits as their goal. Many factors facilitate monopolistic practices in the movie industry. For example, the intangible nature of picture properties, the star system, and the fact that individual theaters are limited to offering one, two, or three pictures on a single bill. Such factors are inherent in the industry and beyond control. However, ownership and trade practices are subject to control; and as a result of occasional brushes with the Sherman Act, certain obvious monopolistic practices were enjoined. But it was not until 1938 that the

long-run trend toward concentration in the industry was in any significant way retarded by legal action. The Department of Justice filed
suits against eight film companies on the charge that they were engaged
in monopolistic practices and in illegal restraint of trade in producing,
distributing, and exhibiting motion pictures.

After about a week of opening skirmishes, the trial was adjourned to
permit negotiation between the Department of Justice and the defendants
for settlement by decree. Five companies reached an agreement with the
department in 1940, but three refused to be parties to the decree. After
eight more years of irregular testimony, intermittent negotiation, two
lower court decisions and one appeal, the Supreme Court held that the
five fully integrated companies were parties to a combination which had
exhibition monopoly in larger cities as its goal. There was no finding of
monopoly or illegal practices in the film production.

RKO and Paramount, apparently tired of the effort, expense, and uncertainty of continued negotiations, sought a consent decree. The Department of Justice insisted on divorcement of theaters from production and
distribution interests, and early in 1949 Paramount and RKO agreed to
the terms of the decree. Loew's, Twentieth Century-Fox, and Warner
Bros. strongly disapproved. But after the Supreme Court upheld a district
court's divorcement of theater holdings from the business of production-
distribution of the three remaining majors, Warners and Twentieth
Century-Fox in 1951 and Loew's in 1952 entered into consent judgments
similar to those of RKO and Paramount.

a coterie of monopolistically inclined corporations

At the time of the final consent decree in 1949, Professor Robert
Brady, an economist, described the movie industry as a "small coterie of
vertically integrated, horizontally co-ordinated, and monopolistically inclined corporations." He said they were "compacted" by contracts, agreements, and "understandings of one sort or another," and submissive to a
trade association possessing "cartel-like powers over various activities of
its constituent membership." According to Brady, members compete
with one another in much the same way that the main branches of
General Motors do. Industry policy and operations are governed by a
selected management group "responsible to banking and real estate
powers" whose interests in turn are interwoven with other monopoly or
semi-monopoly groups "having little to do with the movie industry
directly."

Characterized in the language of Brady, it appears that among the
other media network broadcasting is most nearly comparable in structure
to that of the Hollywood film industry. Only to a much lesser degree is
the structure of newspaper and magazine publishing comparable. The

arenas of competition in publishing are for the most part local or specialized in character. All the media, of course, are marked by instances of both vertical and horizontal integration. But the concentration of control which accompanies integration in the movie industry is much more closely knit than in publishing and broadcasting.

the industry fights back

According to Hellmuth, since the "initial outburst of enthusiasm which greeted the decrees, delays and backsliding which may emasculate the effectiveness of the anti-trust decrees in the long run have developed." The backsliding has occurred on three fronts. Stockholders in divorced theater groups have maintained stock interests in production-distribution units. Exhibitors and distributors (e.g., United Artists) have moved into production. Producer-distributor units have begun to collaborate with their enemy, the television industry, substituting television stations for the traditional exhibition houses.

After a period of consternation and uncertainty in which competition from television was almost wholly blamed for the decline of movie attendance, the motion-picture majors moved vigorously not only to reassert their dominance over the industry, but also to counteract the influence of the new electronic medium. Evidences of their aggressiveness are subscription, or pay-as-you-see, TV; theater TV, which appeals to exhibitors as well as to producers; and direct affiliation of movie interests with television organizations. As Hellmuth points out, the 1953 merger of United Paramount Theaters, the largest theater company, with ABC, the third largest radio-television network, into American Broadcasting-Paramount Theaters is "only the most spectacular affiliation." Among the Big Seven (control of RKO having passed to List Industries, which has interests in textiles, auto parts, and coal), nearly all turn out filmed shows for television, and all have sold film stocks to the networks. Conventional production has been cut back drastically, with the main effort being concentrated in big-budget "blockbusters," which the industry believes the public will abandon free TV to attend. For example, the total estimated cost of the spectacular *Cleopatra* produced in 1963 was about $40 million. Meanwhile, Twentieth Century-Fox entered the petroleum industry when oil was found on its California properties, Paramount went into the manufacture of electrical equipment for computers, and Stanley Warner took a successful plunge into chemicals, drugs, and women's and children's undergarments.

Looking back, it becomes apparent that the mass media together comprise a vast industrial enterprise having certain characteristics common among them and in common, also, with American industry in general.

All serve as adjuncts of the marketing system of an advanced industrial economy. In slightly differing ways, all have a tendency to monopolize the markets they serve or deliver to advertisers. All seek to maximize profits by the familiar means of administered prices, restrictive contracts, discriminatory practices, vertical and horizontal integration, mergers, combinations, informal mutual-interest agreements and dominance of their respective trade associations by its stronger members. Standardization characterizes the products of all, as it does those of conventional mass production and mass distribution industries. Looked at as components of the American industrial order, the media seem to be cut from the same cloth as other big businesses. However, the newspaper, the magazine, radio, television, and the film are widely regarded as something more than mere business enterprises.

References

BERELSON, BERNARD, AND MORRIS JANOWITZ, eds., *Reader in Public Opinion and Communication,* enlarged ed. (New York: Free Press of Glencoe, 1953).

COWLEY, MALCOLM, "The Big Change in Publishing," *Esquire* 54 (December 1960) 309–15.

HEAD, SYDNEY W., *Broadcasting in America: A Survey of Television and Radio* (Boston: Houghton Mifflin Company, 1956).

HELLMUTH, WILLIAM F., "The Motion Picture Industry" in Walter Adams, ed., *The Structure of American Industry: Some Case Studies,* 3rd ed. (New York: The Macmillan Company, 1961).

KREPS, THEODORE J., "The Newspaper Industry" in Walter Adams, ed., *The Structure of American Industry: Some Case Studies,* 3rd ed. (New York: The Macmillan Company, 1961).

MAYER, MARTIN, "Spock, Sex, & Schopenhauer (Soft Bound)," in *Esquire* 57 (April 1962) 101–2, 137–41.

MILLER, WILLIAM, *The Book Industry: A Report of the Public Library Inquiry* (New York: Columbia University Press, 1949).

PETERSON, THEODORE, *Magazines in the Twentieth Century,* 2nd ed., Chap. 4 (Urbana: University of Illinois Press, 1964).

SCHRAMM, WILBUR, ed., *Mass Communications: A Book of Readings,* 2nd ed. (Urbana: University of Illinois Press, 1960).

———, ed., *The Process and Effects of Mass Communication* (Urbana: University of Illinois Press, 1954).

TEBBEL, JOHN, *Paperback Books: A Pocket History* (New York: Pocket Books, Inc., 1964).

6

The Media

and Their

Intellectual Environment

The mass communication system in America, like that in other lands, has been shaped to an extent by what we might call its intellectual environment. The ideas dominant in a society can shape the press just as surely as do the social and economic forces discussed in a preceding chapter. The Soviet press is what it is and operates as it does in large measure because of the amalgamation of ideas which make up Russian communism. The communication system in the United States performs as it does to some degree because of our concept of press freedom and our theory of what the press should be and do.

To understand the press of any society, one must know what that society expects of it. What are its functions? What is its degree of freedom? What do we mean by freedom, anyway? The answers to those questions come only after one has looked at the basic assumptions which the society holds. What view does the society take of the nature of man? What does the society regard as the ideal relation between man and the state? What is the society's idea of truth? Sooner or later, then, the study of a press system leads to questions of philosophy.

The communication system in the United States has a strong English heritage, for the colonists copied the institutions and culture of England. They modelled their newspapers and magazines on those in the homeland. To keep their press in line, they imported the controls that were used in England. Revolting at last, they justified their action by citing their rights as free-born Englishmen. And when, under their newly won freedom, Americans developed a theory of the press, they borrowed liberally from thinkers in England and in Europe.

Methods of Control

The Colonists controlled the press by the methods then used in England and by some that were already losing their effectiveness. However, with the end of the Revolution and the adoption of the Constitution, Americans apparently got rid of most of those controls, although some of them have been revived from time to time.

One was licensing. Publishing was done only with permission of authorities, and all products of the press were submitted for approval before publication. Licensing, through the royal governors, continued in the Colonies long after it had died in England in 1694. It seems to have been abandoned in the Colonies by about 1730. The Supreme Court has interpreted the First Amendment as forbidding prior restraint—that is, censorship before publication.

Taxes, used as a means of control in England, were never imposed extensively on the newspapers in this country. They were tried, primarily as a means of obtaining revenue, under the Stamp Act of 1765, but they met with such strong resistance that they apparently were not revived until the twentieth century. Then, in 1934, the Louisiana Legislature levied a tax of 2 percent on gross advertising revenues on all newspapers in the state with circulations of more than 20,000 a week. The effect was to penalize the newspapers which were opposing the political régime of Governor Huey Long and to exempt the small papers which were supporting it. The Supreme Court in 1936 found the tax a restriction on freedom of the press.

The threat of prosecution for treason seems to have been a potential but little-used instrument of control in the Colonies. However, the wars and international tensions of the twentieth century have revived the opportunities for its use as a means of controlling expression. Early in the nineteenth century, the English courts decided that treason must consist of a more effective and overt act than the mere uttering of words, a position they took for about the next century. No person in this country was tried for treason from the adoption of the Constitution until the trial of Ezra Pound, the expatriate poet, soon after the end of World War II. Pound was one of six Americans prosecuted because of radio broadcasts made for the enemy during the war. The argument that words of themselves constitute treason rests on the belief that messages, widely disseminated by the mass media, can cause greater harm to the state than some overt acts. So far that principle has been applied only in wartime.

The Colonists imported another English control: a ban on reporting the meetings of Parliament. This method, with all its ramifications, seems to have been greatly used in the Colonies so that sessions of the Colonial legislatures were closed to the newspapers. The early constitutional conventions, too, were closed to the press and public. In the nineteenth century, this system of control fell into disuse. Theoretically at least, present-day legislatures still have the power to conduct their business in closed executive sessions, although Congress has seldom done so since 1842. Congress and the state legislatures have found that their own members have relayed secret transactions to the press.

However, conducting governmental business in closed meetings is still a widespread method of withholding information from the press. Congressional committees and state and local governing bodies often go into executive session to keep their transactions secret. One-third of all meetings of Congressional committees are in secret, according to one study, although the rules require that most of them be open to the public. In some cases, Congressional hearings are closed at the request of the executive officials who are to testify, notably in hearings involving foreign policy. Only five states have suitable laws guaranteeing that public bodies at state and local levels will hold open meetings, according to another study; another five states have such laws applying only at the local level.

Moreover, individual executives and administrators at the different levels of government often withhold information from the press and public. Especially since the end of World War II, this tendency seems to have been increasing. Probably it was encouraged by several factors: the war and the Korean conflict, which accustomed Americans to some secrecy in government out of military necessity; the broadened scope of governmental influence on the lives and activities of private citizens; the greater amount of governmental business carried on by appointed individuals and commissions only indirectly accountable to the public; and the feeling that some secrecy is necessary in the struggle between Communist Russia and the Western world. President Harry S Truman in September, 1951, issued an executive order which gave all government agencies, even those without the slightest connection with military security, the power to determine what news and information the public could receive. Although President Dwight D. Eisenhower somewhat ameliorated the situation with a new order, he still made only small improvement in removing the barriers, which continued to exist under his successors.

A number of professional organizations have committees working toward greater access of governmental information. A Congressional subcommittee headed by Representative John E. Moss of California has held hearings on governmental secrecy and sponsored legislation aimed at diminishing it. Individual newsmen have called attention to the dangers to democratic government that can result when citizens are deprived of news at its source. Yet the press as a whole seems to have given little aggressive support to the effort to open up the flow of news about government. Indeed, at least once—early in 1958, just before the United States launched its first successful satellite at Cape Kennedy—representatives of the press voluntarily joined with the military in restricting information to be released to the public.

Threat of prosecution for seditious libel as a means of control also was imported from England to the Colonies, where it was administered by Colonial courts. In general, seditious libel was any published material which, without lawful justification, cast blame on any public man, law, or institution established by law. Its scope was wide, and truth was no defense. In this country, seditious libel was resisted earlier than it was in England. Juries, as in the case of John Peter Zenger in 1735, refused to bring in verdicts of guilty. While their reluctance did not change the law, it reduced the effectiveness of seditious libel as a means of control. Seditious libel probably was no serious threat to Colonial editors after about 1735. It has since vanished as a federal offense, but some states have statutes forbidding it.

Libertarian Philosophy

If the Colonists turned to England for ideas about controlling the press, it is not surprising that they looked there also for ideas in justifying its freedom. Happenings in England and in western Europe in the seventeenth and eighteenth centuries had a profound effect on the American press as it exists today. In the seventeenth century there was emerging a new conception of the nature of man and of his relationship to the state. Scientific and geographic discoveries broadened minds and vistas. The rising commercial class disputed the privileges of the nobility and challenged the supremacy of the monarch. The old order was crumbling. When the seventeenth century began, the authoritarian order seemed secure; when it ended, the Crown was subordinate to Parliament, and liberalism was in the ascendancy. The eighteenth century provided the laboratories in which the philosophies of liberalism were put to practical test.

libertarian government

From the theorists of the seventeenth and eighteenth centuries came the libertarian philosophy which underlies the American democratic form of government.

Under that philosophy the world was conceived of as a vast perpetual-motion machine, going timelessly on according to the laws of nature. God—or some other creator—had put men into a rationally planned universe, then had left them alone to work out their own salvation. That they could do, for the libertarians believed that man is a creature guided by reason, not by passion or narrow self-interest. By using his reason, he could discover the laws of nature which govern the universe, bring his institutions into happy harmony with them, and so build a good and just society.

Men, the libertarians thought, are born with certain natural rights which limit the hand of government and any interference with the individual's liberty and property. Although tyrants might temporarily abridge them, no one can properly take away those rights, for they are God-given, as much a part of the divine scheme as the laws under which the universe operates.

In their natural state, before they voluntarily joined together to form governments, according to the libertarian view, men existed perfectly free and equal. But in that state of nature, their enjoyment of their rights was in constant danger, since the individual was at the mercy of his domineering fellows, who could deprive him by force of his liberty and property.

So, by common consent, men form governments to secure their natural rights. The best way that government can insure those rights is by leaving the individual as free as possible. The best government, then, is that which governs least. When government fails to protect the liberty and property of its citizens, it has failed in its purpose. Then it is the right and duty of the people to establish a new government which does enable them to enjoy their freedom.

The libertarians saw truth as deriving not from authority but from the intellect of men. Man is not to be led and directed towards truth; he is to find it himself with the reason with which he is endowed. With the free play of his intellect, he can discover the all-embracing truth which unifies the universe and the phenomena in it.

As Carl L. Becker has remarked, modern democracy offered long odds on the capacity and integrity of the human mind. It assumes that man is not only a rational being but a moral one. If man is to be free from all but the most necessary of restraints, his moral sense must enforce those obligations to his fellow men which are not specifically covered by law. Human perfectibility, natural rights, and natural reason, then, are three of the key points in the libertarian philosophy.

What is the nature of man? Man is a creature who is guided by reason. He is disposed to seek truth and to be guided by it. What is the ideal relationship between man and the state? Man should be governed only with his own consent. The state, by keeping its power at a minimum, should preserve but not infringe upon man's natural rights. What is the nature of truth? Truth is not the monopoly of the few in power but is discoverable by all men using their natural intellect; it is the key to understanding the natural order of things so that man can form a harmonious society.

libertarian theory of the press

Those same answers are the base on which the Anglo-American theory of the press was erected. Let us briefly summarize the theory.

Under libertarian theory, the press must have a wide latitude of freedom to aid men in their quest for truth. To find truth through reason, man must have free access to information and ideas. Out of the bounteous fare which the press serves him, he can, by employing his intellect, distinguish truth from falsehood. He may find some truth hidden amidst falsehood, some falsehood hidden amidst truth. Yet over the long pull, if man is faithful to his reason, truth will emerge victorious from the unrestrained interplay of information and ideas. Social change will come, then, not from force but from a process of discussion and conversion.

Since free expression carries built-in correctives, according to libertarian theory, there need be few restrictions on what men may speak and write. The great majority of men are moral creatures who will use their freedom responsibly in an honest desire to find truth. One need not worry about the small minority who may abuse their freedom by lying and distorting. Others will find it profitable to expose them—and the lies and distortions will be shown up for what they are since all information and ideas are put to the powerful scrutiny of reason. Therefore, it is unnecessary to exact responsibilities in exchange for freedom; most men will assume them without being asked, and the remainder can cause no great harm. Charles Beard was quite correct in saying that under the Constitution freedom of the press originally was "the right to be just or unjust, partisan or non-partisan, true or false, in news column and in editorial column."

Censorship before publication is an evil for at least three reasons under libertarian theory. First, it violates man's natural right to free expression. Second, it could enable tyrants to perpetuate themselves in power and to make the state a foe of liberty instead of liberty's protector. Third, it could temporarily hinder the quest for truth by throwing off balance the delicate process by which truth ultimately emerges. If man is to discover truth, he must have access to all information and ideas, not just those fed to him.

Even libertarian theory allows some restrictions on expression, however. It sanctions libel laws which protect the individual from defamation. If one is defamed, he may seek recompense in the courts—only after publication, however; only after the writer has had a chance to contribute the offending material to the marketplace of ideas from which truth eventually arises. The theory also condones laws regulating obscenity, although there is confusion over just what constitutes the obscene. The theory has permitted mild sedition laws. Those limitations, however, staked out wide boundaries to the area of free expression.

The boundaries became somewhat narrower after 1919 when Justice Oliver Wendell Holmes expressed his "clear and present danger" doctrine, a test for deciding just when free expression may be denied. What Holmes said in effect was that circumstances alter cases and that in some cases it is quite justifiable, even necessary, to impose restrictions on what people may say and write. His doctrine does not necessarily deny the idea that truth emerges from the clash of ideas; it does reflect the belief that in times of emergency, such as war, society does not have time for the process to work.

Shapers of the Tradition

The libertarian theory of the press, as it developed abroad and in America, drew on the ideas of more men than the few whose names are commonly associated with it. However, some had reputations which gave greater prestige to their teachings or did a better job than their contemporaries of expressing the ideas current among the thinkers of their times. Therefore, we can chart the unfolding of libertarian theory by summarizing the contributions of just a few of those who shaped it.

John Milton

After the Puritans had fought their way to power in the civil wars which tore England in the turbulent seventeenth century, they perceived, as British monarchs had before them, that regulating the press was one means of stifling dissent and maintaining authority. For the Crown's methods of control they substituted their own, one of which was licensing books, pamphlets, and papers. In 1644 a few pamphleteers raised their voices against such regulation, and the most powerful voice was that of the poet John Milton, who had run afoul of authorities with a tract on divorce. His *Areopagitica* has since become regarded as a classic defense of a free press.

Although the *Areopagitica* can be summarized in many different ways, it offers three major arguments against licensing. One is that licensing is the evil child of evil parents. Licensing was invented by the Roman Catholic church, an anathema to the Puritans, and used to prohibit anything which the church found unpalatable. Second, licensing is impractical. It simply will not work. For one thing, it assumes infallible and incorruptible censors; even if such men could be found, licensing would be a waste of their time and wisdom. For another, licensing is not broad enough to control the minds of men, since it merely regulates the current output of the press. To do the job effectively, one must also censor everything which has been printed in the past, cut out the bad parts of good books, and strictly regulate all activities of the citizens. Therefore, licensing cannot keep the truth from winning out in the end. In the meantime, however, it can do great harm by making citizens feel that their government does not trust them and by stifling free inquiry.

That point leads to Milton's third reason: Licensing hinders man's search for truth. Truth will win out in any free and open encounter of ideas, Milton said; the surest way of suppressing falsehood is to have it refuted. But licensing discourages the writing and the arguing, the knowledge in the making, which help men to find truth. It affronts learning, spells an end to teaching, and makes ignorance a virtue.

Perhaps the most effective argument Milton could have used on the Puritan authorities of his day was that licensing is impractical. His most philosophical argument, however, was that truth arises from the free and open encounter of ideas. And this is Milton's most significant contribution to the libertarian theory of the press. What the main stream of the theory absorbed was his idea of the "self-righting process," the idea that free expression carries its own correctives. Grant all men with something to say the freedom to express themselves. In the clash of ideas which ensues, the true and sound will triumph over the false and the unsound. Falsehood may seem to win out temporarily, but if the government does not weigh the balance in favor of either side, truth will be the victor in the end.

Looked at from the twentieth century, Milton's idea of press freedom was narrow. He was the product of his age, although his *Areopagitica* transcended it, and it is unfair to criticize him for sharing the beliefs of his times instead of our own. Nonetheless, the freedom that he advocated was negative, a freedom from government restriction; indeed, his chief concern was simply an end to licensing. He believed that the government should prohibit certain types of publications—blasphemy, atheism, libel— and punish offending printers.

Moreover, Milton put extreme limits on who should be allowed to write without hindrance. He would have denied free expression to those who disagreed with him on fundamentals—Royalists, for instance, and Catholics. In short, he would have denied freedom to anyone who challenged the primary assumptions of public order as it existed in 1644. At least superficially, his idea of press freedom resembles that of the present-day Soviet state, which forbids criticism of the basic assumptions of communism but does permit some criticism of how the work of the party is carried out.

Milton seems to have accepted man's rationality. Yet one cannot help feeling that he was defending free expression for only the educated few, not the London masses, and that his freedom applied only to serious books and discussion, not to the newsbooks, broadsides, and polemics which abounded in his time.

Milton gave the *Areopagitica* a strongly religious cast. Unlike later shapers of the tradition who justified free expression as a natural right, Milton justified it on religious grounds. God—a Puritan God—desired men to have a free press so they could discover truth.

That truth for Milton was something outside of man, an expression of a higher law—the will of his Puritan God. Man once had it, then lost it:

> Truth indeed came once into the world with her divine Master, and was a perfect shape most glorious to look on; but when he ascended and his Apostles after him were laid asleep, then strait arose a wicked race of deceivers, who . . . took the virgin Truth, hewd her lovely form into a thousand pieces, and scatter'd them to the four winds.

From that sad day onward, friends of Truth tried to pick up the scattered pieces so as to reconstruct the whole.

At Milton's end, then, the stream of libertarian theory was narrow; freedom of the press meant little more than an end to licensing so that men could discover the will of a Puritan God. It may seem anticlimactic that the *Areopagitica* had little effect in its own day and that Milton himself later became a government licenser of newsbooks. Yet neither circumstance detracts from the significance of Milton's contribution to libertarian thought. If one reads the *Areopagitica* as a defense of serious books, not of ephemera, his becoming censor does not necessarily reflect a violation of principle. His *Areopagitica,* ignored in its own time, provided a major concept—that of the self-righting process—when libertarians in the eighteenth century broadened the stream of theory.

Newton, Locke, and Smith

In expanding the boundaries of freedom in the eighteenth century, libertarians drew heavily on the works of three men, none of whom wrote specifically about the press. The orderly nature of the universe, natural law, natural rights, the rationality of man, and the hands-off role of government were ideas expressed by Isaac Newton, John Locke, and Adam Smith, and they were used to justify curbing the authority of the state and making the individual paramount.

Unifying work done in physics and astronomy, Isaac Newton in 1687 gave man a new picture of the universe. In that picture, as we saw when discussing libertarian government, the universe was an orderly machine, timeless, unchanging, running on according to certain discoverable laws of nature.

Building on Newton, John Locke gave libertarians their picture of man and his relation to government. Locke, in vindicating the scientific achievements of his age, set out to show that all knowledge comes from experience, from the senses. While the human intellect does have limits, its powers are great enough to secure happiness for mankind. He proved to the satisfaction of libertarians that man is distinguished by his capacity for creative thought.

In his essays on civil government, phrases from which ring out in the American Declaration of Independence, Locke advanced a system of natural rights which, like Newton's discoveries, rest on the unchanging laws of nature. Men in a state of nature are free and equal with certain inalienable rights. They form governments by their own consent to protect those rights, and a government which does not protect them has violated its purpose and should be dissolved in favor of one that does.

The libertarian theory of the press took two of its vital propositions from Locke: the rationality of man and free expression as a natural right. Man's rationality became inextricably bound up with the self-righting process of Milton. By putting all discussion, spoken or written, to the powerful test of reason, man could discover truth. Newton had given a glimpse of the majestic truth that man could discover—the enduring laws of nature. Mortal man could discover those laws, bring his institutions into harmony with them, and thus found an earthly paradise of justice and order.

Free expression became accounted one of man's natural rights, and no one has the authority to deprive him of it. Indeed, it is the right on which all other rights depend, for if men are free to speak their minds, they can rally support whenever the government acts unjustly or arbitrarily.

In 1776, Adam Smith showed how economics fits both into Newton's orderly world and into Locke's system of natural rights and self-government. He contributed two more propositions to the libertarian theory of the press.

One was that government should assume a negative role in man's affairs, should take a position of laissez faire or "hands off," lest it upset the delicate workings of nature's laws. The idea was an appealing one to libertarians, who had long eyed the government as the chief threat to freedom. Here was good reason why the press should be obliged to make its own way in the marketplace. Here too was good reason why the government should not sponsor media of its own in competition with private media. This tenet of libertarian theory was reflected in a talk by George E. Sokolsky, newspaper columnist, in 1947:

> The American press can only be free as long as it is solvent and competitive. Freedom depends upon solvency. . . . I was

always opposed to RFC loans to newspapers because the RFC
. . . was and is an agency of government. . . . Newspapers that
are insolvent are bound to become subservient to their protectors.
And a newspaper should be protected from failure by nothing
but circulation and advertising.

Smith's second contribution was his theory that as each person works
for his own gain he serves the welfare of the community. The libertarian
press has applied this idea in various ways. The idea lies, for instance,
behind the remark of the editor who said that his readers vote for his
newspaper with their coins every time he brings out a new issue. According to this line of thought, the press is accountable to the public, and the
public controls the press in its own interests by the choices it makes. If a
newspaper, magazine, or broadcasting station serves what people regard
as the public interest, they will give it their patronage, and it will
flourish. If it fails to serve the public interest, they will not patronize it.
In consequence, it will wither and die. By working for his own personal
gain, then, the publisher or broadcaster automatically gives the public
the sort of media it wants and needs. Smith's idea also can be used to
justify the publication of virtually any material in a different way. The
argument can be put something like this: "Helping to find truth is in the
public interest. Many ideas and much information are needed for the
discovery of truth. What I publish for my own personal profit serves the
cause of truth and hence the public interest."

Mansfield and Blackstone

Even in the eighteenth century, when the libertarian movement came
to full flower, some shapers of the libertarian tradition held views of
press freedom almost as narrow as Milton's. Two such men—Lord Mansfield and Sir William Blackstone—were responsible for this basic principle: The government shall not restrain the press before publication.

Lord Mansfield sat as chief justice on the King's Bench in England
from about 1750 to 1790. He held that the government does not have the
right to suppress any material before it is published. However, it does
have the authority to punish publishers of material which causes damage,
as determined by the common law and Parliament. The publisher is free
from censorship before publication; he may publish whatever he wishes,
but must bear full responsibility for the abuse of his freedom.

Mansfield's ideas were picked up by Sir William Blackstone, a jurist
influential in setting the law of his day. He worked them into his famous
Commentaries.

By libertarian standards, both men had a narrow view of press freedom.
They granted law-makers the authority to decide what materials consti-
tuted abuses and to set the punishments for offenders. In effect, then, they

gave law-makers the authority to decide what should be published. What they did was to substitute the many opinions of the law-makers for the single opinion of the censor. Under such a system, the government could easily stifle ideas. It could simply declare the publication of certain materials an abuse of freedom. Or it could make penalties so severe that fear of punishment would discourage publishers from bringing forth certain ideas.

What has survived in libertarian theory of the press is their basic principle that there should be no censorship before publication. The courts have continued to uphold that principle, sometimes with references to Blackstone. In an important decision in 1931, for instance, the United States Supreme Court declared unconstitutional a Minnesota law aimed at suppressing scandal sheets. The court said that the law infringed upon free expression by providing for censorship before publication. Further, persons harmed by the offending materials had ample recourse after publication.

In the United States, the legislatures still have the power to decide for just what abuses publishers shall be punished after publication. However, two important safeguards protect free expression. One safeguard lies in two Constitutional amendments: the First Amendment, which forbids Congress to pass laws restricting free expression, and the Fourteenth, which makes the First Amendment binding on the states. The second safeguard is the Supreme Court, which interprets the Constitution.

The principle that there should be no censorship before publication is intimately bound up with Milton's self-righting process. Even if a man is later punished for what he says or writes, at least he first has the chance to make himself heard and so help the quest for truth.

Camden and Erskine

Mansfield and Blackstone, by giving the legislature a strong control of the press, were at odds with a growing and influential body of libertarians who believed in a minimum of government. Lord Camden and Sir Thomas Erskine were among the Englishmen who had drunk heavily of Locke's philosophy of man's reason and natural rights, and the two men broadened the stream of libertarian theory by arguing that the power of the government to interfere with the press was severely restricted. Across the Atlantic, their position was shared by Thomas Jefferson, an important figure in shaping the bent of ideas about press freedom in America.

Camden and Erskine believed that the authority of government is limited by natural law and natural rights. Because free expression is a natural right, the government should not restrict the press either before or after publication so long as the material is aimed at peaceful change.

Even to save itself, the government should not interfere with any publication which would change the existing order by peaceful means or by appeal to the intellect. Here the scope of freedom is far, far broader than that pleaded for by John Milton, who would have spared the existing order from questioning.

Thomas Jefferson

In America, Thomas Jefferson also had optimistic faith in man's reason and pessimistic distrust of government. He wrote no unified work on the press, but his letters are full of scattered references to it. From them one can piece together his ideas of press freedom and the role of the press in a democratic society. His beliefs arose quite naturally from his political philosophy.

Like the philosophers of the Enlightenment, Jefferson believed that the universe had been created in accordance with some orderly plan. Men had been given reason so that they could discover that plan and bring their lives and institutions into harmony with it. He put strong faith in the rationality and morality of mankind; men are good unless ignorance or bad institutions corrupt them. Because men are essentially reasonable, because they have certain natural rights, they should live under only a minimum of government as they walk their way in peace and contentment. But even under the best form of government, Jefferson knew, those in public office may become so corrupted by power that they will stifle the freedom of the people. Therefore, the citizens must be alert to any attempts to curtail their liberty.

The role of the press followed from that picture of man and the state. As Jefferson saw it, the press has two major functions: to enlighten the public and to safeguard personal liberties.

"The press," Jefferson wrote in 1823, "is the best instrument for enlightening the mind of man, and improving him as a rational, moral, and social being." Democracy places a heavy burden on the individual citizen. Self-governing, he must be enlightened to govern himself wisely. The press is an important auxiliary of government, for it is a means of giving the citizen the facts and ideas which he needs for proper self-government. Jefferson himself summarized this viewpoint in an often-quoted passage from a letter to Edward Carrington:

> The basis of governments being the opinion of the people, the first object should be to keep that right; and were it left to me to decide whether we should have a government without newspapers, or newspapers without a government, I should not hesitate a moment to prefer the latter. But I should mean that every man should receive those papers, and be capable of reading them.

The press should also be a check on government, Jefferson thought. Freedom of the individual is the core of democracy, but even a democratic government can trample on the rights of its citizens. An important function of the press, Jefferson believed, is to safeguard personal liberties, to serve as a watchdog to sound the alarm whenever individual rights are threatened or infringed. As a result, public officials who rule despotically can be deposed peaceably by public opinion instead of violently by revolution. The role of the press as watchdog was on Jefferson's mind when he wrote George Washington in 1792:

> No government ought to be without censors; and where the press is free, no one ever will be. If virtuous, it need not fear the fair operations of attack and defense.

That same idea was with him in 1816:

> If a nation expects to be ignorant and free, in a state of civilization, it expects what never was and never will be. The functionaries of every government have propensities to command at will the liberty and property of their constituents. . . . Where the press is free, and every man able to read, all is safe.

To perform as enlightener and watchdog, the press must have the widest possible freedom, and that Jefferson granted it. Like Erskine and Camden, he believed that the government should not hinder the press even to save itself. He apparently did favor libel laws to protect individual citizens from unwarranted attack. At first he seems to have thought that private citizens should have the right to sue for libel but that public and political figures should not have such protection. By 1803, however, he seems to have favored granting public figures the same libel protection as private citizens. Even so, his theory imposed only the barest of restraints on the press.

the eighteenth-century libertarians

The concept of freedom of the press held by Jefferson, Camden, and Erskine was the predominant one in the late eighteenth century when the American Constitution was being written. Although eighteenth-century libertarians sometimes differed on minor points, they agreed on fundamentals. How had they changed libertarian theory since Milton?

They had changed the basis of press freedom. While Milton had justified freedom of the press as the will of God, they justified it as an inherent, natural right of man.

They had broadened the concept. Indeed, in the late eighteenth century the stream of libertarian theory was as wide as it was ever to become before the problems and complexities of the twentieth century were to narrow it once more. While Milton had seen press freedom as simply freedom from licensing, the libertarians saw it as an absence of government interference in virtually every form. Milton denied free expression to those who disagreed with him on fundamentals. Not so the libertarians; for them, freedom meant the right to question even fundamentals. The form of government itself was not to be spared from questioning, and the state could not intervene even to save itself. As we have seen, Milton approved of restrictions on certain types of content—atheism, for example, and blasphemy. The libertarians, with their strong faith in reason, permitted publication of virtually everything, although they did sanction mild sedition laws, libel laws, and laws regulating obscenity.

They had a different conception of the truth which free inquiry was intended to disclose. While Milton equated truth with the will of a Puritan God, the libertarians saw truth as a revelation of the laws which governed the operation of the harmonious universe.

John Stuart Mill

In America throughout most of the nineteenth century, the stream of libertarian thought remained wide. Before and during the Civil War, some restrictions were imposed on the press. But the libertarian tradition strongly predominated throughout the century, and viewpoints of all sorts were tolerated, even those which questioned or attacked the beliefs of the majority.

Shortly after mid-century, an English scholar fed two more ideas into the stream of libertarian thought. For one thing, in his essay "On Liberty," John Stuart Mill justified free expression on grounds other than natural rights—on utility. For another thing, he emphasized that the majority could tyrannize the minority, could stifle minority thought, just as surely as government, the traditional enemy of liberty.

For Mill, liberty is the right of the mature individual to think and act as he pleases so long as he harms no one else by doing so. Harm to others is the sole justification for restraint. For its own protection, society may try to advise, instruct, and persuade the individual; it may, indeed, ostracize him. But it may not restrain him for his own good.

Mill rested his case for freedom not on natural rights but on utilitarian principles. All human action, he said, should aim at creating the greatest happiness for the greatest number of persons. That happy state will come about most surely if the individual is free to think and act as he pleases. The individual needs freedom to bring his capabilities to their fullest flower, Mill argued; and as each individual blossoms and blooms, society as a whole benefits.

Four major arguments underlie Mill's case for free expression. First, if we silence an opinion, for all we know we may be silencing the truth. Second, a wrong opinion may contain a grain of truth necessary for finding the whole truth. Third, even if the commonly accepted opinion is the whole truth, people will hold it not on rational grounds but as a prejudice unless they are forced to defend it. Fourth, unless commonly held opinions are contested from time to time, they lose their vitality, their effect on conduct and character.

Fighters for liberty commonly regard the government as their chief enemy, Mill said, and think that they have won the battle when they have thrown off the yoke of government. Yet the majority can tyrannize just as surely as government by imposing its collective opinion on the individual:

> There needs protection also against the tyranny of prevailing opinion and feeling; against the tendency of society to impose, by means other than civil penalties, its own ideas and practices as rules of conduct on those who dissent from them; to fetter the development, and, if possible, prevent the formation, of any individuality not in harmony with its ways, and compel all characters to fashion themselves upon the model of its own.

Oliver Wendell Holmes

In twentieth-century America the atmosphere that encouraged dissent which had made the eighteenth and nineteenth centuries times of disputation was diminishing. In the first years of the new century, the states passed a rash of laws forbidding criminal anarchy—the overthrow of the government by force, violence, or other unlawful means—and in World Wars I and II the federal government put limits on what people could speak and write.

Libertarian theory was somewhat narrowed by Justice Oliver Wendell Holmes of the Supreme Court, who believed that some limits must be set to the free expression guaranteed by the Bill of Rights. Just where the limits should be drawn, he thought, involves a fine balancing of the rights of the individual and the protection of society.

Like Milton and the eighteenth-century libertarians, Holmes saw the interplay of ideas as the way to truth. But his truth seems to have been a pragmatic one. Since the majority of reasonable men can be counted on to choose whatever is best for them at a given time, they will choose truth. The truth they seek, Holmes seems to have said, is not a unified, cohesive whole which explains all of nature and human affairs. Rather they choose a succession of little truths—"whatever proves itself to be good in the way of belief," as William James put it—in a continuous process of refining, maturing, and perfecting. Truth, then, is that which endures.

Free expression provides men with the divergent opinions which are necessary if they are to decide what is best for them. It is, moreover, a good safety valve in democratic society.

Yet government must protect the majority as well as the minority, Holmes thought, so it must draw some line between what it permits and what it does not. Speech is sometimes a form of action and, if criminal, should be punished. What matters is not whether the words in question are mere theory or actual incitement. What matters is the circumstances. Words allowed at one time under one set of circumstances might not be allowed at another time under a different set. "The most stringent protection of free speech would not protect a man in falsely shouting 'fire!' in a theatre and causing a panic," he wrote in the case of Schenck vs. United States, and he added: "The question in every case is whether the words used are used in such circumstances and are of such a nature as to create a clear and present danger that they will bring about the substantive evils that Congress has a right to prevent."

The "clear and present danger" doctrine sets as wide bounds to freedom as possible while allowing the government to protect itself in emergencies. The danger must be urgent, the possibility of harm immediate. Although the doctrine has been criticized, it has been the test by which the courts have judged most attempts to restrict freedom of expression since World War I.

The Electronic Media

While libertarian theory was evolving, the major media were the printed ones, and their contributions were, primarily, to enlighten the public, service the political system, and serve as a check on government. The electronic media of the twentieth century—motion pictures, radio, television—brought new problems: How much freedom should be granted to media which appeal less to man's critical faculties than to his suggestibility? How much freedom to media which have entertainment, not information and discussion, as their chief objective? Or to media which, like radio and television, are limited in number by the availability of channels?

motion pictures

Motion pictures in the United States have never enjoyed the breadth of freedom granted the printed media. For more than half a century, a number of states and municipalities have had official movie censorship boards. Chicago was among the first in 1907. Then came New York in 1909, Pennsylvania in 1911, and Kansas in 1913. The Pennsylvania law set the pattern from which most of the subsequent censorship laws were designed. No movie film could be shown in that state without the approval of the state board of censors. The United States Supreme Court in 1915 upheld the Pennsylvania law—and similar laws in Kansas and Ohio —as a reasonable exercise of state police power.

Censorship of the movies seems to have been tolerated for a number of reasons. From their beginning, the movies were looked on primarily as an entertainment medium. In their infancy they were linked with vaudeville houses, where they sometimes rounded out the bills, and as they matured they became associated with the legitimate stage. In England, where much of the libertarian tradition developed, the theater was regarded as an institution quite properly coming under government control on political and religious as well as moral grounds. The excesses of the film industry in the United States immediately after World War I created a climate of opinion favorable to restrictions. Producers tried to outdo one another in luring the public with risqué titles, lurid advertisements, and passionate love scenes. The stars themselves became involved in a succession of highly publicized off-screen scandals. Public pressure for governmental regulation was strong, and the movies had no tradition of freedom to prevent it.

Except in a few isolated instances, the motion-picture industry itself has done little fighting to enlarge its freedom. Aiming at a mass market, the major producers have been much more interested in giving the public what it wants than in championing the producers' right to dissent from majority opinion. They have cooperated with both official and unofficial censors, and they have tried to keep screen fare antiseptic by a voluntary production code.

In 1952 the Supreme Court in *The Miracle* case moved motion pictures a step closer to freedom by holding that a state may not ban a film on the censor's conclusion that it is sacrilegious. Motion pictures come under the protection which the Constitution gives the press, the court ruled, and their importance as an organ of public opinion is not lessened by their preoccupation with entertainment. However, the court said that the Constitution does not authorize absolute freedom to show every kind of movie at all times and places. Since sacrilege was the sole standard involved in this case, the court did not pass on other standards whereby states could ban films.

Nevertheless, the 1952 decision did establish that the movies are entitled to the protection of the First Amendment, an important victory that was consolidated and extended in later cases. Two years later the court held that New York could not ban *La Ronde* and in 1955 that Kansas could not ban *The Moon Is Blue.* In 1959 it rejected a ban that New York had imposed on a movie version of *Lady Chatterley's Lover,* which the censors said seemed to advocate immoral ideas. Justice Potter Stewart remarked that the Constitutional guarantee is not confined to just majority opinions: "It protects advocacy of the opinion that adultery may sometimes be proper, no less than advocacy of socialism or the single tax."

In 1963 four states—Kansas, Maryland, New York, and Virginia—and some twenty-five municipalities still had censorship boards, but the recent court decisions had considerably weakened their authority.

broadcasting

In the early 1920s, when commercial broadcasting was in its infancy, one new radio station after another began sending its signals into the airwaves. The only laws regulating broadcasting then were those designed for radio telegraphy, and they were powerless to keep chaos from the airwaves. Cacaphony filled listeners' earphones and speakers as amateurs cut in on the programs of professional broadcasters; as ships' radios punctuated musical programs with the dots and dashes of Morse code; as commercial stations tried to crowd competitors from their wave lengths.

The broadcasting industry itself turned to government for help in bringing some order from all the confusion. The eventual result was the Communications Act of 1934, which created the Federal Communications Commission to regulate broadcasting in the "public interest, convenience, and necessity." That act had been preceded by the Radio Act of 1927, which in general was its model.

Congress gave the FCC the authority to license broadcasting stations, to assign wave lengths, to decide hours of broadcasting for individual stations, and to suspend or revoke the licenses of stations not serving the public interest.

On the one hand, the FCC is a regulatory agency. Its authority to regulate broadcasting stems from the assumption that the airwaves belong to all the people. A broadcaster may use them only under license from the FCC after showing his qualifications for serving the public interest. While his license may be renewed at the end of its three-year term, it also may be suspended or revoked if the FCC decides that he has failed to serve the public interest. Rarely, however, has the FCC used its power to revoke a broadcaster's license. The agency's power to assign frequencies is based on two aims of Congress: first, to prevent the chaos which characterized broadcasting in the 1920s and second, to make broadcasting service available to the widest possible segment of the population.

On the other hand, the FCC is also a judicial agency, for it has been given the power to decide just what constitutes the public interest. The scope of its judicial powers, however, is yet to be determined. The law specifically forbids the FCC to censor broadcast content, apart from such items as profanity, obscenity, and information about lotteries. Yet since it is charged with making sure that stations operate in the public interest, the FCC has taken the position that it must necessarily concern itself with over-all program content. Indeed, its famous *Blue Book* set forth certain standards of desirable programming. Broadcasters have argued that any interference with content runs counter to libertarian principles and that the FCC should do no more than regulate frequencies.

To what extent the FCC may concern itself with the over-all performance of stations has never been settled conclusively by either Congress or the Supreme Court. The Supreme Court has indicated that broadcasting is protected by the Constitutional guarantees of free expression. But it also has upheld the government's right to regulate the use of the airwaves and to decide the composition of the traffic on them.

Government regulation of broadcasting represented a break with the traditional theory of freedom of the press, however much Congressmen and others tried to keep it in accord with libertarianism. It foreshadowed a major change in thinking about what the mass media should be and do in society.

References

BECKER, CARL L., *Freedom and Responsibility in the American Way of Life* (New York: Alfred A. Knopf, Inc., 1945).

——, *The Heavenly City of the Eighteenth-Century Philosophers* (New Haven, Conn.: Yale University Press, 1932).

BRINTON, CRANE, *The Shaping of Modern Thought* (Englewood Cliffs, N.J.: Prentice-Hall, Inc., 1963).

——, "Natural Rights," in *Encyclopedia of the Social Sciences,* Vol. 11 (New York: The Macmillan Company, 1937), pp. 299–302.

CHAFEE, ZECHARIAH, *Free Speech in the United States* (Cambridge, Mass.: Harvard University Press, 1948).

JENSEN, JAY W., "Toward a Solution of the Problem of Freedom of the Press," *Journalism Quarterly* 27 (Fall 1950) 399–408.

LINDSAY, A. D., "Individualism" in *Encyclopedia of the Social Sciences,* Vol. 7 (New York: The Macmillan Company, 1937), pp. 674–80.

MOTT, FRANK LUTHER, *Jefferson and the Press* (Baton Rouge: Louisiana State University Press, 1943).

PERRY, RALPH BARTON, "Liberty and the Limits of Government" in *Puritanism and Democracy* (New York: Vanguard Press, Inc., 1944), pp. 421–27, 512–15.

RANDALL, JOHN H., *The Making of the Modern Mind: A Survey of the Intellectual Background of the Present Age,* rev. ed. (Boston: Houghton Mifflin Company, 1954).

SIEBERT, FREDRICK S., THEODORE PETERSON, AND WILBUR SCHRAMM, *Four Theories of the Press* (Urbana: University of Illinois Press, 1956).

7

The Social

Functions

of the Media

In America and especially in England, the struggle for free
expression was long and bitter, and its outcome might have
been in doubt except for the success of liberalism in reshaping Western life and thought. The ideas of liberalism
were applied to the press, just as they were to other institutions. As the libertarian theory of the press evolved, the
media became responsible for performing certain social
functions. Some are of longer standing than others; some
have been modified with the passage of time. But taken
together, they comprise a widely accepted statement of
the role of the press in a democratic society.

Libertarian Functions

The mass media have two major tasks under original libertarian theory, according to F. S. Siebert in *Four
Theories of the Press*. The first is to inform; the second is
to entertain. Eventually, a third—advertising, or sales—developed as the press sought financial independence.

Basically, of course, the underlying purpose of the media
is to help discover truth, to assist in the successful working
of self-government by presenting all manner of evidence
and opinion as the basis for political and social decisions,

and to safeguard civil liberties by providing a check on government. In sum, then, libertarian theory seems to recognize at least six social functions: public enlightenment, servicing the political system, safeguarding civil liberties, profit-making, servicing the economic system, and providing entertainment. No one medium is responsible for all, of course; they are the functions of all the media working together. And they are functions grounded in the theoretical assumptions of liberalism discussed in the preceding chapter. One gets a picture of what libertarian theorists thought the media should be and do by looking at how they defined those functions and how they expected them to be carried out.

Libertarian theorists universally regarded public enlightenment as a major function of the press. From the time of Milton onward, they saw the press as an important partner in the search for truth. The press can feed man the information he needs to formulate his own ideas; it can stimulate him by presenting the ideas of others. The press, in short, is one of the most pervasive and inexpensive of educators.

Akin to that first function of the press is the second—servicing the political system. Democratic government places heavy responsibilities on both the citizen and the press. It assumes that the people can do a better job of governing than any leader can. To govern himself wisely in congregation with others, the individual citizen must be aware of the problems and issues confronting the state and of their possible solutions and consequences. In a government resting on public opinion, then, the press furnishes the people with the information and ideas that they need for making sound decisions.

The third function of the press—safeguarding civil liberties—stems quite naturally from the second. The idea of individual autonomy is the heart of libertarian theory. John Stuart Mill expressed the idea this way: "The only freedom which deserves the name, is that of pursuing our own good in our own way, so long as we do not attempt to deprive others of theirs, or impede their efforts to obtain it. Each is the proper guardian of his own health, whether bodily, or mental and spiritual." As each individual pursues his own good in his own way, as he freely develops his capacities, the libertarians thought, society would be enriched.

However, the individual's freedom is threatened from many quarters. The libertarians generally regarded government as the traditional and chief foe of liberty; even in democratic societies, those in office might use their power capriciously and dangerously. Therefore, libertarians assigned the press the task of maintaining a constant check on government, of playing the watchdog to warn the public whenever personal liberties are endangered. Jefferson especially made much of that point. "The functionaries of every government have propensities to command at will the liberty and property of their constituents. . . ." he wrote in

1816. "Where the press is free, and every man able to read, all is safe."
All is safe because the press can arouse the citizenry against the offenders.
For, as he wrote a few years later, "This formidable censor of public
functionaries, by arraigning them at the tribunal of public opinion,
produces reform peaceable, which otherwise must be done by revolution." The press, then, must protect not only its own freedom but the
freedom of all citizens.

Libertarian ideas on economics lend strong justification to the fourth
function of the press—making a profit. According to libertarian theory,
only a free press, operating under a private-enterprise system as conceived
by classical liberal economists, can enlighten the public, service the
political system and safeguard civil liberties. Only a free press, beholden
to neither government nor any faction in society, can serve the cause of
truth and, ultimately, the rights of individuals and the public interest.
Therefore, if the press is to be free to present views and information
without fear or favor, it must be a private, independent business enterprise.

This line of thought has been used also to justify large communications
units, including monopolies and chains and cross-media empires. The
argument is that a large prosperous organization can better withstand
pressures than a small marginal one.

Today, according to disciples of traditional libertarian theory, a free
people should strongly resist the government's entry into the communications field. Media owned outright by the government would be more
interested in perpetuating the party in power than in encouraging a free
trade in information and ideas. Media subsidized by the government
would threaten the autonomy of privately owned communications. Moreover, with no compulsion to earn a profit, media of either type would
have an unfair economic advantage over the traditional commercial press.
Therefore, they would inhibit the operation of the self-righting process
inherent in a competitive market of ideas and opinion.

In linking press autonomy with profit-making, libertarian theory has
borrowed freely from Adam Smith's concept of "the invisible hand" in
classical economics. In the economic marketplace, each individual working for his own gain ultimately contributes to the wealth of all. In the
marketplace of knowledge, each individual freely expressing his ideas and
opinions furthers the inevitable emergence of truth. Public benefit is
virtually guaranteed by the profit motive, which results in a press finely
geared to the wants and interests of the community. As the late George
Sokolsky once expressed it, "The battle for circulation becomes a battle
for the truth." His explanation of that remark is in the best libertarian
tradition:

> Some newspapers and some journalists may become subservient
> to base purposes but in a competitive system, the truth will out.

What one seeks to suppress, another will publish. The error of one reporter is corrected by another. The fallacy of one editor is made right by another editor. The attempt to serve some private cause is exposed by a competing newspaper or news service.

By serving his own personal interest in making a profit, then, the publisher, as if by deliberate intent, gives the community the sort of newspaper it wants and needs.

Contemporary critics of libertarian theory have challenged this. Instead of the invisible hand at work, they see a sort of Gresham's Law of Journalism under which bad publications tend to drive out the good. For, they argue, a press system devoted to the irresponsible pursuit of profit results not in publications serving the wants and needs of the community but in publications ill-equipped to meet the demands of a complex industrial society. The saving point in traditional theory, which critics more or less disdain, is the libertarian's contention that man is essentially moral; that if the pursuit of profit does not result in responsible journalism, the publisher's innate moral sense eventually will.

Servicing the economic system, the fifth function of the press, is intimately bound up with the task of profit-making. It became an accepted function of the media with the rise of modern advertising. From its infancy, the press to some degree served the economic system. In their news columns, the Colonial papers carried information about commerce and shipping; in their advertising columns, they carried announcements of merchants and traders. Mercantile dailies, newspapers devoted to specialized commercial information and announcements, were an important segment of the press even after Ben Day and his followers in the 1830s began turning out mass-oriented papers heavy with human interest.

However, as industrialization brought mass production and mass distribution, the media became more than ever linked to the economy and its operation. As always, the media report happenings in the business and industrial world, but today they do it on an unprecedented scale. Some two thousand business, technical, and trade publications cover new ideas and new developments in the specialized areas they serve for some sixty million readers. General newspapers and magazines carry an impressive load of material about business and economic affairs. Perhaps even more important, through advertising the media play an important role in bringing together the buyers and sellers of goods and services. By doing so, according to C. H. Sandage, they contribute to a high level of consumption, help to allocate the nation's resources, stimulate product variety, and help to make possible prices that are favorable to consumers.

The sixth function of the press, providing entertainment, began soon after Caxton introduced printing in England in 1476. Today, producing entertainment is one of the main tasks of all the media; indeed, some observers say that it is the principal function. Certainly, that is true of commercial broadcasting, the Hollywood film, and much magazine and book publishing. And even newspapers, following the lead of the news magazines and certain radio commentators of the thirties, have more and more packaged news as entertainment.

Although based on the assumptions of eighteenth-century thought, libertarian theory was modified without damage to its basic values as the media developed. Even today it is a powerful factor in the formulation of policy of public communication. It conceived of free expression as a natural right essential to individual autonomy and of a free press as indispensable to that prerequisite of a free society. Showing a strong faith in the rationality and essential goodness of men, it takes for granted the existence of a self-righting process inherent in a free and open market-place of knowledge and opinion. Its ultimate and morally persuasive appeal is to a transcendental order of values. Truth (the will of God or the laws of nature) is discovered by rational, moral men in the contest between it and falsehood. Freedom lies in the knowledge of truth and living in accordance with the book of nature (or the word of God). The center of its attention, as in libertarian thought in general, is the individual. The freedom of the press is a universal, personal right. The right to publish is subject only to individual reason and conscience and to the minimal restraints of a free society composed of autonomous individuals with similar and equal rights. Comprehensive and impressive in stature, libertarian theory helped to order the development and shape the character of America's contemporary media of mass communication.

The Social-Responsibility Theory

Although libertarian ideas still guide thinking about the press system in America, a new theory has begun to emerge. It has been called the social-responsibility theory, and it rests on this proposition: Whoever enjoys freedom has certain obligations to society. Therefore, the press, which is guaranteed freedom by the Constitution, is obliged to perform certain essential functions of mass communication in modern society. To the extent that the press assumes those obligations, libertarian theory will suffice. If the press is remiss, other agencies, including government, must make it live up to its responsibilities.

This new theory has arisen as critics, in recent years, have challenged the libertarian theory of what the press should be and do. They have questioned not only the performance of the press but also the underlying assumptions of libertarian theory regarding the nature of reality, of man, of society, and of freedom. The revolution in thought wrought by Darwin with his theory of evolution, Einstein with his theory of relativity, and Freud with his theory of the subconscious has undermined the very foundations of libertarian theory. The ideas of evolution and modern physics have challenged the Newtonian picture of the universe as a timeless, unchanging order. Modern psychology, with Freud and behaviorism, has laid siege to the fortress of rationalism. Contemporary political science, attacking the tradition of natural law, has declared the doctrine of natural rights to be merely a persuasive slogan of an outmoded ideology. Economists and social scientists, questioning the radical individualism of libertarians, have raised doubts about even the possibility of a free and open marketplace of either commodities or ideas. The self-righting process has been widely rejected as a notion without foundation in reality; the free exercise of individual will has been forcefully attacked as often harmful to the community.

Moreover, critics assert, certain social forces and certain developments within the media themselves have so altered the environment of public communication that the media cannot be and cannot do what libertarian theory prescribes. Most critics cite the three forces described in Chapter 3 —the rise of democracy, the economic and technological revolution which produced America's modern industrial culture, and the continuing urbanization of American life. Some mention two others. One is the development of markets for the mass consumption of mass-produced goods. The other is the development of modern advertising, publicity, and public relations for market exploitation. All those factors, the critics say, have so transformed the character and functions of the media that much of traditional libertarian theory is either obsolete or misguided.

grafting new theory onto the old

Like its predecessor, the social-responsibility theory is a composite of ideas. In one sense, it still consists of ideas, beliefs, and values which have been grafted onto the roots of traditional theory. For instance, social responsibility accepts the traditional functions of enlightening the public, servicing the political system, and safeguarding civil liberties. However, it reflects the belief that the media have not performed those tasks as capably as they should in a modern industrial democracy. The social-responsibility theory also accepts the functions of servicing the economic system, providing entertainment, and making a profit. But it would subordinate those tasks to the more important ones of promoting democratic processes and public enlightenment. Thus the social-responsibility theory accepts the six social functions traditionally assigned to the media. However, it does not accept the way in which some owners and operators have interpreted those tasks or the way in which the media in general have fulfilled them.

In another sense, the social-responsibility theory is quite new. Its major premise is that freedom, including the freedom of the press, cannot be defined apart from a responsibility for its exercise. The media, which enjoy a protected and privileged position under American laws and customs, have an obligation to society to carry out certain essential functions of mass communication in a complex, modern industrial democracy. If the media assume their responsibilities and make them the basis of operational policy, remedies may be unnecessary to insure the fulfillment of contemporary society's needs. But, as some social-responsibility theorists warn, in the areas where the media do not assume those responsibilities, other social agencies, including government, must see that the essential tasks of mass communication are carried out.

The First Amendment to the Constitution made no demand that publishers accept responsibility in return for their freedom. Nor did the framers of the Constitution intend it to. To them, as to all libertarians of the time, freedom of the press meant the right to be true or false, fair or unfair. The aim was to promote untrammelled discussion, tempered only by reason and conscience. There was no need to exact responsibility, for the system carried its own built-in correctives. In the free play of ideas and opinions open to the inspection and judgment of rational men, truth inevitably would arise victorious, and society inevitably would progress.

The twentieth century, however, has brought a gradual shift away from that radically individualistic conception of freedom of the press. Somewhere between the bitter partisanship of the early press and the ostensible objectivity of today's, faith diminished in the happy notion that unrestrained liberty coupled with man's reason and conscience would assure a press adequate to society's needs. Some readers began to demand certain standards of press performance, threatening to enact legislation if the media did not meet those standards. Chiefly of their own accord, publishers began to link responsibility with freedom. And, over the years, a remarkable change took place in the media's definition of free expression.

a new definition of freedom of the press

Today, especially in their public appearances, publishers and broadcasters commonly speak of "the public's right to know" and "the responsibility of the press." What this amounts to is a shift in the theoretical foundation of freedom of the press from the individual to society. What was once looked on as a universal, personal right to free expression is now described in terms of public access, of the right to know.

Exactly when publishers began to link responsibility with freedom is hard to say. In the early days when publishers were mainly printers who ran their newspapers as sidelines, they could scarcely be expected to give much thought to the ethics of journalism. And in later years when editors were frankly partisan and wedded to political interests, they could scarcely be expected to put the public interest above their own. By the middle of the nineteenth century, however, some newspapermen were men like Horace Greeley, who thought that the newspaper should ignore the trivialities of the penny press and the political bondage of the partisan press. The newspaper should not be politically neutral, but neither should it be subservient to any political party or faction. Rather it should furnish political leadership by setting the public good above party allegiance. At mid-century, too, there were men like Henry Raymond of *The New York Times*, who thought that the newspaper should be free of party but not of principle, that it should give its readers the broadest possible coverage, and that it should actively promote the community welfare. Later in the century men like William Rockhill Nelson of the Kansas City *Star* saw the newspaper as an aggressive force for community betterment. In all those views there were traces of a growing sense of social responsibility.

In the twentieth century, professions of public responsibility have become more numerous and more explicit. Increasingly, publishers have spoken of the duties imposed on the press by its growing professional spirit and its important role in the progress of society. In 1904 Joseph Pulitzer took nearly forty pages of the *North American Review* to defend his proposal for a college of journalism. But, as more than a plea for journalism education, his article asked publishers to place duty to the public above duty to the counting room.

> Commercialism has a legitimate place in a newspaper, namely, in the business office. . . . But commercialism, which is proper in the business office, becomes a degradation and a danger when it invades the editorial rooms. Once let a publisher come to regard the press as exclusively a commercial business and there is an end of its moral power.

Journalism needed moral and courageous men to give newspapers their ideals; for as Pulitzer put it, "Without high ethical ideals a newspaper not only is stripped of its splendid possibilities for public service, but may become a positive danger to the community."

As the decades passed, other publishers in similar words reminded their fellow journalists of the responsibilities which went with freedom. As newspaper ownership became increasingly concentrated and as the number of competing dailies declined, editors and publishers spoke of the special responsibilities of ownership in one-newspaper communities. In time movie makers and broadcasters, too, picked up the theme of public responsibility.

codes of performance

This sense of responsibility has been represented by codes setting ethical standards for the media. In 1923 the American Society of Newspaper Editors, a national organization, adopted its Canons of Journalism, which call upon newspapers to act with responsibility to the general welfare, truthfulness, sincerity, impartiality, fair play, decency, and respect for individual privacy. The canons are more attuned to libertarian theory than are the codes of the motion picture and broadcasting industries. The newspaper, some three centuries old when the code was adopted, was deeply attached to the liberal movement of the seventeenth and eighteenth centuries which led the battle for press freedom. Thus, the newspaper canons share the libertarian's faith in the rationality of man and in his ability to find truth and to distinguish right from wrong by the power of his reason and the dictates of his conscience. The canons also share the traditional faith that the self-righting process will operate in a free marketplace of knowledge and opinion. What is new in the canons is their acknowledgment that freedom of the press carries a responsibility to the public welfare.

In contrast, the codes of the electronic media are spiritually attached to the emerging values and beliefs of the social-responsibility theory. They reflect not only the intervening changes in intellectual and social climate but also the dark cloud of government intervention and regulation. To ward off government interference, the motion-picture industry set up a system of self-regulation under a voluntary code in 1930. The radio code of 1937 and the television code of 1952 were written under conditions of existing government regulation, which required them in any case to perform "in the public interest, convenience, and necessity." All three codes see the film and broadcasting industries as devoted primarily to producing entertainment, although they do make some references to the educational functions of those media. All three codes also reflect the changing image of man as not altogether rational in his behavior and as highly susceptible to moral corruption. The broadcasting codes are largely concerned, as a matter of social responsibility, with promoting public morals and conforming to accepted standards of good taste in programming and advertising. Only as if by afterthought do they deal with promoting democracy by enlightening the public. The movie code, which is merely negative, sets minimum standards of acceptability, not of responsibility. It does acknowledge, however, that the film can contribute to "correct thinking" and is concerned with safeguarding public morals.

Today the publishers of many American newspapers seem to feel a strong responsibility to the national interest and to the communities they serve. The movie industry, working under a system of self-regulation encouraged by threats of local boycott and censorship, professes to serve the public interest as it conceives it. Broadcasters, required by law to serve the public interest, also perform according to what they regard as the public welfare. True, performance of the media still falls far short of genuinely serving the public interest as some critics see it. Nevertheless, the avowal of duty to the public of itself represents a break with traditional theory. And self-regulation of the movies and government regulation of broadcasting, however negative and passive, are even sharper departures from the libertarian tradition. They are in far closer harmony with the assumptions and goals of the social-responsibility theory.

the commission on freedom of the press

The changing attitudes of owners and managers toward the functions and operations of the media reflect a general drift toward collectivist conceptions of reality, of man, and of society. Those conceptions are the foundation of the social-responsibility theory of the press. However, not until the report of the Commission on Freedom of the Press in 1947 were those attitudes and conceptions organized into what amounts to a new, integrated theory of the press. The commission, a group of distinguished private citizens headed by Robert M. Hutchins, conducted its studies under grants by Time Inc. and Encyclopaedia Britannica, Inc., to the University of Chicago. Social-responsibility theory is spelled out in *A Free and Responsible Press,* by the commission as a whole, and in *Freedom of the Press: A Framework of Principle,* by William E. Hocking, a commission member.

So far, social responsibility as defined in those volumes has remained little more than a theory. However, it is significant for two reasons. It reflects a conviction that contemporary thought and the conditions of modern society have outmoded libertarian theory. And it suggests a direction which future thinking about the press may take. Already, despite disavowals, much of the theory has found its way into the ideology and behavior of the mass media.

The commission has listed five things which contemporary society requires of the press. Together they provide a new conception of what the media should be and do as well as a measure of their performance. But these requirements did not originate with the commission; it drew them largely from the professions and practices of those who operate the media.

truth and meaning in the news

The first requirement of the media in contemporary society, according to the commission, is that they provide "a truthful, comprehensive, and intelligent account of the day's events in a context which gives them meaning." They should be accurate; they should not lie. Moreover, they should identify fact as fact and opinion as opinion and separate the two as much as possible. In simpler societies, the commission says, people could often compare accounts of events with other sources of information. Today they can do so to only a limited degree. Therefore, it is no longer enough to report *the fact* truthfully—as, for example, an accurate account of a statement made by a politician. It is now necessary to report the *truth about the fact*—presumably the motives and interests of the politician and the political situation in which he made the statement.

The media themselves appear to agree with the commission's dictum that they should be accurate and should separate news and opinion. Most newspapers try to adhere to the principle of objective reporting and to relegate expression of opinion to the editorial page. Quite apart from the newspapers' growing sense of professionalism, of course, economic considerations led to the development of objective reporting. The omnibus newspaper, which seeks to attract everyone and to alienate no one, found in the technique of reporting events and ideas without comment or interpretation a way to have its cake and eat it too. But philosophical principle was also involved. By separating news and opinion, by giving opposite sides of an issue, by reporting without comment what happened or what was said, the newspaper saw itself as helping the self-righting process by making it easier for the reader to discover the truth about things. Broadcasters took much the same view of their interests and responsibilities. Newscasters, depending heavily upon wire-service copy turned out according to newspaper standards, seldom deliberately violate the principle of objectivity. There are exceptions, of course, just as in the newspaper columns. But most newscasters, when they do make comments on the news, are careful to label them as such and to separate them from straight news.

With respect to the commission's demand that the media tell the "truth about the fact," the situation is somewhat different. Many newspapers and broadcasting stations are reluctant to go beyond telling what happened or what was said. To give the reader or listener the facts necessary to an understanding of the *why* would be to run the risk of introducing bias and distortion into the straight-forward account of events as they happened, of statements as they were uttered. In addition, to give the background of events and put them into context can be costly, not only in manpower and time but in audience reaction. The major elements of the newspaper's market might not find the "truth about the fact" palatable, even if it were attainable. Nevertheless, some media leaders are promoting "interpretative" and "depth" reporting. In public-affairs reporting, interpretation is widespread.

common carrier of ideas

A second requirement of the media, says the commission, is that they serve as a forum for the exchange of comment and criticism. What this means is that the media should regard themselves as "common carriers" in the realm of public discussion, even though not subject to the legal obligations of common carriers such as railroads. The commission does not expect the media to give space or time to everyone's ideas; but without giving up their own proper function of taking a stand, they should as a matter of policy carry views contrary to their own.

Behind this requirement is the concentration of media ownership in fewer and fewer hands. The individual citizen finds access to the facilities of public expression more and more difficult. Therefore, the media must act as a common carrier of viewpoints that otherwise might not find public circulation.

On this requirement, too, the media seem to agree with the commission. For example, Norman Isaacs, managing editor of the Louisville *Times*, has written: "The one function we have that supersedes everything is to convey information. We are common carriers. The freedom of the press was given for that purpose—and that purpose alone." Another newspaperman, Grove Patterson, defined one of the social responsibilities of the press as making sure that "newspapers are representative of the people as a whole and not of special interests." The failure of some editors, publishers, and owners to make their papers truly representative of the people lies in their erroneous belief that freedom of the press belongs to them alone, he said, and added, "A free press is vastly more than a meal ticket for publishers."

Broadcasters, too, speak in their code of exerting every effort to insure equality of opportunity in the discussion of public issues. The television code suggests that stations "give fair representation to opposing sides of issues which materially affect the life or welfare of a substantial segment of the public."

The media, of course, could be expected to oppose any laws compelling them to accept all applicants for space and time or any move by government to regulate their rates. Likewise, they could be expected to oppose anyone who demanded, as a right, that they disseminate his ideas. But in principle and in broad practice, the media accept the commission's conception of their role as common carriers of news and views. This makes sense on two counts. It helps them to appeal to as many people as possible in their audiences. And it helps them to expedite the self-righting process in the marketplace of knowledge and opinion.

a representative picture of society

The third requirement is that the media give a representative picture of the various groups which make up society. That is, they should accurately portray all social groups and not perpetuate stereotypes. The reason is that people are guided in their thinking by favorable or unfavorable group images. If the images are faulty, they contribute to faulty judgments. In giving a true picture of any group, the commission urges, the media should take into account its values and aspirations as well as its weaknesses and vices. If the portrayal is sensitive, the public will gradually acquire respect for and understanding of the group.

The media seem to subscribe to this requirement in principle, too, although they sometimes violate it in practice. Workers for the print media no doubt would say that they try to portray social groups accurately —and individuals and events as well—as part of their broader task of reporting the day's news truthfully and impartially. The codes of performance of the electronic media ask respect for national feelings and the sensitivity of racial and religious groups.

This attitude is easily understood. Once again, it makes good sense to treat one's readers and listeners with respect, to recognize the values, aspirations, and common humanity of all segments of one's market. Philosophical reasons for such policy are hard to come by in libertarian theory, which assumed and approved of social as well as intellectual competition, of the conflict of group interest and will. Reasons for this policy may be readily found, however, in the ascendant twentieth-century conceptions of reality, of man, of society, and of freedom. For these conceptions emphasize social equality over personal liberty, foreswear the ruptures caused by social competition, and seek to socialize individual interest and will. There is little reason to think that media owners and managers are immune to the new climate of ideas any more than they have been to contemporary political, industrial, and social forces.

clarification of the goals of society

The fourth requirement offered by the commission is that the media present and clarify the goals and values of society. The commission does not suggest sentimentalizing and manipulating the facts to create a rosy picture. Rather it asks for realistic reporting of the events and forces which work against social goals as well as of those which work for them. The media are an educational instrument, perhaps the most powerful one we have; therefore, they must "assume a responsibility like that of educators in stating and clarifying the ideals toward which the community should strive."

Aside from the question of whether or not educators would agree with such a statement, media practitioners probably would accept this requirement with little hesitation. Indeed, the media in practice, despite isolated objections from time to time, meet this requirement quite naturally. True, their content shows a sense of conflict regarding goals and values, especially the political and the economic. But they do show a strong tendency to close ranks when the traditional goals and values of society are at stake.

In general, the news columns, editorial pages, magazine articles, radio and television shows, and feature films all tend to support and reinforce the accepted goals and values of society. This is not surprising. There is a natural tendency of men to conform and there is also the practical necessity of pleasing one's customers. But some influence should be attributed, too, to honest, more or less independent belief in the commonly accepted goals and values of society. In any event, both the principle and the practice encouraged by the commission's recommendation clearly run counter to the radical individualism and competitive ethos of the libertarian tradition.

full access to information

The final requirement which the commission urges is that the media provide "full access to the day's intelligence." The citizens of a modern industrial society, the commission says, need a far greater amount of current information than a people needed in any earlier time. Even if the citizens do not always use all the information they get, the wide distribution of news and opinion is essential to government carried on by consent. Moreover, information must be available to everyone because leadership changes so often and so freely that any citizen may suddenly find himself holding the power of decision.

Media leaders surely agree. They are eager, for economic reasons, to reach as wide an audience as possible, but they also accept the obligation which the social-responsibility theory imposes of maintaining what the commission calls "freedom of information." As the media sought to conquer larger and larger markets and became more and more imbued with a sense of social responsibility, the idea that the public has a *right* of access to information, a basic right to be informed, became a foremost tenet of editors, publishers, and broadcasters.

This social-responsibility doctrine represents a break with traditional thinking in two ways. First, libertarian theory assumed that full access to the day's intelligence would be the natural consequence of a free and open marketplace of knowledge and opinion. No provision was made for guaranteeing the flow of information when individuals chose to be silent. But of what benefit is the right of free expression without full access to the information that ought to be conveyed? Hence, the media see themselves as active agents in breaking down the barriers of secrecy and silence. The American Society of Newspaper Editors, the journalism fraternity Sigma Delta Chi, and other professional groups formed committees to champion the public's right to know and to help open up the sources of news at all levels of government. Such respected journalists as James Reston, James Pope, and Erwin Canham have warned repeatedly of the dangers to democratic government of censorship by suppression of information.

Second, libertarian theory saw the media as instruments of individual—as opposed to public—will and interest. No person was barred in principle from either acquiring or using the media for individual ends. Indeed, libertarian theory encourages the selfish use of the media on the assumption that conflict in ideas, as in society, is of itself good. Today, however, the media are more and more seen as instruments of public, not individual, will and interest. With their operation and ownership resting in fewer and fewer hands, the media are exhorted to act as agents not of the individuals who own and manage them but of the public, which bestows its largess of freedom.

The Objective Theory of the Press

Both libertarian theory and the social-responsibility theory are "normative" theories of the press. In this sense, they are not merely *descriptions* of what the media are and do; they are also *prescriptions* of what they ought to be and do. Therefore, they have been likened to ideologies, which seek to rationalize or justify the behavior of media and to exhort them to perform certain desirable social functions.

Thus libertarian theory assumes that men, like atoms in the mechanical order of nature, are independent and autonomous entities in perpetual collision of will and interest. Accordingly, the most desirable social system is one in which the conflict of individual will and interest is resolved by a built-in mechanism: in politics, for instance, by multiparty competition and a governmental system of checks and balances. Similarly, the most desirable communication system is one in which the conflict of ideas is encouraged and resolved by competition in a free and open marketplace of knowledge and opinion. All that is needed to insure the enlightenment of the public and the successful working of democracy is the vigilant protection of the right of the individual to free expression.

The social-responsibility theory, on the other hand, assumes that men are not free and independent entities; rather, they are bound to society by countless moral and psychological threads. Hence, the most desirable social system is one in which men recognize their responsibilities to society and act accordingly. In politics, this means putting the public welfare before individual will and interest, or at least taking the public welfare into account before making judgments and decisions. In the communication system, it means that the media have a duty to the public to perform certain social functions in return for society's protection of their freedom. The free and open marketplace of knowledge and opinion can result only to the extent that free expression is tempered by a sense of responsibility to society.

Although the theories are in some ways opposed, being normative, they have one important similarity. Both are grounded in a particular ideology and prescribe what the media ought to be and do according to that ideology.

The so-called objective theory of the press is quite different in perspective and intent. The term here, as in its use with other social theories, has a dual meaning. First, it refers to a concern with objects outside of one's self. Thus, the media are looked upon as having, in some sense, an existence of their own apart from the motives and intentions of men. Like other institutional orders, they are specifically human inventions. But they tend to develop "objective" functions as contrasted with the "subjective" functions assigned to them by their creators. Sometimes these objective functions are neither intended nor regarded as desirable. Therefore, they are not recognized, much less acknowledged, by normative theories. Nevertheless, they do exist, and it is with their analysis and description that objective theory is chiefly concerned.

Second, the term "objective" refers to an impartial, disinterested way of looking at things. The media are considered without benefit of ideology, since the avowed aim of objective theory is to determine what they actually do, not what they ought to do. For what the media actually do may be quite different from, or something other than, what men might wish them to do. This does not mean that the descriptions or prescriptions of normative theory are rejected out of hand. Objective theory recognizes that the prescriptions of normative theory may have an important, even decisive, influence on the character and operation of the media. Then, too, objective theory accepts much of the description of the media in normative theory as valid. But it tries to describe the characteristics and functions of the media that normative theory ignores.

some objective functions of the media

The objective theory of the media originated more recently than either the libertarian or the social-responsibility theory. It probably dates from World War II, when social scientists took a renewed interest in the mass media as instruments of propaganda in modern society. Like the normative theory, it is a composite of ideas contributed by persons in many fields. Today the objective theory finds its main support among academicians of one sort or another—historians, psychologists, sociologists, political scientists, economists, and some journalism educators. Few people actually within the media are attracted to it, probably because they find normative theories more palatable and more useful.

Even some of the scholars most dedicated to the objective theory have let prescriptions typical of normative theory creep into their writings. For example, H. A. Innis, the Canadian historian, not merely describes but deplores the ephemeral character of media content, which he considers a serious threat to continuity and stable political relations. Joseph Klapper warns against the threat of cultural stasis and calls upon the media to cultivate a critical spirit. Nevertheless, scholars have begun to analyze from a viewpoint relatively free from ideology and cultural bias, and in recent years the outlines of an increasingly objective theory of the media have become clear.

Objective theory largely takes the media as it finds them. Its analysis and description proceed from an attitude of noncommitment to any form of ideology (except that of scholarship). Its claim is a theory that both corrects and supplements the normative theories of the past and present.

The media are seen as a mode of social interaction. That is, they facilitate interaction of various sorts: among individuals; between individuals and institutional orders of society; among the institutions themselves. All this they do by the symbolic transfer of meanings, values, and beliefs. Characteristically, they purvey the ethos of the social order in which they operate. Yet they also provide the means for response and for potential challenge to that order. On the one hand, then, reflecting the tension of values and interests in society, they tend to reinforce the status quo. On the other, offering a means of challenge, they tend to disrupt it. Which of those tendencies is stronger at a given moment depends upon the stability or instability of the society's power structure.

The media are taken as a system of human communication. They constitute an institutional order comparable to those of politics, industry, art, science, religion, education and the like. They interact with other institutional orders; they influence them and are influenced by them in the formulation of public policy. And the media are a source of social power as well as a means for its exercise.

Historically, communication systems invariably have been adjuncts of other institutional orders, not autonomous orders in themselves. That is, the requirements of other institutional orders have largely determined the basic policy and behavior of the media. In the United States, the requirements of the industrial order primarily decide media policy and behavior. In Russia, the needs of the political order govern the media.

Just how free the media are, therefore, depends upon the institutional structure of the society in which they operate. In his *Freedom of the Press in England,* Fred Siebert has shown how the arena of freedom can contract or expand, depending on how the political order dominates the policy and behavior of the media. The extent of government control, he says, depends upon the relationship of government to those subject to it. The more directly accountable the government is to those ruled, the more freedom the media will have. As the stability of the government and the structure of society come under increasing stress, restraints on the media are enforced more vigorously and freedom contracts.

A similar situation exists when the industrial order dominates the policy and behavior of the media. Then the industrial order will exert control. How much and in what way will depend on how stable the position of the industrial order is in the power structure of society. For the industrial order, like other institutional orders, is always under the threat of government intervention. Thus, in the United States, where the media operate chiefly as an adjunct of the industrial order and the government exercises only minimal sovereignty, freedom of the media is largely determined by the requirements and demands of the industrial order.

As adjuncts of other institutional orders, the media are generally used as agencies of social control. Consciously or unwittingly, the dominant institutional order, or a combination of the most dominant, uses the media to stabilize the social order and to consolidate the existing power structure. Sometimes, of course, the media may be an agency of change— as, for example, in revolutionary situations. But historically the media move with shifts in the locus of power. Regardless of temporary upheavals in the social order, they continue to perform their objective function of social control.

As a mode of social interaction and an agency of social control, the media are a kind of pseudo-environment which stands between man and the external world and which envelops him in an ersatz reality. As such, they may confront man as much with mystification as with enlightenment. Much the same can be said of the other institutional orders, of course. For politics, industry, religion, and all the rest are no less pseudostructures which man has invented to help him deal with the problems of existence. The media as a system of human communication take on a new and greater significance in a world where, as C. Wright Mills has said, "primary experience" has been replaced by "secondary communications": the printed page, radio, television, and film. The media played a major part in transforming the social order into a mass society. More than that, according to Mills, they are an increasingly important means of power for the élite of dominant institutional orders. They not only filter man's experience of external reality; they also help to shape his experience. They tell him who he is, what he wants to be, and how he can appear to be that way to others. They provide a rich fund of information about the world of events. But because they provide it in the language and images of stereotype and wishes, they often frustrate the individual in his efforts to connect his personal life with the realities of the larger world. Therefore, as man depends more and more on the media for knowledge and guidance, he becomes more and more vulnerable to manipulation and exploitation by the dominant orders of society.

This conception emphasizes a fundamental difference between the two normative theories of the media and objective theory. Libertarian theory, for instance, regards the media as agencies of individual expression. If left unrestrained, they will free men from ignorance and enable them to govern themselves in harmony with the realities of nature and social existence. The social-responsibility theory agrees, rejecting only the selfish use of the media. It asks that owners and managers accept their duty to society in performing the task of public enlightenment. Objective theory, however, regards the media generally as comprising an institutional order whose policy and behavior are determined by the dominant orders of society. The media together, then, according to this theory, work on behalf of the dominant orders as an agency of social control by manipulating the pseudo-world which they convey and perpetuate.

This objective view does not necessarily invalidate the others. It is a different angle of vision, a way of looking somewhat coldly at the media in terms of social processes.

Anyone who wants to understand the *what* and the *how* and the *why* of the mass media, then, ought to know something of what objective theory has to say. Although ideological theories are always based on reality, they also are usually somewhat myopic in their description of it. And while ideological theories may give direction and substance to man's existence, he can never really understand himself or the world until he lifts the veil of ideology and looks on the realities behind it. That is no less true for the student of the mass media than for the student of politics, economics, or religion. The literature of objective theory is both scattered and scarce, but it is well worth investigating. For no one can fully understand the media without getting some grasp of their character and functions beyond the descriptions and prescriptions of normative theory.

References

CARR, EDWARD HALLETT, *The New Society* (London: The Macmillan Company, 1956).

CHAFEE, ZECHARIAH, *Government and Mass Communications* (Chicago: University of Chicago Press, 1947).

COMMISSION ON FREEDOM OF THE PRESS, *A Free and Responsible Press* (Chicago: University of Chicago Press, 1947).

GERALD, JAMES EDWARD, *The Social Responsibility of the Press* (Minneapolis: University of Minnesota Press, 1963).

GIRVETZ, HARRY K., *From Wealth to Welfare: The Evolution of Liberalism* (Stanford, Calif.: Stanford University Press, 1950).

HOCKING, WILLIAM, *Freedom of the Press: A Framework of Principle* (Chicago: University of Chicago Press, 1947).

JENSEN, JAY W., "Freedom of the Press: A Concept in Search of a Philosophy" in *Social Responsibility of the Newspress* (Milwaukee, Wis.: Marquette University Press, 1962).

————, "A Method and a Perspective for Criticism of the Mass Media," *Journalism Quarterly* 37 (Spring 1960) 261–66.

LEVI, ALBERT W., *Philosophy and the Modern World* (Bloomington: Indiana University Press, 1959).

ORTEGA Y GASSET, JOSE, *The Revolt of the Masses* (New York: W. W. Norton & Company, Inc., 1932).

PETERSON, THEODORE, "The Social Responsibility Theory of the Press" in Fredrick Siebert, Theodore Peterson, and Wilbur Schramm, *Four Theories of the Press* (Urbana: University of Illinois Press, 1956).

———, "The Social Functions of the Press," in Nelson B. Henry, ed., *Mass Media and Education* (Chicago: University of Chicago Press, 1954).

SCHRAMM, WILBUR, *Responsibility in Mass Communication* (New York: Harper & Row, Publishers, 1957).

SIEBERT, FREDRICK S., "The Role of Mass Communication in American Society" in Nelson B. Henry, ed., *Mass Media and Education* (Chicago: University of Chicago Press, 1954).

8

The

Audiences

of the Mass Media

On September 3, 1919, President Woodrow Wilson climbed into his dark-blue private railroad car and set out on a campaign to convert the American people to their country's participation in the League of Nations. Most Senators opposed the League, but Wilson had faith that the citizens themselves would support it if he could but present his case to them. In the next twenty-two days, he traveled more than eight thousand miles in seventeen states and made forty formal speeches. Hugh Baillie, who covered the tour for United Press, remarked thirty years later in his memoirs, *High Tension:* "If he'd had radio and television to carry his message and personality to millions rather than to thousands, the history of the world might have been different. With television, I am convinced, Wilson would have carried the country for the League."

As recently as 1919, then, a speaker ordinarily could talk to only as many persons as could assemble within range of his voice. Today the marvel of broadcasting enables him to reach far-flung millions simultaneously. Before World War I, virtually no American homes had radio receivers; today 98 percent of all American homes have sets and so do three-fourths of all automobiles on the road. In recent years television has enabled millions to see events which once could be witnessed by a mere handful. Very few American homes had television sets in the late 1930s. Ninety-two percent of all households have them now, and as many as 54 million persons may be tuned in at the same time to a top-rated program.

The printed media, too, as a result of technical improvements, have come to count their audiences in the high thousands or millions instead of in the hundreds. At one time the book, patiently hand-lettered in the monks' scriptoriam, was available only to the few who had access to the table to which it was chained. Today books reach more than 30 percent of the population in the United States. Paperback editions are as available as razor blades and cigarettes—and are not much more expensive. Newspapers, which in the early nineteenth century sought out the cultured few, now reach almost everyone in the United States except the very young. Total daily circulation is almost 60 million, or well over a copy a day for each household in the nation. Magazines are read regularly by at least two-thirds of all Americans. *Life* alone reaches about one in every four adults; so does the *Reader's Digest*.

Within the memory of persons still living, the motion picture has developed from a curiosity which could be viewed by only the few who could peek into a cinescope into a medium which reaches about half the population.

Audiences Attracted to Various Media

Figures showing the size of the media audiences are dramatic and impressive, but they also can be misleading. They can easily give the impression that each newspaper, each magazine, each book, each movie, each broadcast program tries to reach all the people. But newspapers are restricted by geography. With rare exception, they concentrate their circulation efforts within the trade area served by the community in which they are published. The audiences of individual radio and television stations are also restricted, their boundaries being limited by the station's wave length. And all the media are restricted by the tastes, interests, and motivations of the public.

Therefore, as the introductory chapter indicated, mass communication does not mean communication for everyone. On the contrary, mass communication involves a selection of *classes*—groups or special publics, which of course might be quite large numerically—within the *masses* (or to put it less invidiously, within the larger public which is the total population). The media and their audiences come together through a process of mutual selection. The media tend to select their audiences by means of content. For their part, the audiences tend to select among and within the media, also on the basis of content.

The audience attracted to one medium may be quite different from that attracted to another, although obviously there will be a great deal of overlapping. Television counts among its fans many who would never leaf through a book, let alone own one. Newspapers have readers who rarely attend a movie.

Even within a single medium, the audience may differ widely in composition from one unit to another. The typical magazine is not edited for everyone; it is aimed at some homogeneous body of readers within the total population, for readers sharing a common profession, common interests, common tastes. Thus *Sunset* magazine makes its appeal primarily to middle-class home owners on the West Coast, *Hot Rod* to devotees of souped-up automobiles, *Parents'* to fathers and mothers seeking guidance in rearing their children, and *Diplomat* to high society in Washington, D.C., and other metropolitan centers.

newspapers

Reaching all but the very young, newspapers attract a highly heterogeneous audience. About 98 percent of all readers read something on the front page, about 58 percent some item on any other given page. But after the front page, subject matter is more important than page number in determining what is read, for different readers seek out different things in the newspaper.

Age, education, sex, and socioeconomic status—all are factors in determining just what will be read, according to studies conducted by Wilbur Schramm and David M. White. In general, young people are likely to use the paper for entertainment, older readers for information and views of public affairs. Adults do more news reading than young people, who seem to be introduced to the paper by its pictorial content and then branch out to its crime and disaster news. The more educated a person is, the more likely he is to use the paper for information; the less educated, for entertainment.

The amount of newspaper reading also tends to increase with education. Men tend to read newspapers at greater length and with greater intensity than women, and they are more likely to use them for information rather than entertainment. Higher economic status is generally accompanied by an increase in the reading of public affairs news as well as by an increase in the reading of sports and society news. However, higher economic status does not bring with it a decline in picture and cartoon reading.

broadcasting

Before the advent of television, radio ranked with the newspaper as the most universal of all the media. Perhaps the most distinctive characteristic of its audience was that it had no distinctive characteristic; radio appealed to all types, although tastes in programs and extent of listening varied. About 95 percent of all American adults listened at least fifteen minutes a day, and the heaviest listening was after 6 P.M. Now television is rapidly becoming a medium as universal as radio was in its heyday. Like radio, it has so broad an appeal that it reaches all segments of the population.

The great popularity of television has been largely at the expense of radio. Radio listening has dropped off sharply since the television set became a fixture in American living rooms. In 1949 the typical American family had its radio on for an average of about four and a half hours a day; now it is approximately two hours a day. In that same period— when the TV set was becoming a fixture—the family's television viewing jumped from almost nothing to more than four hours a day, a figure which has increased to about six hours.

Since television came along, the circumstances under which people listen to radio and their purpose in listening to it seem to have changed. Out-of-home radio listening apparently has increased, to judge from the greater sale of automobile and portable sets. Unlike television, which requires fairly close attention, radio can be heard with the so-called third ear. There is some evidence that people now use radio as a personal companion while driving to work or doing the housework or reading, whereas they watch television as a member of a family group. Having lost to television its preëminence as an entertainment medium, radio appears to have become somewhat more selective in seeking its audience. It now beams its programs at little publics within the population, as with its disc-jockey shows aimed at teen-agers.

Despite its many losses to television, radio is still far from dead. Although listening has fallen off, manufacturers turned out more than one and a half times as many radio sets in 1957 as they did in 1949. By 1964, Americans owned more than 185 million radio sets. For most families, radio is a necessity, not the luxury that television is sometimes considered. And even in the homes of avid television fans, radio continues to perform a useful role. When television fails to carry an event of great interest, people still rely on radio, as when 12,225,000 families tune in on a championship boxing match.

motion pictures

Television has hit motion pictures only a slightly lighter blow than it dealt radio. Movie attendance has dropped precipitously since television made the living room a private theater. More than half of a national sample interviewed in 1957 reported that their movie-going had declined in the previous few years, and they mentioned television more often than any other reason. One in three said that it had kept him from attending movies in the previous month. Projecting those figures, survey statisticians estimated that television was costing theaters as many as 89 million admissions a month. In fact, according to UNESCO studies, annual attendance dropped from 2,300,000 in 1952 to 2,165,000 in 1961. There also was a decline of movie-making. The industry made 344 major feature films in 1953. Ten years later, production was cut in half.

Most published studies of movie audiences were made before television producers had driven many moviemakers from the vast sound stages of Hollywood. The motion picture audience may have changed since then, but the changes are probably more quantitative than qualitative. In other words, while fewer patrons now occupy theater seats than in the days before television, they are by and large like the former patrons.

Pretelevision studies showed that the movie audience was predominantly a young one. Today, too, the movies evidently depend upon youth for their support. The great majority of movie-goers are under the age of thirty, more than half are under twenty, and almost a third are under fifteen, according to an elaborate study of audiences which the Opinion Research Corporation made for the Motion Picture Association of America. Adults of fifty or older seldom attend at all. Whatever their age, the unmarried attend more regularly than married people.

Content aside, it is not hard to explain why the movies are chiefly a medium for young people, for whom movie-going is a social activity. The mere act of going to the movies may be as important to them as the picture on the screen; groups of two or more account for about four fifths of all admissions. Then, too, the young are barred from some types of recreation—nightclubbing is an obvious example—and have not become involved in activities like P.T.A. and lodge meetings which eat into the time of settled adults. In many communities there are few places that a young couple on a date can go besides the movies. The lure of the movies for the unmarried can be similarly explained. Apparently, this group finds the social experience of movie-going preferable to solitary use of the other media.

Those who go to the movies frequently represent only a small part of the total population, but they are important to the movie industry. Only about 15 percent of the population attends once a week or oftener, yet they account for approximately 62 percent of theater admissions.

books

Books attract people who are above average not only in education but also in their heavy use of serious content of the other media—the "culturally alert" of their communities, to borrow Bernard Berelson's phrase. Books are more likely to attract young adults than old ones, people living in urban communities than in rural ones, people of high income than low. Book readers are more likely than people who do not read books to be critical of the other media.

Studies of reading have shown consistently that book reading and education go hand in hand. As the level of formal education declines, so does the extent of book reading. Some of the other characteristics of the book audience can be explained partly by this one factor of education. For instance, while young adults read more books than old ones, age might not be the governing consideration, since the older the population group, the less formal education it has had. Similarly, the greater amount of reading by urban dwellers might be explained by the higher level of education in urban areas. Obviously, however, more than education is involved. The resident of a rural area has less ready access to books than a city dweller. The person of low income cannot easily spare money for books.

General Principles

Although their audiences overlap considerably, each of the mass media has a general tendency to draw its most devoted following from a somewhat different sector of the total population. From the many studies which have been made of audiences, four general principles of communications behavior have emerged; and while they are subject to a number of exceptions, as are most generalities, they are valuable.

all-or-none principle

Paul Lazarsfeld and Patricia Kendall have remarked on what they call the all-or-none aspect of communications behavior, the tendency for the person who is above average in exposure to one medium to be above average in exposure to all. They found that a radio fan was also likely to be a movie fan; on the other hand, those who seldom went to the movies were not likely to use their radios very often. They found, too, that regular book-readers were more likely than other people to be frequent moviegoers.

There has been some study of this all-or-none tendency in magazine readership. Investigating overlapping magazine audiences, Lazarsfeld and Wyant found that anyone who reads one magazine is likely to read several. An audience study made by the Magazine Advertising Bureau a decade later underlined the same point; about half of all magazine readers read four or more magazines, 32 percent read two or three, about 18 percent read only one.

Studies since the advent of television have not negated this principle. They indicate quite clearly that pioneer set owners tended to be more media-minded than nonowners. That is, those who first acquired television sets had read the most magazines, had listened most to radio, had gone to movies most frequently. Studies also suggest that, after the initial novelty wore off, television did not (except for movies) seriously cut into the use of other media. What it did seem to affect was the reasons for use of other media. People apparently use television mainly for entertainment and escape. When it came along, they turned to it for those things instead of to the movies, comic books, and light fiction. Thus television seems to have displaced the printed media as a source of entertainment and escape, but it does not seem to have affected them as a source of serious, useful information.

One explanation for the all-or-none principle comes from Lazarsfeld and Kendall, who see two things at work—interest and opportunity. A man interested in escapist material may find it in books, in magazines, and on the air. Similarly, one interested in current affairs will perhaps seek information in newspapers, magazines, books. In short, a person can best satisfy his interest by using more than one medium. On the other hand, one who has little opportunity to use a medium—because of the demands of his job, hobbies, or other activities—will probably have little opportunity to use any.

education principle

In general, studies indicate that the better-educated a person is, the more use he will make of the media, although this principle has more exceptions than the others.

The amount of newspaper reading tends to increase with education, as does serious use of the paper. The typical magazine reader is likely to have well over five years' more schooling than the person who does not read magazines. Moreover, the number of magazines read by each one hundred persons in the population rises swiftly as the level of education goes up. The better-educated read more books than the rest of the population.

However, education is not a sure guide to the use of the electronic media. A safe generality seems to be this: Most reading is done by the college-educated, and the greatest fans of television, radio, and movies come from among the high-school educated.

economic principle

Another general principle is that the use of the media increases as income increases, although this seems to apply more strongly to the printed than to the broadcast media.

Not only does newspaper reading increase with economic status, but so does attention to serious content such as editorials or material about public affairs, social problems, economics, and science. Those of high income are more likely to be magazine readers than those of low. About 90 percent of those in the high-income group are magazine readers; only about half of those in the low-income group are. Those with large incomes tend to read more magazines as well. The number of books read also increases as income goes up.

Before World War II, Lazarsfeld found, as economic status declined, people had a greater preference for radio over the printed media. Recent studies suggest that those in the middle-income group are more likely to be television and movie fans than those in the upper or lower-income groups. Leo Bogart has suggested two plausible reasons for this finding. One is that broadcast programs, aiming at the largest possible audience, are directed at the great middle segment of the population. The other is that those with above-average income and education have greater resources for occupying their leisure time.

age principle

As Americans become older, they tend to use the media more for serious purposes and less for entertainment. Older newspaper readers are more likely than younger ones to read letters to the editor and public-affairs reports, less likely to occupy themselves with comics and sports news. They are great readers of editorials; for those over sixty, editorials rank second only to news pictures in readership, whereas scarcely anyone under twenty turns to the editorials. In radio listening, older adults seem to favor such serious fare as newscasts, discussions of public issues, classical and semi-classical music, religious programs, and quiz shows, the last perhaps because they are considered educational. On the other hand, the older readers apparently have little interest in drama, comedy, mysteries, and popular music. The pattern is only slightly different in television. Older viewers are more likely than the young or those in their middle years to favor newscasts, forums, music, and quiz shows; less likely to favor dramatic programs, whose greatest appeal is to those between thirty and fifty; and less likely to favor mysteries. On the other hand, the elderly do like televised comedy-variety shows, sports, and films.

The extent to which people use the media does not increase steadily with age. Rather, it tends to drop off in the later years. The amount of news reading, rising swiftly through the teens, hits its height between the ages of thirty and fifty and then tapers off gradually. Older adults read fewer books and magazines than young adults. Movie attendance, at its peak in a person's late teens, drops off sharply after age thirty; studies made before the advent of television suggest that those under thirty comprise about 70 percent of the movie audience.

Verifying Sizes of Audiences

Advertisers have become increasingly interested in the audiences they are paying to reach. To assure himself of his money's worth, the advertiser needs the answers to many questions. Does the newspaper or magazine actually reach as many readers as the publisher says it does? How great is their interest in the publication? How strong is their loyalty to it? Are they really the best possible prospects for the product or service? How many sets are tuned to a given television or radio program? How many people are clustered around each set? Under what conditions do they watch or listen and with what degree of absorption? What programs were they watching before this one? How desirable are they as prospective buyers?

printed media

In the nineteenth century, advertisers looked to circulation as a measure of the audience of newspapers and magazines. One of the first attempts to verify circulation claims was made in 1847, when a neutral publisher and a paper dealer were called in to settle a dispute between the New York *Tribune* and the New York *Herald*. After checking the number of copies issued and the amount of paper consumed by each newspaper, the referees adjudged the *Herald* the circulation winner, 28,946 to 28,195.

But that was unusual. Ordinarily an advertiser was fortunate if he learned even the claimed circulations. Some publishers regarded circulation as a business secret, never to be shared with advertisers. Others made outrageous circulation claims. Rather than endorse possible exaggerations, the issuer of one directory of periodicals in 1870 simply omitted circulation figures. About that time George P. Rowell, the pioneer advertising agent, was working painstakingly to get accurate figures for a directory he published. He gave special recognition to publishers who supplied affidavits certifying their circulation data.

Even fairly reliable circulation figures were open to several interpretations. They could refer to all copies distributed, including those given away and those sold in bulk, or could refer just to those sold at regular prices. Nor could the advertiser tell much about the quality of the circulation—how it was obtained and how willing the subscribers were to pay for the publication.

The Association of American Advertisers in 1899 made the first effort to verify circulation claims on the basis of uniform standards, but it quickly encountered a host of difficulties, among them a reluctance of publishers to cooperate, a shortage of funds for operation and necessary experimentation, a lack of standardization in publishers' bookkeeping and auditing methods—and even the absence of an accurate definition of the term "circulation." The attempt ended in failure in 1913 with the association in debt to some of its backers. But other advertising groups were proceeding with parallel programs, and the Audit Bureau of Circulations emerged in 1914.

The ABC, as it became known, has for decades provided advertisers with essential circulation data about a lengthening list of newspapers, consumer magazines, business publications, and farm papers. Its bylaws hold:

> The objects of the Audit Bureau of Circulations shall be to issue standardized statements of the circulation of publisher members; to verify the figures shown in these statements by auditors' examination of any or all records considered by the Bureau to be necessary; and to disseminate circulation data only for the benefit of advertisers, advertising agencies, and publishers.

By listing such points as methods by which circulation was obtained, authorized prices for subscriptions, premium offers, and market zones, the Bureau helps the advertiser assess the quality as well as the quantity of audience. Other agencies which now perform similar functions are Verified Audit Circulation Company, Office of Certified Circulation, Canadian Circulations Audit Board, and Business Publications Audit of Circulation, Inc.

broadcast media

In February 1953, the water commissioner of Toledo reported that he could rate the popularity of television programs by fluctuations in water pressure. Pressure stayed high while people remained close to their sets; it plummetted at program's end as viewers walked out on the concluding commercial to go to the bathroom. By applying what he called the Program-Popularity-through-Pumpage-and-Pressure Index, the commissioner concluded that "I Love Lucy" was the most popular television show. As early as 1935, the British Broadcasting Corporation had known that it could gauge audience size by water pressure, and twenty years later the management of a large apartment house on Long Island could estimate the appeal of certain television shows by demands on the hot-water boiler.

These are intriguing but crude and limited methods of determining the audience reached by a given radio or television program. How *can* one measure the size of the broadcast audience? Broadcasts offer nothing so tangible as a subscription list to count, for they are beamed into the great unknown.

When radio was in its infancy, broadcasters urged listeners to send in postcards. This mail response may have given some notion of how far the signal carried but it gave only the sketchiest information about how many people received it. Then research workers, applying statistical techniques to obtain representative samples of the population, devised methods for gauging audience size. Four used during the happy heyday of radio have been adapted to estimate the number watching television programs today. These methods are the recall, the coincidental, the mechanical recorder, and the diary.

The *recall method* was first used by Archibald Crossley in 1929. Interviewers ask a carefully selected sample of listeners what programs they heard or viewed during a stated period. They also try to learn the listening or viewing pattern of other members of the household. They may refresh the respondent's memory with a printed list of programs. Pulse, Inc., a commercial agency, has used this method for its surveys.

The *coincidental method* involves telephone interviews. While a program is on the air, interviewers call a sample group of people in various cities to ask whether they are viewing or listening and if so to what program. From this information, researchers can estimate the size of the audience attracted to a given program or to some part of it. Obviously this can cover only listeners or viewers with telephone service, but the researchers take the ratio of telephone installations to set ownership into account in making their estimates. C. E. Hooper pioneered in developing this method for determining radio listenership and continued to use it in combination with the diary method for information about television audiences.

The *mechanical recorder method* uses devices attached to receiving sets to enable researchers to learn the listening or viewing habits of those in rural homes and those without telephones. Special instruments installed in a number of representative households tell when the set is on and to what station it is tuned. One disadvantage, apart from the high cost, is that the audimeter tells only when the sit is tuned to a particular station, not how many are watching or listening—if indeed anyone is. However, proponents say that they have found that actual listening and viewing closely correspond to the number of sets in use. A. C. Nielsen devised this method and first used it in the early 1940s to measure radio listening. Later he installed audimeters in television sets.

With the *diary method,* individuals chosen to comprise a representative sample are asked to keep a record of all listening or viewing over a specified period. They may be asked to include information about which other members of the household watched or listened to the programs. They record all this data on a standardized diary form, which they send periodically to the central agency for tabulation.

These surveys can disclose two types of information: the average number of listeners or viewers for the duration of the entire program and the total audience of a program, including those who tuned in for only part of it.

Bases of Selection

So ubiquitous are the mass media that Americans are engulfed by many times the communications they can possibly heed. Inevitably they are highly selective.

The typical American helps himself to only minute portions of the bountiful fare. He chooses only about one-fourth of the assortment of news presented him by his daily paper. To that paper he gives only about forty minutes a day, although he would have to spend three or four times that much to read it completely. When radio was in full flower, he spent less than three hours a day listening to his choices from the more than one hundred hours that were available. He listened only to about half of the items in a fifteen-minute newscast. The average television set, which is in use about six hours a day, carries only about one-third of the programs available in even a single-station city and about 4 percent of the programs broadcast in a large city such as Los Angeles.

Consider some of the selections that the typical American makes. First, of course, he decides whether or not he will use the mass media at all. Then he chooses the medium to which he will give his attention; that is, he decides whether he will watch television, listen to the radio, read a newspaper or magazine or book, or go out to a movie. Having chosen one medium, he selects from among its offerings. He decides whether he will watch a television drama or a variety show, whether he will read newspaper editorials or the comics, whether he will read the major articles in his picture weekly or scan the photographs.

He chooses the circumstances under which he will use the medium. He may elect to read his newspaper while the television set is blaring, while his children are playing spaceship around his armchair and while his wife is trying to engage him in a one-sided conversation from the kitchen. He may read his magazine on a jolting commuting train or in the peace and quiet of his bedroom at day's end. And he also decides the degree of attention that he will give to the material he selects.

Why do people make the selections they do? If an editor or producer knew precisely why, he would have an inestimable advantage over his competitors. A good many factors come to play in the selections one makes among and within the media, of course. Different people make different selections, and one person makes different choices under different sets of circumstances.

Wilbur Schramm of Stanford University has offered a tentative answer to the basic question of why people select as they do. He has advanced two general principles of selection—least effort and promise of reward—as being in accord with existing research, even if not yet proved conclusively.

least effort

By least effort, Schramm means just what the term implies: that the reader, viewer, or listener takes the route of least resistance in his choice of communications. In everyday affairs, least effort seems to play an important part in governing human behavior. Indeed, George Zipf of Harvard has written a thick book documenting what he calls the "principle of least effort." Simply stated, Zipf's principle is that in solving his immediate problems a person looks at them against a background of what he regards to be his future problems. He tries to minimize the work he must devote to solving both his immediate and his probable future problems. Least effort, Zipf believes, is fundamental to all human action, and he shows it at work in individuals and in society. In communications behavior, as Schramm sees it, a number of factors contribute to least effort.

One is availability. All other things being equal, one helps himself to whatever communication medium is most readily at hand. A family is more likely to watch television in its own living room than to get out the automobile, drive to a far-off theater, hunt for a parking space, pay admission, and attend a motion picture. That same family will choose a program with a clear, sharp picture over a program with a blurred, wavy one. What is more, some members of the family will not be especially interested in the program on the screen, but will watch because it is less effort to watch than to leave the set. A patient waiting in a dentist's office will pick up a copy of *National Geographic* from the end-table instead of walking to the corner drugstore for a newspaper. From an early study of the extent to which factory workers and students actually read about the subjects that most interested them, Douglas Waples concluded that accessibility is "perhaps the most important single influence" upon reading, except for readers with highly specialized interests.

Expense also is related to least effort. A family which has just spent $300 for a new television set probably cannot afford a membership in the Book-of-the-Month Club, a daily subscription to *The New York Times,* and subscriptions to a half-dozen magazines all at once. College students on limited budgets probably are more likely to buy books in inexpensive paper covers than in hardbound editions. However, the alacrity with which even low-income families have bought television sets suggests that expense is not an insurmountable barrier to using a particular medium if the promised reward seems great enough.

Time is another factor involved in least effort. Leisure time comes at different periods for different people. Some men find the commuting train a good place to read the newspaper. Others consider the automobile ride to and from work a good time to listen to the radio. Daytime hours when the family is away are a good time for many housewives to listen to the radio. The television set is an electronic babysitter in many households just before the evening meal.

Role, habit, and custom also may influence media choices, according to Schramm, for it is easier to continue behavior patterns than to change them. Eliot Freidson has suggested that one selects media content from habit or under pressure from one's social groups. Communications behavior, in fact, becomes a part of social behavior, and some selection of media fare is really just a habitual social act. For example, only about one person in five in a movie audience may have made any conscious effort to choose that particular movie. A young man may take his date to the movies on Saturday night simply because going to a movie is what the young people in their group do on Saturday night. A midwestern couple may read the Sunday edition of *The New York Times* because others in their social group do. A family may subscribe to a magazine out of habit long after keen interest in it has died.

promise of reward

Schramm suggests that promise of reward means that a person chooses from the available communications whatever he thinks will give him the greatest reward. His selection is based on his knowledge of what communications are available and on his needs of the moment, as he sees them. One's needs result from a whole complex of factors, including environment, personality, social position, and physiological situation at the moment. Obviously, then, needs will change in the same person from time to time and will differ greatly from one person to another.

Schramm classifies rewards into two general types: immediate and delayed. Content which pays its rewards at once may relax tensions or help in simple problem solving. It includes stories dealing with accidents, corruption, crime, disaster, society affairs, and sports, in all of which the reader gets a vicarious thrill without the strain of actual participation. Content which pays its rewards in the future may promise information useful for social effectiveness. Instead of reducing tensions, it may increase them. But it prepares one for meeting needs and problems. This may include material about economic and public affairs, health, social problems, and the like.

Distinctions between immediate and delayed reward content are often hard to make, Schramm recognizes. Although the division of rewards into those two categories generally holds, and although a person's reading habits tend to cluster around one or the other, one may find an immediate reward in what ordinarily would be regarded as remote-reward material and vice versa. Indeed, he might get both rewards from a single item. Ordinarily a serious drama review would be considered to hold a delayed reward for the star fullback, for instance, but if his girlfriend played the leading role on opening night his reward might be immediate.

In a study of news reading reported in the *Journalism Quarterly*, Herbert Kay takes issue with Schramm on some points. He sees limitations in classifying news items on the basis of reward apart from their readers; the reader-item relationship must be taken into account, he believes. The chief fault of Schramm's position, he thinks, is the assumption that material gives either immediate reward or delayed reward but only rarely both. All reading must promise some immediate reward, Kay contends, for it promises to answer the essential question, "Why?" News reading always carries the immediate reward of emotional satisfaction. The distinguishing characteristic of delayed-reward material is that it carries intellectual or material satisfaction as well as emotional satisfaction.

Reasons for Using the Media

Why do people pay attention to the mass media at all? A cynic might say: because there is no escape. A more accurate reply is probably that the mass media satisfy certain needs. In recent years there has been a growing amount of research—still unfortunately small—which provides some clues to these gratifications.

As one would expect, different people make different uses of the media. Age, sex, education, socioeconomic status—such things tend to influence the reasons for which people turn to the media. So do much more subtle factors—attitudes, aspirations, hopes, fears. Not only do these predispositions help to govern the use a person makes of the media; they also help to govern how he interprets what he finds there.

newspapers

To say that people read newspapers to become informed is to oversimplify a situation involving complex and subtle motivations. It is true that people read to become informed, but they want to become informed for varying reasons: to achieve prestige, to escape boredom, to feel in contact with their environment, to find reassurance for their behavior, and to adjust to their roles in society.

On June 30, 1945, the deliverymen of eight major newspapers in New York City went on a strike that lasted for more than two weeks. While most New Yorkers were without their daily papers, Bernard Berelson and a team of research workers moved in to find out just what doing without the newspaper means. They found that the newspaper plays several roles.

To some readers the paper is important in its traditional role as a source of information and ideas about serious public affairs. They use it not only for the raw facts of current events, the researchers found, but also for the interpretations of editorial writers, background writers and columnists. Yet other readers are apparently less interested in the content itself than in the use to which they put it—bolstering their own ego. They use the newspaper because it enables them to appear informed about issues and events in conversations with other people. It is a source of social prestige.

Some readers find the newspaper an indispensable tool in the routine of daily living. They feel a little lost, sometimes almost helpless, without its advertisements for local stores, radio and movie schedules, financial information and stock market reports, weather forecasts, recipes, and fashion tips.

Readers also use the newspaper for social contact. It gives them, through its gossip and advice columns and human-interest stories, glimpses into the lives and problems of others. In a small town, one may know many of his neighbors; in a large city, as one reader expressed it, the newspaper "makes up for the lack of knowing people."

Then, too, readers use the newspaper to escape from their everyday world. It is an inexpensive vacation away from the cares, problems, frustrations, and boredom of daily routine. More than that, it is a socially acceptable form of escape.

Reading has value per se in American society, Berelson concluded, and the newspaper shares in that value as the most inexpensive and convenient purveyor of reading matter. It is a source of security in an insecure world, and reading it has become for many people a "ritualistic or near-compulsive act."

Some thirteen years after Berelson's study, New York newspapers again suspended publication because of a deliverymen's strike. New Yorkers had an almost universal feeling of loss over the absence of their papers, according to a survey conducted by the Department of Journalism at New York University. Their daily routine was scarcely disturbed by their lack of newspapers; they turned to radio as their chief source of news and to television as a poor second. But no other medium really took the place of newspapers; without them, New Yorkers felt "out of touch with the world" and had "a distinct feeling of loss." The questionnaire returned by one Manhattan housewife neatly summarized the findings of the entire survey. After the question asking if the absence of newspapers had affected her daily routine, she wrote, "No." Alongside it, in large letters, she added, "I Just Miss Them."

broadcasting

Radio and television content affords a variety of lures. Social contact, counsel in daily living, self-glorification, escape from boredom—all are served by broadcast fare.

In the days of radio's glory, Herta Herzog of McCann-Erickson sought to learn what gratifications listeners found in daytime serials. For some women, she found, the programs were a source of emotional release. Listeners welcomed the chance to cry over the misfortunes of others or to share in their triumphs, to compensate for their own troubles, or to magnify their own problems by identifying them with those of the heroes and heroines. Secondly, women liked the opportunities for wishful thinking that the programs afforded. By identifying themselves with the fictional characters, listeners could compensate for their own inadequacies and failures.

Finally, for many women the serials were a source of advice on meeting life's problems and on proper modes of behavior. The less formal education women had had or the more they regarded themselves as worriers, the more help they found in daytime radio serials. They were aided in social relationships—getting along with other people, handling husbands or boyfriends, rearing their children. Said one listener, "Bess Johnson shows you how to handle children. . . . Most mothers slap their children. She deprives them of something. That is better. I use what she does with my children." Listeners also learned how to meet the threats of a hostile world. They learned to adjust to such tragedies as a death in the family or a son's going off to war. They learned how to react when trouble came. "When Helen Trent has serious trouble she takes it calmly," one listener commented. "So you think you'd better be like her and not get upset." Some listeners considered the programs so valuable that they sometimes referred friends seeking advice to specific programs.

It is easy to find fault with this sort of help. Basically, the listeners learned to cope with adversity in three ways: by wishful thinking which promised that everything would work out all right, by projecting blame to others, or by applying some convenient formula. Whether or not those measures are adequate for solving one's personal problems is certainly questionable, but thousands of listeners evidently thought that they were.

The gratifications which listeners found in radio soap operas no doubt explain some of the popularity of television's daytime serials. Similarly, a study of radio quiz programs which Miss Herzog conducted and reported in Lazarsfeld's *Radio and the Printed Page* helps to explain the appeal of television quiz shows.

According to Miss Herzog, people tune in on quiz shows because of four major appeals: the competitive, the educational, the self-rating, and the sporting. The listener can satisfy his competitive urge by pitting his knowledge against that of the actual contestant or that of someone who is listening with him. He may show off by simply displaying his knowledge before others clustered around the set. If he fails to answer some questions, he is more than compensated by his correct answers to others. What listeners regard as the educational aspects of the quiz program have greater attractions for them than the competitive aspects. They see the answers as contributing to diversified knowledge, more easily obtained from the quiz show than from reading, and useful in everyday conversation.

Furthermore, the quiz program gives the listener a chance to find out about himself, and he usually comes off better than he had expected. A good score can compensate for life's failures and can soothe his feelings for being so indolent about furthering his education. While the sporting appeal seems less important than the others, according to Miss Herzog, listeners take pleasure in trying to pick the winner. If one chooses a contestant better educated than himself, his self-esteem is enhanced by his identification with the winner. If one picks a contestant much like himself and roots for him to win, he may vent his aggressions against those better educated.

In 1959, when eight of the ten television shows with the largest audiences were westerns, many observers tried to fathom their tremendous popularity. Thomas W. Moore, program director for the American Broadcasting Company, had an uncomplicated explanation: "The western is just the neatest and quickest type of escape entertainment, that's all." But that explanation was too simple for many observers.

Dr. Ernest Dichter, a pioneer in motivational research, explored their psychological appeal in *Broadcasting* magazine. Westerns are typical folk art with unchanging characters writ larger than life, he said. They provide rootless Americans an emotional identification with their country and its past. By having the hero single-handedly solve problems justly and with dispatch, they help to allay the frustrations that the viewer feels as an impotent individual in a complex and threatening society. They give him a sense of security by portraying a world of perfection and order in which the wicked are punished and justice triumphs. For women they have an added appeal: They help to satisfy a craving for independence by picturing woman as sharing the decisions and hardships necessary to creating a good society.

magazines

To learn what motivates women to read magazines, *Good Housekeeping* commissioned Social Research, Inc., to conduct a study covering six women's magazines and two general magazines. The study, published under the title "Women and Advertising," pictures what it calls the "middle majority housewife." She moves in a small world, physically and socially, and her home is its center. Even in her own community, she seldom travels beyond her own neighborhood; her social circle consists largely of her family and a few close friends. She views the outside world with distrust and anxiety. She wants to hold it at bay, although she knows she cannot control it, for it can strike suddenly with disastrous effect. Whatever happens outside of her own little world she evaluates by its impact upon her home. Within that home, she regards herself as the central figure, the one who primarily, and properly, manages the family. She wants nicer things and more security than her own parents had, although she is not impelled to alter the basic pattern of her existence. Her home-making tasks are arduous, but she is compensated in part by praise and affection from her family. It is from them, not from outsiders, that she craves approbation. She does not care for the recognition that comes from participation in civic and charitable organizations. On the contrary, she does not think that women should be active in affairs outside the home, except possibly in those that impinge directly upon it, such as P.T.A.

What part do the women's magazines play in her life? According to the study, they are important in three overlapping areas of her existence—social orientation, realistic concerns, and personal experiences.

From stories, articles, and advertisements, she gets ideas for relating herself to the people in her world and for strengthening her position as the central figure in the household. She learns how to get along with members of her own family, with her friends, and with the outsiders whom she is likely to meet, such as teachers and doctors. She finds answers to a host of questions which her dealings with others raise: How much should her children watch television? How should she prepare them for a stay in the hospital? How should she entertain guests, and what should she serve them? What is a proper wardrobe for her husband?

The magazines also teach her how to do all sorts of practical things not closely involving other people—her "realistic concerns," to use the phrase of the study. They teach her the practical skills of cooking, sewing, and housekeeping. They help her to formulate her goals and some give her an idea of what she can reasonably expect from life. They give her information about the ways and costs of attaining her goals, about her own world and that of other housewives. and about the outside world which she fears and mistrusts.

The magazines also enter into her personal experiences, into her private set of values and judgments. They help her to ward off a feeling of loneliness. They provide her the stuff of creative daydreams in which she explores ways of life unfamiliar to her. They bolster her self-esteem by underscoring the importance of her work and contributions. They assure her that the virtues and values she cherishes are the right ones.

By guiding their readers in daily living and by supporting their moral and ethical code, the women's magazines seem to afford gratifications similar to those of daytime radio serials. So do the confession magazines. Indeed, Herta Herzog noticed some overlapping of audience: "If a magazine is especially preferred by daytime serial listeners, it is of one of two types: either its content is noticeably similar to that of the daytime serial (the 'true story') or it centers about home life."

Perhaps the greatest similarity in audience and appeal is between the daytime serial and the confession magazine. Readers of the confession magazine ordinarily do not read the "white-collar" women's magazines. Indeed, according to the publishers of confession magazines, such women read little not written in their vernacular; apart from daytime serials, which can treat but one behavioral problem at a time and that only over a period of several weeks, only confession magazines deal in the problems, lives, and language of these women.

Who are the readers of confession magazines? According to the publishers, they are women who have been moved by the redistribution of income into a middle-class setting. They find their new setting and their roles in it strange and uncomfortable. They may live in the same general neighborhood as their white-collar sisters and share economic equality with them, yet they move in an entirely different social orbit and have an entirely different outlook on life.

They differ in many ways from readers of the white-collar women's magazines, according to a report prepared for Macfadden Publications by Social Research, Inc. The reader of confession magazines is less confident than the reader of the service magazines that she is the center and prime force in her household. She wants to be a good mother to her children, but she sometimes doubts that she is. She sees her husband as more domineering, self-sufficient, sexually active than the middle-class reader does. And she sees herself as having two roles—that of mother to her children, that of wife to her husband—and the conflict of roles sometimes disturbs her. She is primarily interested in people, not in ideas and institutions. Although her world, too, is a moral one, she does not want to live up to all values, standards and patterns of behavior propagated by the white-collar women's magazines.

According to such students of the confession magazine as Wilbur Schramm and George Gerbner as well as Social Research, Inc., the confession magazines not only entertain the reader but also help in resolving her problems and conflicts. She feels a strong identification with the first-person stories, which strike her as highly authentic and true to life. The stories address her in her language, treat problems in her social context, and apply her standards. They reassure her that other women have similar problems and manage to surmount them. They give her help and advice on countless topics, as Schramm has noted:

> Ought she confess that episode out of her past? How can she handle a husband who always wants to sit at home in the evenings? And so forth. And still more important, the reader can get from these magazines a comforting sense that this is not a world of chance or caprice, but rather of order and justice. If she makes a mistake, she can do something to rectify it. Her neighbor, who seems to be getting away with murder, will be caught up with in good time. . . . It is a comforting pattern of justice and free will.

There are hypotheses about the gratifications provided by other types of magazines. Joseph Gusfield, a sociologist at the University of Illinois, has suggested that perhaps much of the attraction of *Playboy* is to young people moving up the socioeconomic ladder because it depicts the attitudes and behavior patterns they expect to share once they have reached the next level. One writer has hypothesized that a reason for the popularity of men's magazines such as *Argosy* and *True* is that they reassure the reader that the individual is still a potent force in a world which seems to be governed largely by complex, bewildering, impersonal forces.

Unfortunately, research so far has been fragmentary and for the most part limited. What images do people have of the media they use? What roles do the various media play in the lives of their users? What cravings do they satisfy? When research turns up answers to these questions, students will have not only a clearer idea of why people pay attention to the mass media but also of their indirect effects.

References

BERELSON, BERNARD, AND MORRIS JANOWITZ, eds., *Reader in Public Opinion and Communication,* enlarged ed. (New York: The Free Press of Glencoe, Inc., 1953).

BOGART, LEO, *The Age of Television: A Study of Viewing Habits and the Impact of Television on American Life* (New York: Frederick Ungar Publishing Co., Inc., 1956).

DEXTER, LEWIS ANTHONY, AND DAVID MANNING WHITE, eds., *People, Society, and Mass Communications* (New York: The Free Press of Glencoe, Inc., 1964).

Rosenberg, Bernard, and David Manning White, eds., *Mass Culture: The Popular Arts In America* (Glencoe, Ill.: The Free Press of Glencoe, Inc., 1957).

Schramm, Wilbur, ed., *Mass Communications: A Book of Readings,* 2nd ed. (Urbana: University of Illinois Press, 1960).

————, ed., *The Process and Effects of Mass Communication* (Urbana: University of Illinois Press, 1954).

————, "The Nature of News," *Journalism Quarterly* 26 (September 1949) 259–69.

————, Jack Lyle, and Edwin B. Parker, *Television in the Lives of Our Children* (Stanford, Calif.: Stanford University Press, 1961).

9

The Media

as Informers

and Interpreters

Like many a later dictator, Julius Caesar championed the common people against the rich and powerful. One of his weapons was the first daily newspaper in the Western world, the *Acta Diurna*. Established in 59 B.C., it was a daily record of senatorial and other public actions. Copies of the *Acta Diurna* were duplicated by scribes, then posted on the walls of the forums and sped by private messenger to all parts of the empire to focus public attention on the Roman Senate. As the official organ of Caesar's successors, it served the imperial government until the fall of Rome in A.D. 479, some four and a quarter centuries after its birth.

The Roman Empire was able to expand over vast territories and endure for as many years as it did at least partly because of its highly developed communications system, which included the *Acta Diurna*. Significantly, one of the reasons Rome fell was that its frontiers had pushed too far for its media of information and interpretation. Technology was not sufficiently advanced to cope with the range, speed, and output required for continuous and effective communication over an empire that at its greatest stretched from Mesopotamia to Scotland.

Journalism in Varying Governmental Situations

This is more than a mere fact from history. It is central to understanding the American experience. For the first consideration in assessing the role of the mass media as informers and interpreters is the heavy hand of official authority, which is not easily lifted. Tracing the development of American journalism against the social, political, and economic background which shaped it will emphasize this overriding fact. It should do much more; it should demonstrate that journalism develops *with* a society—now leading by a bit, now following slightly, now in step—never very far from the march of a national culture.

response to a social need

The need for information and interpretation of a new life became compelling with the expansion of the Colonies. Growing steadily since 1607, the population had reached 250,000 by the end of the century. Agriculture, manufacturing, trade, and commerce—all had increased. With the growth of seaports in Boston, New York, and Philadelphia, shipping and general commercial news became important to success in business. Colonists along the seaboard wanted to know what was happening in England, the West Indies, and other colonies. Wars and rumors of wars between European nations might drive up the price of tobacco or cut off the demand. Were pirates menacing sea trade? Were Indians on the warpath? Slowly, colonial authorities established a mail system; a weekly service began in 1692 between New York and Boston.

The need was apparent, but the growth of newspapers was severely retarded by the traditional attitude of government toward the press. Although the Colonies were originally established by trading companies and other independent groups, the trend was toward making them royal wards. Strong control over the press was exerted by governors and other authorities. Since the Puritans governed Massachusetts Bay, the first two presses in the Colonies were controlled by the church and turned out religious tracts and official printing. An effort to set up commercial papers in the middle of the seventeenth century resulted in a law providing for a board of three members to license the press and to examine all material before publication.

In Philadelphia, the Quakers maintained strict control. The first printer was William Bradford, who published laws and almanacs—and showed everything to the government before publication. In 1689, he published a speech by a critic of Quaker policies. Although he was acquitted by a jury, Bradford's presses were long kept in custody.

Then, in 1690, came Benjamin Harris' *Publick Occurrences,* an independent paper which died after one issue. Not until 1704 was a private publisher, John Campbell, able to establish and maintain a private paper of continuous publication. Campbell's *Boston News Letter* succeeded only because the editor promised never to offend the government.

the growth of the Colonial press

In the first quarter of the eighteenth century, five newspapers emerged in the Colonies: three in Boston, one in Philadelphia, and one in New York. All were in seaports—the first cities large enough to support them—as soon as the economic and cultural situation favored their growth. Publishers were mainly postmasters or were closely allied with the government. As a result, they seldom criticized authorities, and the press in the Colonies (as in England) was identified with the State. Early publishers accepted pre-publication censorship and close control without protest. Many were political office-holders first, newspapermen second; usually they shared the attitudes and had the same beliefs as the colonial governors and proprietors. Until 1721, when the Massachusetts assembly refused to approve a licensing law requested by the governor, there was virtually no opportunity for competitors to challenge the existing papers. Thereafter, more papers appeared in Massachusetts and in other colonies.

Inevitably, strong-minded editors began to attack government. One touched off the most famous legal case in the history of the struggle for freedom of the press in America. A group of wealthy opponents of New York's governor financed John Peter Zenger's *New York Weekly Journal*, which was first issued in 1733. Eventually, Zenger, a German immigrant who was actually little more than the printer and was used as a front, was indicted for "raising sedition." Unable to meet bond, he was jailed. New York lawyers were too fearful to defend him; Andrew Hamilton of Philadelphia, a friend of Benjamin Franklin, took over the case. Although the jury's task, according to custom, was only to decide whether Zenger had published criticisms of the governor—not whether the material was in fact libelous—the jurors found him not guilty. The verdict had no real effect on the law of the land, but, as Edwin Emery and Henry Ladd Smith point out in *The Press and America*, the trial did enunciate a principle: "After the Zenger trial, few juries would condemn the accused simply because of criticism of government." The case helped to spread the idea that popular will was stronger than the men who made and enforced laws, and promoted the belief that the newspaper properly had the function of criticizing capricious and arbitrary government.

the Tory-Patriot conflict

By 1750 the newspaper was an accepted social institution—a permanent part of the American cultural scene. More than a dozen papers were being published in six American colonies by mid-century. Significantly, the majority had progressed from weak, inconsequential organs with a circulation of only a few hundred to powerful propaganda agencies, some with circulations as large as 3,000. In the rapidly developing Tory-Patriot conflict, the press became the most effective channel of information and interpretation. Papers increased in number; on the eve of the Revolution there were forty-eight. In addition to increasing in number and circulation, they were published more frequently. For propaganda, the editors used political essays, crusading features, cartoons, and headlines. Expanding circulation brought more advertising, and newspaper publishing, even without political subsidy, became a profitable business.

The Colonists increasingly recognized the need of newspapers to help them fight the Crown and the Crown's agents. Royal governors, seeing the temper of the times and the people, made few attempts to punish publishers for sedition and libel. When they did, juries refused to find the defendants guilty. As the revolutionary tide came to its crest, the Crown lost all control over the papers with Patriot sympathies. This encouraged more publishers and political groups to enter the quickening conflict between the Crown and its colonies.

During the period of increasing tension preceding open rebellion, many Colonial editors crystallized the economic and political resentments of the Patriots. Others remained on the Tory side and propagandized valiantly for the British. In general, the editorial policies of newspapers reflected the political attitudes of the people in the towns where they were published. Boston, the center of revolutionary activity, supported Sam Adams' *Boston Gazette,* perhaps the most important of the Patriot papers, and Isaiah Thomas' *Massachusetts Spy,* which catered to the laboring man. Not all papers in Boston were Patriot, of course, but the Tory press was merely negative rather than aggressive.

New York was the center of Tory sympathy. At least five newspapers there, reflecting the aristocratic backgrounds of prosperous and conservative merchants, were Tory to the core. Patriot papers, although in the minority, did exist; for example, John Holt's *New York Journal* took up the cause of Alexander MacDougall, the "Sam Adams of New York," and made him a Patriot hero.

Newspapers throughout the Revolutionary period were mainly Patriot in most of the Colonies. From 1765 to 1782, there were thirty-nine Patriot papers, with varying life spans. In the same period, less than half that many could be called Tory papers—and some of these were neutral with Tory leanings, such as the *Boston Chronicle* and the *Boston Evening Post.* To whip up hatred for the British, the Patriots ran atrocity stories much like those in the Allied press in World War I—British rapes of Colonial women and mistreatment of children. Freedom of the press meant freedom to print one's own views.

the revolutionary press

The Tory and Patriot newspapers of the Revolutionary period had much in common besides their rabid partisanship. Both were beset by problems of gathering and reporting news under conditions which made the former slow and the latter unorganized and spotty. Editors relied heavily for news on other papers that were just as haphazard. The favorite sources were letters, official and semi-official messages, conversations, and rumors. Each editor did develop some local news and, with widely separated papers contributing small parts to the mosaic, the press as a whole was able to present a sketchy picture of the Revolutionary struggle.

Coverage of the Revolution in the columns of the *Boston Gazette* was fairly typical. Letters and reports George Washington sent to Congress were reprinted, frequently in full. A newspaper in a locality where battles were fought was a source for other papers. Typical of the reporting of the time was a *Gazette* war dispatch reporting Washington's crossing of the Delaware:

January 6, 1777

The following is a copy of a letter from Major General Heath forwarded by express by Jonathan Trumble, Esq., Governor of the State of Connecticut, to the President of the Council of State, received last Saturday afternoon:

"By Col Chester, this moment arrived his Excellency, George Washington, who was at Newton, I have the Pleasure to acquaint you, that early on the morning of Thursday last, his Excellency in Person at the head of about 3000 of our troops, crossed the Delaware, at Trenton, consisting of about 1600 men; and after a brisk action of thirty-five minutes, entirely routed them, taking 1 colonel . . .

"Our troops behaved with the greatest bravery. This Signal victory, at this time, will be productive of the best consequences. Ardour glows in every face, and I hope she shall soon return all our losses."

Transmitting this item—from the time of the battle of Trenton to its publication in the *Gazette*—required eleven days. (In contrast, during World War II British broadcasters described air force bombings about one hour after the bombers returned to their bases, and American newspapers carried pictures the day after a mission.)

Patriot and Tory papers lifted items from one another. Both tried to minimize victories reported by the other, and at the end of their accounts, editors usually appended a paragraph of reassurance to set their readers straight. When Tory Hugh Gaine's *Mercury* claimed that the rebels had lost "4 or 5,000 killed and wounded" in a battle for the city of New York, the *Gazette* countered with, "Our readers will very much question the truth of the above account when they are assured that a letter from a person of distinction in New York has been intercepted, the writer of which has proved that the regular army in the late encounter have lost 200 men and 100 officers killed."

When news arrived after publication, penny broadsides were sometimes issued. During the war, the *Gazette* and other papers published essays to bolster the courage of their readers. Perhaps the most important of these was Thomas Paine's *The American Crisis,* which began in the *Gazette* on January 13, 1777.

When rebel troops took over a Tory town, or vice versa, the opposition's editor was forced to flee, although he usually managed to continue publication. Newspapers were severely handicapped, too, by the lack of presses, type, paper, and printers. Paper was in short supply; pleas were made to housewives to save rags for paper making and prizes were offered for the largest rag collections. The shortage often limited the size of editions and affected the regularity of publication. Some printers and papermakers, being no less patriotic than farmers, shoemakers, and butchers, went into the army, leaving publishers without the means to report the news regularly.

rise of the political press

The end of the war brought marked changes. Many old papers folded, but, according to Frank Luther Mott, some forty survived the war. Although only about a dozen that had been influential during the Revolution survived to the end of the century or beyond, the period 1783–1800 was one of tremendous growth. The mid-eighties saw the birth of some sixty new papers; altogether, more than 450 were established in the two decades before the turn of the century, although few survived for more than a few years. Daily publication became more frequent. The mercantile class demanded more and more commercial news, especially of ship sailings and cargo information. Then, too, the period following the Revolution continued to be one of political ferment, and daily publication was essential to effective partisan propaganda. Indeed, the press became so extremely partisan in the Federalist-Republican conflict that it suffered harsh infringements with the passage of the notorious Alien and Sedition Acts.

The struggle over ratification of the Constitution brought forth two principal political factions, which furnished the basis for the modern two-party system. The great battle was between the Federalists, who favored a strong, central government, and the Antifederalists, who wanted a mere league of more or less independent states. The press took sides; both factions had newspapers that were "bought and paid for." The Federalists encouraged John Fenno, a Boston schoolteacher, to set up the *Gazette of the United States,* which first appeared in 1789. It reached a peak circulation of 1,400, but never made expenses and existed on regular financial aid from the Federalists. Naturally, it applauded the program of Alexander Hamilton and jeered at Jeffersonian views. Recognizing the *Gazette of the United States* as Hamilton's mouthpiece, Jefferson encouraged Philip Freneau to start the *National Gazette* in Philadelphia, which had become the seat of the government (and the home of Fenno's Federalist paper). Both editors wildly attacked each other and the personalities associated with the Federalist and Antifederalist factions. There were also privately owned papers on either side of the political line, some drawing financial support from the factions they represented. In the heat of partisan politics, the political press indulged in violent and often extremely personal criticism and attack.

bright spots in a dark age

The period from 1800 to 1833 has been described by Mott as the "Dark Age of Partisan Journalism." Many newspapers sank to new lows of virulence, invective, and bias. Given the bitter conflict between the Federalists and Antifederalists and the severe strain of the War of 1812, it was difficult for any newspaper to be neutral. But dark as the period was from the twentieth-century view of ethics and social responsibility, there were some bright spots.

In addition to the political press there was another type: the mercantile or commercial paper, edited for the readers of the business and professional classes, which had its beginnings in the Colonial period. Moreover, the period from 1800 to 1833 was characterized by rapid growth in the number of newspapers of all kinds. The population was rising sharply. Cities, though still small, were becoming the centers of commerce and politics; mail service ran from Maine to Georgia; the American frontier pushed from the Atlantic seaboard into the fertile Mississippi Valley and beyond to the Great Plains. Farms dotted the wilderness; towns and trading centers sprang up along travel routes, and wherever people went, the newspaper went. Presses were relatively portable, and equipment was cheap. The total number of papers published simultaneously in the United States shot up from about 200 at the start of the period to 1,200 at the end. Dailies increased from 25 to 65, and total circulation rose even more rapidly; by the third decade of the century, the United States had more newspapers—and those newspapers had larger total circulation— than any country in the world (a distinction it still holds).

There were significant developments in magazine publishing. Five magazines had been established during the Revolutionary period. Among them was Philadelphia's perceptively edited *Pennsylvania Magazine,* which first offered the writings of Thomas Paine. With the turn of the century, the magazine industry began to flourish. Mott estimates that several hundred quarterly, monthly, and weekly magazines were printed at one time or another between 1800 and 1840. Most were published only briefly, but a few managed to last for a generation. Among the latter was *Niles' Weekly Register,* an early equivalent of the modern news magazine.

Broader News Coverage

America in the 1830s was still largely rural; only about 10 percent of the population lived in urban centers. But the consequences of urbanization and of industrialization, enfranchisement, and free public schools were already being felt. As Emery and Smith point out, the press became "more and more counted upon to supply information, inspiration, agitation, and education" to meet the demands of a society founded on the rule of opinion.

a press for the masses

Despite generations of literary dependence on the Old World, the American publishing industry by 1820 could list more than 50,000 titles, including books, magazines, and newspapers. Sales, according to Merle Curti in his *Growth of American Thought,* increased by more than $1,000,000 in the decade beginning in 1820, when publication grossed about $2,500,000.

The press was an important factor in fashioning the mass democracy which issued from the Jacksonian revolution. Newspapers not only helped to crystallize public opinion in support of the democratic revolution; they also, for the first time, began to notice a new type of citizen: the urban laborer. Indeed, some newspapers were published solely in the interest of the previously neglected laboring class. The first labor paper, the *Journeyman Mechanics' Advocate* of Philadelphia, appeared in 1827.

Technological developments were making possible larger circulations. In 1813, the printing press operated by a hand lever was displacing the screw-type press of Gutenberg's day. In 1825 the steam-driven cylinder press capable of turning out 2,000 copies an hour began replacing the hand-lever press and, in 1832, the double-cylinder press made possible 4,000 copies an hour. The growth of ink manufacturing plants, type foundries, and paper mills also contributed to newspapers of relatively wide circulation. All the ingredients were available for the production of a cheap paper that the masses could afford to buy.

Edited for the masses, the penny press emphasized local news, "domestic tragicomedy," crime and sex, and "human interest copy." It stood in remarkable contrast to the "respectable" six-cent dailies which filled their columns with political and factional controversy and were, generally speaking, beyond or outside the interest, understanding, and means of the great mass of a growing population. As the penny papers published tales about boys who whistled in their sleep, stories about murder and suicide, and hoaxes about men and buffalo on the moon, circulation climbed by the thousands. Benjamin Day's New York *Sun* hit a circulation of 19,360 in 1835, the largest of any daily paper in the world. The penny papers introduced changes that decisively shaped the development of the modern newspaper. Distribution was characterized by street sales, which had an important bearing on news policy. Large circulations made them attractive to advertisers, and newspapers became dependent upon advertising for the greater part of their revenue.

Significantly, it was in 1841 that what might be called the first advertising agent appeared. Forerunners of today's giant advertising agencies, these men bought large quantities of newspaper space at lower than usual rates and then resold them to advertisers. Eventually, in order to offer their customers something in the way of additional service, they helped advertisers with copy, illustrations, and planning.

James Gordon Bennett: "news," not "views"

New York was the center of the penny papers, but Boston and Philadelphia also had them. By 1835, when the popular press was firmly established, still another important development took shape: the rise of the newspaper as an independent purveyor of news. By giving the cheap newspaper a wider appeal than that of any other penny papers, the New York *Herald*, founded by James Gordon Bennett, was to transform American journalism. Self-proclaimed "genius of the newspaper press," Bennett publicly declared his paper free of every political clique or faction. What Willard G. Bleyer called in the history of American journalism the *views*paper became in Bennett's *Herald* a *news*paper, although the development he began was less a movement toward the modern ideal of objectivity in news coverage than it was a shift away from unabashed political partisanship. Moreover, Bennett created the truly sensational tradition in which William Randolph Hearst and many others were later to operate. Thus, his brand of journalism was a kind of bridge between the picturesque sensationalism of the penny press and the shocking yellow journalism of Hearst at the end of the century. As much as any single man, Bennett helped to create the newspaper stereotype of cynicism and hard-boiled ruthlessness, tastelessness, and lack of principle.

As circulations soared and advertising revenues grew, editors and publishers were able to experiment with novel types of news and news gathering, and to improve their production facilities—thus making possible still greater circulation and advertising support. Bennett, in particular, made the most of the opportunities present in the "new journalism." The *Herald* was brimming with advertising and, year by year, its content was broadened to gather in new readers. He appealed to the business class by developing a financial section and putting his best staff men on the Wall Street beat. He offered sports news long before other editors recognized its appeal. He built up a "Letters" column and helped to develop the critical review and society news. Accused in 1840 of blasphemy and faced by a boycott of the *Herald* by rival publishers, he defeated his opponents characteristically: recognizing in the protest the existence of a neglected public worth cultivating, Bennett put his best reporters on the church beats and covered all the important religious meetings. By full and able coverage of the city's religious life, he soon had won over his erstwhile enemies.

The *Herald* was thus a forerunner of the modern "omnibus" newspaper, which—like broadcasting and film—appeals to a broadly based market and tries to provide "something for everybody." There was, however, no abatement in the flood of sex, sin, and crime that had won Bennett his initial success. His objective plainly was to continue to attract the masses; but he aimed also at the more prosperous and educated reader, formerly the target of papers edited along class lines.

Horace Greeley: "The masses aren't asses"

Despite Bennett's success, a reaction developed against the sensational journalism of the popular press. Many complained that the advertisements and editorial content of the penny papers were unfit for family reading. Dissatisfaction of this sort no doubt contributed to the success of Horace Greeley's New York *Tribune*, which, after 1841, carried on the transition from the sensational penny papers to the general newspapers of mass circulation.

Until the appearance of Greeley on the New York publishing scene, there is not much evidence that editors of the popular press were motivated by anything other than profits and demands of their egos. But Greeley, who was perhaps the earliest example in American journalism of the "socially responsible" editor, possessed an uncommon faith that the common man could be attracted by reason as well as by emotionalism. The first issue of his *Tribune,* selling for one cent in competition with the penny papers, was intended to attract mass readership. He devoted it mainly to serious discussion and reporting, but did not insult the common man by trying to write down to him. The *Tribune* subsequently offered its readers stories, as Emery and Smith point out, "just as sensational as those of its rivals, but that type of journalism was not its hallmark."

Even the *Sun* and the *Herald,* in order to keep pace with the growing literacy and expanding interests of their readers, offered more substantial material as time went on. Other penny papers gradually followed suit. By the time of the Civil War, the popular press had left much of the semi-literate public behind.

war and slavery: the revival of partisanship

The anti-slavery controversy and the eventual war between North and South again split the press. Partisan journalism, on the wane, was revived. The war also had other clear effects. It brought military correspondence to its highest development. It accustomed newspapers to huge expenditures in the gathering, transmission, and presentation of news. Never had a war of such magnitude been covered so comprehensively, so accurately, and with such zeal. Disturbed social and political conditions made the period one of personal journalism and editorial ascendancy. New and better practices in news production became well established, and mechanical and technological improvements became essential. *The New York Times*, for example, was forced to buy additional presses and, in 1861, to adopt the process of stereotyping to keep up with the demand for copies. The scarcity of labor led inevitably to increased substitution of machines for men, to the introduction of mechanical devices and the invention of processes that sped production. The conflict established the Sunday newspaper, which had appeared from time to time during the preceding half-century but did not catch on until the war made news an everyday necessity. Later, some papers experimentally dropped the Sunday edition, but were forced to return to it. The war also introduced wartime censorship for the first time in the United States. Finally, it begat a generation addicted to regular newspaper reading and later confronted the press with the problem of satisfying the hunger for news and maintaining war-inflated circulations.

Many newspapers were still closely allied with the major political parties after the war. The partisan political press, as a clearly distinguishable type, did not die until the 1870s. But the general trend was continuing toward a press independent of direct political affiliations. Henry Raymond of *The New York Times*, for example, announced that a newspaper's aim should be the good of the community. A paper should be partisan only if by supporting a party it advanced the public interest.

The contribution of Raymond, who left a reputation as one of the great journalists of the century, was a conscious attempt to develop "objective" reporting—still the basic editorial formula of the newspaper he founded in 1851. There was a minimum of personal invective in the *Times;* it seldom painted things black and white as had Greeley; and it substituted accuracy for wishful thinking, even when Raymond himself was deep in politics.

The Beginnings of Modern Journalism

From the end of the Civil War to the turn of the century, the United States passed through a period of change affecting every facet of the national scene. Mechanization, industrialization, and urbanization brought great cultural, political, and social changes that were reflected in the nation's press.

Manufacturing production in the United States increased sevenfold between 1865 and 1900. As mass-production techniques were introduced into other fields, publishers applied the same principles to reach ever increasing audiences. Mass production and mass distribution meant increased advertising revenues. Moreover, the potential circulation was waiting. Between 1870 and 1900, the United States doubled its population; the number of urban residents tripled. During the same period, the number of weekly publications tripled, from approximately 4,000 to more than 12,000. Both in number and in total circulation the daily newspaper rose more rapidly than the cities which spawned it. General-circulation newspapers increased from less than 500 in 1870 to more than 2,000 in 1900. Circulation totals for all dailies reached 15 million by the turn of the century.

With the growth of the great cities, newspapers were needed for contact with the manners and values of urban life. The newspaper of the late nineteenth century reflected the desires, the aspirations, the successes, and the failures of a nation on the move. The daily newspaper more and more became a cohesive force binding together urban populations of diverse national and ethnic backgrounds. The nation was rapidly being unified by the extension of economic interdependence and a parallel improvement in communication facilities; the American newspaper became the chronicler of the national scene and the interpreter of the new environment.

The growing public looked mainly to the nation's newspapers to try to grasp and adjust to a rapidly developing industrial society. Not only did the successful newspaper of the period emphasize news rather than views, but those that were partisan and outspoken usually crusaded in what they considered to be the public interest.

yellow journalism and the tabloids

The nineteenth-century democratization of journalism produced many popular, well-balanced, and sober newspapers. But, especially in the great cities, it also led in its extreme form to the exploitation of a reader segment previously unsought even by the penny papers. As Ralph Casey has put it, "The 'yellow journals' of Hearst and Pulitzer reached down in the nineties to a substratum of readers." And again, in the twenties, the "jazz journalism" of the tabloids "tapped lower levels of taste and intelligence than other papers cared to reach." Circulations were achieved by "popularizing" the product, with entertainment overshadowing reporting and interpretation. As Emery and Smith have written, "Yellow journalism, at its worst, was the new journalism without a soul." While popularization is necessary if mass readership is to be achieved, it did not have to become mere sensationalism, a "shrieking, gaudy kind of journalism which lured the reader by any possible means."

Although the press for the masses reached its nadir in the periods of the "yellows" and the "tabs," it used editorial practices to which the people would not eternally respond. The most sensational journals eventually were compelled to modify their editorial methods, and even during the heyday of sensationalism, both in the 1890s and the 1920s, there were always sober and intelligent newspapers.

In Pulitzer and Hearst emerged the figure of the industrialist in American journalism. This does not mean merely that newspaper publishing had become big business and that Pulitzer and Hearst were tycoons. This was true enough, but it does not distinguish their style of journalism from that of many other prosperous publishers. The industrial producer regards news not so much as information to be discovered and reported, but as a commodity to be manufactured, packaged, and marketed like other consumer goods. Both Pulitzer and Hearst consciously oriented their newspapers to the sensation-hungry millions. If the events at hand were not sensational enough, they set about making news that was. Where there was smoke, they saw fire, and they described it to their readers as a holocaust. While the early penny papers had appealed to the baser emotions, they had depended largely on the appeals of the curious, the mysterious, and the bizarre. They did not, as did Pulitzer and Hearst, calculatingly dramatize those aspects of crime, sex, and violence certain to arouse the baser emotions.

It must be acknowledged that Pulitzer made some worthy contributions. Although he revived the tradition of sensationalism, he also provided excellent, sometimes brilliant, coverage of significant news. He injected the editorial page with a vigor of style and an aggressiveness of policy that generally had been lacking since the days of Greeley. He was instrumental, too, in extending the scope and variety of the Sunday newspaper, printing in his New York *World* the first colored comics. Finally, by advocating professional education for journalism, by endowing a school of journalism at Columbia University, and by establishing the Pulitzer Prizes, he gave a powerful thrust to the idea of better-educated and better-trained newspapermen.

press associations

Many less dramatic, but far more significant, developments shaped the character of information and interpretation. News coverage was greatly improved nationally by the expansion of communication facilities. Between 1880 and 1900, for example, the number of miles of railroad tracks doubled, while those of telegraph lines quadrupled. The Bell System's telephone lines spread steadily from city to city; the post office began rural free delivery; the Atlantic cable linked the United States to London; and another cable was laid eastward to the Orient.

Founded in 1848, the Associated Press, by extending its franchise beyond New York, had become by the turn of the century the main source of national and international news. The rise of the press association was one of the most important developments in the history of journalism. AP expanded in the twentieth century and got strong competition from United Press and International News Service (which merged with UP to make United Press International). Dedicated to rapid, thorough, accurate, and impartial collection and dissemination of news, the news agencies greatly enhanced the ability of the media to inform and interpret. While contributing to the increasing standardization of American journalism, they also improved newspapers by providing editors and readers with a continuous coverage of domestic and world events better than any previously available.

The Associated Press now serves more than 5,000 newspapers and radio stations around the globe. It produces one million words a day—the equivalent of seven or eight novels of average length. Its communication system of leased teletype circuits, submarine cables, Morse wireless channels, and radio-teletype channels circles the world. In the United States alone, AP operates nearly 400,000 miles of teletype and more than 20,000 miles of wirephoto circuits. It estimates that about 100,000 persons participate in the production and transmission of an average day's news report. Every hour, every minute, somewhere a paper is going to press or a newscast is going on the air. For the news agencies, there are no breathing spells between editions. Edition time is always now.

feature syndicates

Also important was the development of feature syndicates which supply on a contract basis articles, columns, poetry, fiction, serial stories, garden news, recipes, dress patterns, photographs, illustrations, and comic strips. The syndicate springs from an innovation in 1861 by the editor of a small Wisconsin paper, Ansel N. Kellogg. He supplied small country papers with "insides" (commonly known as "boiler plate")—that is, whole papers with the inside pages already printed, or inside page-fillers that could be inserted into the regular edition. After 1875, when the first stereotype plate was introduced, he syndicated the plates in various lengths—column, half-column, half-page, full-page, and so on.

In 1884, Irving Bacheller began a similar service for metropolitan papers. By 1920, the syndicate was a well-organized business and an integral part of American journalism. Today, there are nearly 200 syndicates of various kinds in the United States. Perhaps the best known is King Features, organized in 1896 by Hearst to sell features he was using in his own papers and to devise new ones for the Hearst chain. In its time, King features has syndicated such writers as William Jennings Bryan and the late George Bernard Shaw. Today, it distributes such widely-read columns as those of Louella Parsons and Walter Winchell.

Newspaper Enterprise Association (NEA), another giant, sells a complete feature service, including a women's page, a sports page, a comic page, a page of canned editorials with cartoons, one or more pages of general news features, and numberless pictures sometimes presented as a "picture page." This canned material may be seen in the content and make-up of newspapers throughout the country—and may result in a paper in Maine so closely resembling one in Texas as to be scarcely distinguishable. Most syndicate copy is "soft," as compared with "hard" news stories, and superficial or intellectually innocuous. However, while encouraging lazy editors to substitute prefabrications for locally produced news, syndicated material does make available information and interpretation which costs hundreds of thousands of dollars to produce and which few single papers could afford to develop themselves. Thus, millions of readers are exposed to ideas and events they might otherwise not have encountered. In many cases, the syndicates and the press associations have virtually made metropolitan papers out of small-city dailies.

Broadcasting as Informer and Interpreter

The possibility that broadcasting would ever become a medium of information seems to have occurred to no one during the early days of radio. Through the years of technical development that followed Marconi's first brief transmission of a wireless message in 1895, radio was considered a future competitor with the telegraph—an instrument to be developed for point-to-point communication—and a scientific novelty. Hobbyists assembled their own receiving sets, listened, and proudly reported distances. *How far* was the status symbol, and listeners compiled logs with lists of the farthest distant stations they could receive.

Even when radio was young, the process of making it an information medium seems to have been inherent from the beginning. Donald E. Brown of Arizona State University has traced the development of broadcast news through four stages.

Sarnoff's vision

In 1916, David Sarnoff, a twenty-five-year-old with a bent for science, wrote a memo to a superior in the company in which he was employed: "I have in mind a plan of development which would make radio a 'household utility' in the same sense as the piano or phonograph. The idea is to bring music into the house by wireless." Sarnoff also spoke of the possibility of transmitting lectures, baseball scores, and events of national importance.

From the vantage point of today, it seems incredible that no one followed through immediately on Sarnoff's proposal. But there were two handicaps: The primitive radio sets were not widely distributed, and World War I diluted the interest in broadcasting. News was almost incidental. It is true that Presidential election bulletins reporting the Wilson-Hughes race were read over Dr. Lee de Forest's experimental station in New York in 1916, but they excited little attention. Only in 1920, when two stations reported Presidential election returns, was there any real hint of the future.

the press–radio war

Radio grew phenomenally during the early 1920s, setting the stage for bitter warfare with the nation's newspapers. Fearful that the new medium might take over the news function, some publishers brought pressure; the Associated Press warned its newspaper members, some of which owned radio licenses, that broadcasting AP news was contrary to the association's bylaws.

Actually, the radio stations of that time had little interest in public affairs. In the fourteen-month period beginning in January 1922, the number of stations increased from 30 to 556, but the increase was in entertainment. Few broadcasters even attempted meaningful news reporting. They were eager for the new and different to feed the millions who had suddenly become intrigued with the novelty of radio, but the focus was on special events, not on the ordinary run of the news.

Then, in the late 1920s, a few stations began to consider themselves competitors with newspapers. By 1933, the competition between press and radio had become full-scale war. One network news executive organized what he called the "Scissors and Paste-Pot Press Association" to combat the withholding of press-association news from broadcasters.

Eventually, radio won the right to share the reports of worldwide news-gathering systems, first through United Press in 1935. The importance of radio as a news medium was emphasized in 1936 with one of the most dramatic broadcasts in history: the announcement by King Edward that he was renouncing the British throne for "the woman I love."

the zenith of radio news

Radio news reached its zenith beginning in 1938. Americans listened tensely to detailed, on-the-spot coverage of the Munich crisis. War clouds gathered over Europe; millions were made instantly aware of the troubled present by reporters and of the disturbing future by commentators. In Europe, Edward R. Murrow of the Columbia Broadcasting System was fashioning a great reportorial staff. At home, Lowell Thomas, Boake Carter, Elmer Davis, H. V. Kaltenborn, and a host of other authoritative voices suddenly became national celebrities.

By the time the United States entered World War II, radio was firmly established as a major medium of information and intepretation. Surveys indicated that broadcast news ranked very high with listeners and that the American people had confidence in radio reporting and commentary.

the rise of television news

The development of television, which had been halted by World War II, came rapidly during the late 1940s. Television newsmen, many of them trained in radio, borrowed radio techniques—and cut heavily into radio listening. News remained one of radio's primary assets, but the nature of news programs changed considerably. Many small communities got their first radio stations, and local news was emphasized. In fact, most radio stations cut back significantly on national and international events and issues, trying to find a formula that would enable radio news to survive in the age of television. Newscasts became shorter; the traditional fifteen-minute news program was down to five minutes; mere headline reports became common.

Because of the nature of the medium, television news emphasized features—especially the human-interest stories—at the beginning. Gradually, as TV newsmen developed competence and confidence, daily news programs grew from fifteen minutes to half an hour. By the beginning of the 1960s, newscasters—Howard K. Smith, Edward P. Morgan, Walter Cronkite, Eric Sevareid, and the team of Chet Huntley and David Brinkley—had achieved greater celebrity than the radio commentators of the 1930s. News and commentary over television had become so important by the mid-1960s that NBC News was producing a quarter of the broadcast hours on that television network: straight news programs, documentaries, discussions, and programs such as Senate hearings and national elections and political conventions.

The Varying Roles of the Media

In their fierce competition for advertising dollars and public attention, the media have developed varying roles. As *information* media, radio and television are primarily useful in signalizing events, making the immediate—and usually sketchy—reports that announce a happening. When broadcasters give full attention to an important subject or a momentous event, as in the case of documentaries and special-events reports, they must scant other news. This leaves an important role for the newspaper, which supplies many more details than the newscast and covers many more stories than the broadcast documentary or special report. In turn, newspaper reports leave a role for magazines, which are chiefly devoted to fleshing out the information that has been shown only in silhouette through broadcasting and newspapers and to reporting matters that the faster media have missed in the rush of meeting deadlines. Magazine writers also take advantage of their wide-spaced deadlines to fashion articles more graceful and unified than most writers for TV, radio, or newspapers have time to achieve. As a consequence, the interpretative writing used to discuss the meaning of events is more advanced in magazine journalism. The writers of books of nonfiction are a step farther; they have the leisure to draw full-bodied portraits and to set their writing in a fully meaningful context. Much the same point can be made regarding informational films, which aim at establishing themes with timeless relevance.

The media do not always work within the boundaries of these roles, and it must be obvious that they seldom take full advantage of their best qualities. Broadcasting is swift, but it sometimes misses important aspects of quick-breaking events. Newspapers are large, but they sometimes ignore significant stories. The long periods that go into the writing of magazine articles, books, and film documentaries do not prevent the worst of them from exuding a helter-skelter, thrown-together quality. All in all, though, each medium has a clear and substantive role in supplying information and interpretation.

References

BIRD, GEORGE L., AND FREDERIC E. MERWIN, eds., *The Press and Society: A Book of Readings*, rev. ed. (New York: Prentice-Hall, Inc., 1951).
BRUCKER, HERBERT, *Freedom of Information* (New York: The Macmillan Company, 1949).

CATER, DOUGLASS, *The Fourth Branch of Government* (Boston: Houghton Mifflin Company, 1959).

COHEN, BERNARD, *The Press and Foreign Policy* (Princeton, N.J.: Princeton University Press, 1963).

DAVIS, ELMER H., *But We Were Born Free* (Indianapolis: The Bobbs-Merrill Co., Inc., 1954).

GRAMLING, OLIVER, *AP: The Story of News* (New York: Farrar, Straus & Giroux, Inc., 1940).

GREENBERG, BRADLEY, AND EDWIN PARKER, eds., *The Kennedy Assassination and the American Public* (Stanford, Calif.: Stanford University Press, 1965).

JOHNSON, GERALD W., *Peril and Promise: An Inquiry into Freedom of the Press* (New York: Harper & Row, Publishers, 1958).

LIPPMANN, WALTER, *Public Opinion* (New York: Harcourt, Brace & World, Inc., 1922).

MORRIS, JOE ALEX, *Deadline Every Minute: The Story of the United Press* (Garden City, N.Y.: Doubleday & Company, Inc., 1957).

MOTT, FRANK LUTHER, *The News in America* (Cambridge, Mass.: Harvard University Press, 1952).

RIVERS, WILLIAM L., *The Opinion Makers* (Boston: Beacon Press, 1965).

SNYDER, LOUIS LEO, AND RICHARD B. MORRIS, eds., *A Treasury of Great Reporting*, 2nd ed. (New York: Simon and Schuster, Inc., 1962).

10

The

Media

as Persuaders

Wherever he turns today, the American is surrounded by sales talk—subtle, slick, and shrill. The editorial in his evening paper, sandwiched between the sales messages of department stores, urges him to vote for the incumbent mayor. A vocalist interrupts his favorite dramatic program on television to sing the praises of a shampoo which gives hair a halo. Perhaps 50 percent of the pages in his favorite magazine coax him to buy compact automobiles, gleaming refrigerators, king-size cigarettes, decay-fighting toothpastes, astringent mouthwashes, and detergents which clean whiter than white. His automobile rushes him past billboards extolling this brand of motor fuel, that brand of salt.

Much of the persuasion comes from advertisers, public-relations specialists, and other special pleaders, who use all of the mass media to make their sell, hard or soft. The nation's daily and Sunday newspapers alone in 1963 used more than 4 million tons of newsprint to carry advertising messages. Some of the persuasion comes from the media as advocates in their own right. Some comes as a by-product of content intended primarily to inform or entertain.

growth of persuasion

The American has become the target for all sorts of special pleading because he is called on to make manifold decisions, some of them trivial, some of them important, in his various roles as citizen, consumer, and member of many little publics.

His opinion in politics has become important. The growth of population, extension of the franchise, and women's suffrage all helped to expand the electorate. Popular education gave to the great majority of citizens the opportunity of acquainting themselves with the issues and problems of government, of observing the gaps between the actual and ideal in society. The direct primary and the increased number of elections added to the responsibilities of the individual citizen.

The functioning of the economic system has come to rest in large measure on the behavior of the consumer. Persuading people to buy goods was scarcely a necessity in the eighteenth and nineteenth centuries. The economy was one of scarcity, and the major problem was producing enough goods to maintain a subsistence level. But persuasion is an important factor in the operation of the modern economy. Production is far beyond the level of satisfying basic needs. The growth in population and the redistribution of income since the turn of the century have given producers a greatly expanded market. Moreover, the redistribution of income has given most Americans a margin of buying power to be used at their own discretion. Once he has paid for the necessities of living, a consumer can dispose of his extra income as he sees fit. True, many things which were once luxuries have now become necessities or near-necessities. But even among them the consumer has choices. He can buy a new automobile now or wait for next year's model; he can buy a new automatic washer this year or, at the risk of a repair bill, make the old one do for another year.

The complexity of twentieth-century existence; the advances in transportation, which shrank the world; the growth of the mass media, which broadened the horizons of the average man—all have widened the area of opinion. Should parents be strict or permissive? Should we discontinue testing atomic weapons? Should a former Communist be allowed to hold public office? What policy should our government take toward Egypt? Should we have a high tariff or a low one? What should the government do to help the farmer?

As the American has been called upon to make an ever larger number of decisions, more and more people have become anxious to help him make what, from their point of view, is the correct one. Reformers urge him to support their causes. Editorial writers and publicists ask him to share their opinions. Charitable organizations want him to support their work. Advertising men and public-relations specialists want him to favor their clients. Politicians want his vote. Every one of them wants a decision favorable to himself.

types of persuasive content

The mass media carry three broad types of persuasive content. One is advertising, which is treated along with public relations in the next chapter. Second is intentional advocacy—editorials, editorial cartoons, columns, and interpretive articles which are intended to lead the reader to a conclusion. Third is content which is intended primarily as entertainment or information but of which persuasion may be a by-product.

The informational content of the media is probably more influential on public opinion than the avowedly persuasive. That is, news stories may be a greater force in shaping public attitudes than editorials and political columns. They record events, and the events a paper reports probably change more minds than what it advocates. Hadley Cantril has generalized in his *Gauging Public Opinion:* "Opinion is generally determined more by events than by words—unless those words are themselves interpreted as an event." In addition, events tend to solidify changes in public opinion produced by words. Without some bolstering event, the change in opinion may be short-lived.

However, as Bernard Berelson has pointed out, those generalities call for two comments. First, it may be hard to distinguish between "events" and "words." Is a major speech by the President an "event" or just "words"? Second, many events exert their influence not of themselves but with the aid of words. That is, the importance of an event in persuading the public may be sharpened considerably by the interpretations given it by television commentators, editorial writers, and political columnists.

The relative emphasis given to information and entertainment on the one hand and frank advocacy on the other has varied with the time and with the medium. Newspapers, for example, have changed over the years from organs of political warfare to organs of information and entertainment. Some publications today by their very nature are organs of advocacy, even though they may be heavy with other content. The labor press and the company publication, which get somewhat disproportionate length in this chapter because they are specifically treated nowhere else in this book, are cases in point.

Before considering the effectiveness of the media as persuaders, consider how they have been deliberately used to shape public opinion.

Newspapers

Since 1890 at least, observers have been speaking of the declining influence of the newspaper on public opinion. Among other things, they point to the failure of newspapers to get their candidates elected to public office. In the 1940 presidential campaign, more than two-thirds of the newspapers in the United States supported Wendell Willkie, who was defeated; in 1944 and in 1948, a high proportion of the dailies supported Thomas Dewey, who was defeated both times; in 1960, Richard Nixon won the support of most newspapers and lost the Presidency.

What these figures show is not that the newspaper has lost in influence, say its defenders, but that it has gained in fairness. True, newspapers have supported candidates who have been defeated. But their defeat, the defenders say, simply underscores the fact that other candidates have been treated so fairly in news columns that readers could make up their own minds. And one cannot know, of course, whether the winning candidates might have won much more decisively with newspaper support.

Whatever its influence on public opinion, the newspaper has clearly changed over the years from a politically partisan advocate into an organ which has the dissemination of objectively written information as its goal.

partisan organs

Throughout much of its lifetime in America, the newspaper has been an important weapon in political warfare. Its usefulness in controversy was demonstrated as early as the American Revolution. In the period of Colonial dissatisfaction with British rule, the newspaper became a major medium for whipping up sentiment for independence; during the war itself, it was an important champion of the Patriot cause, as the previous chapter has shown.

After the war, when the Federalist and Republican parties emerged to align political differences, newspapers became recognized as political organs instead of just a means by which printers could earn a living. One contemporary, John Fenno, gave this capsule description of the press of his time: "The American newspapers are the most base, false, servile, venal publications that ever polluted the fountains of society—their editors are the most ignorant, mercenary automatons that ever were moved by the continually rustling wires of sordid mercantile avarice."

Newspapers were vituperative, biased, and bought. Their role as instruments of partisan conflict had its roots in the part they had played in the Revolution. It also grew out of the bitter differences between those who favored a strong central government for the nation and those who wanted a loose federation of states.

official organs

Inevitably it became the tradition for the President and his administration to have their official newspaper, a practice which reached its high point from 1832 to 1837 during Jackson's term of office. The official newspaper, as exemplified by Jackson's organ, the Washington *Globe*, had certain distinguishing characteristics. Although it was close to the party in power, it was privately owned and highly profitable, since it drew subsidies from government funds. In those lean years when the party was out of office, the paper made its own way, as best it could, with some aid from the party. The newspaper was the medium through which the President addressed the public, and other papers recognized it as his mouthpiece.

The official newspaper began to wither when the creation of the government printing office took politics out of the letting of printing contracts, when individual papers started to send their own correspondents to Washington, and when the telegraph enabled Presidents to reach a far wider audience much more quickly. The last flicker of the official organ came in 1860. President Lincoln declined to name a party organ.

transition to independence

Then came a gradual transition from partisan to independent newspapers. The Confederate and Northern causes both had their adherents among the press, and even in the North there were papers which backed the Confederacy and tried to undermine the war effort. They were the so-called Copperhead Papers, which extended from east coast to west. They were so harmful to the prosecution of the war, General Grant said, that he would have preferred an additional hundred thousand troops in the Confederate army.

Between about 1870 and the end of the century, newspapers generally moved from under party domination. The editorial page had become a separate department starting in the 1850s, and more and more editors spoke of and practiced independence. True, some of them at first meant simply an end to party control so that they could be free to criticize party leaders and policies from within. Yet an increasing number believed that the newspaper, in working for the good of the community and society, should stand above party loyalties. As the century ended, Joseph Pulitzer and others were demonstrating the value of news as a commodity. They were architects of the modern independent paper.

The end of political subsidy for the press grew out of a number of circumstances. The Civil War had shown the public's hunger for timely and detailed news accounts; thereafter, the most successful papers were clearly those which concentrated on news undistorted by partisan loyalties. News gathering techniques had improved. Editors could expand the scope of their coverage beyond business and politics. More than that, the developing press services furnished news to papers all over the nation, and they could not easily color it to fit organs of varying political complexions. Competition for advertisers as well as readers dictated the change. Advertisers, growing in importance to newspapers, did not wish to alienate customers by patronizing violently partisan organs. Then, too, from mid-century onward newspapers were attracting personnel of higher education and attainments.

contemporary persuasion

The change of newspapers from partisan persuaders to objective chroniclers was affirmed by the Canons of Journalism adopted by the American Society of Newspaper Editors in 1923: "Promotion of any private interest contrary to the general welfare, for whatever reason, is not compatible with honest journalism."

To promote the general welfare as they see it, newspapers have continued to crusade through editorials, cartoons, photographs, and interpretive articles. The catalog of their causes is long. Silas Bent has summarized hundreds of campaigns up to and through the 1930s in his book *Newspaper Crusaders*. They have used their influence to promote traffic safety, parks and playgrounds, new and improved city charters, diversification of farm crops, fluoridation of city water supplies, recreation centers for young persons, pardons for the wrongly convicted, community hospitals, smoke abatement measures, reduced utility rates, municipal auditoriums, mental health programs. For two years in succession, in 1957 and in 1958, Pulitzer Prizes were awarded to southern editors who stood up to local pressures during the crisis over integration.

Periodically newspapers have flushed out crime and political corruption, which often have been entwined. Shortly after 12:30 on a July night in 1926, Don Mellett, the young crusading publisher of the Canton, Ohio, *Daily News,* went out to park his automobile while his wife put on a pot of coffee for some visitors. A volley of shots rang out. When his wife reached him, Mellett was dead, shot through the head from an ambush.

Mellett died fighting two things. One, some newsmen still say, was the three-to-two circulation lead of his opposition, the *Repository.* That fight led to the second—which did push his circulation towards that of his competitor—a campaign against public officials in Canton who were in league with criminals. The city seemed in need of reform: wanted criminals could hide out in safety, gangland murders went unsolved, a policeman held a monopoly on the sale of perfume to prostitutes.

Under Mellet the *Daily News* hounded the police, attacked their chief, reported crimes prominently and lengthily. Mellet was presumably shot by enemies made during his crusade, but a mystery still surrounds his death. Although three men went to prison for their part in the murder, no one but the killers knows just who the murderer was. Nor is the exact motive known; other editors have gone unharmed for crusades at least as fiery as Mellett's. One explanation is that he was shot for what he was about to publish, not for what he had published. However, for a short time, at least, Mellett's campaign cleansed the city. A more lasting memorial is a series of lectureships bearing his name. Each year for more than a quarter of a century now a distinguished lecturer has spoken on some aspect of the press to keep Mellett's crusading spirit alive in other newspapermen.

Some of his spirit does exist even among small-town newspaper editors. Personal threats and a burst of pistol shots through the window of his newspaper plant in December, 1955, did not halt a campaign which C. E. Townsend had undertaken in Granite City, an Illinois community of about 30,000. His semi-weekly *Press-Record* exposed gambling, prostitution, and underworld influences for several years and eventually effected a clean-up of Madison County. "I am opposed to organized vice because of its corrupting influence on government," Townsend said in 1958. "In my time, I have seen plenty of public officials corrupted in Madison County." Convinced that a newspaper need not be neutral to be fair, Townsend has conducted campaigns which contributed to a $2,200,000 bond issue for school buildings, a new post office building, a city zoning plan, and other community developments. For his community service, the Illinois Press Association chose him as its Illinois Editor of the Year.

Large dailies, less subject to direct community pressures, no doubt find crusading and exposés less uncomfortable than do small-town papers. In mid-May of 1956, a man walked into the offices of the Chicago *Daily News* to suggest that the paper look into the activities of Orville E. Hodge, state auditor. A team of reporters, led by George Thiem, went to work. Hodge concealed records, secretly removed files from his office, instructed his employees to give out no information. Yet by June 4 Thiem had uncovered enough for his first story. It was followed by others which told how Hodge had padded his payroll and diverted state funds, more than $1,500,000 in all, to his own use. Resigning under the attack, Hodge was tried, found guilty, and sentenced to ten years in prison on federal charges, twelve to fifteen years on state charges.

Magazines

In crusading and in the original reporting which is sometimes its substitute, newspapers in recent years have lost ground to magazines, Louis B. Seltzer of the Cleveland *Press* has complained. Whether in fact they have or have not, magazines since the end of World War II do seem to have given some emphasis to what might be called public-service articles, many of which have overtones of advocacy.

public service articles

Public service articles defy definition. They take many approaches, and they cover a great many topics. They include, on the one hand, *Collier's* postwar exposés of politics in Kansas City, and its articles about crime in American cities which called for "getting the police back on the beat." They include, on the other hand, *Life's* controversial five-part series "Crisis in Education," and its more recent articles on Congressional pork-barrel projects. They include the graphically detailed "Blast in Centralia No. 5," which appeared in *Harper's Magazine* with the subtitle, "A Mine Disaster No One Stopped," and which by implication at least was a strong plea for changes in the Illinois system of mine inspection. They include *Look's* article in 1956 to gain understanding for mentally handicapped children, and its articles on vocational education in 1963 and 1964. They include the articles that *Redbook* was running in 1958—articles close to being exposés, on such subjects as the "shocking truth" about the fruits and vegetables one buys. And they include *The Reporter's* articles on wire-tapping, "The China Lobby," and "The Foreign Legion of U.S. Public Relations," a notable exposé.

No really suitable term fits all these articles, although some of them bear a kinship to the muckraking articles of the turn of the century. Among themselves, editors of one magazine call them "exposés," but the staff is not entirely satisfied with that term, for the authors try to present the case, if one exists, for whatever they are exposing.

Even in public service articles, magazines generally have engaged in comparatively few outright attempts at persuasion. Rather, they have tried to arouse the public's awareness or its conscience by means of interpretive information, or by setting forth a fresh viewpoint on a controversial situation. There was little overt attempt to convert the reader in the meticulously detailed articles which John Bartlow Martin wrote about prison riots and mental hospitals for the *Saturday Evening Post,* even less in Ben Bagdikian's notable pieces in 1963 and 1964 on poverty, also published in the *Post.* Nor did William Bradford Huie do much arguing for justice in an article for *Look* in which he wrote that a jury had freed the murderer of Emmett Till, a northern Negro boy killed while visiting a southern town; he was content to rest his argument on his facts and interpretation.

Only infrequently since the days of the muckrakers have large-circulation magazines sounded clear calls for action to correct abuses. *Sports Illustrated* did in the opening article of a two-year campaign to clean up "boxing's dirty business." Its subtitle called the welterweight champion-ship fight "one of the most brazen frauds of modern times" and asked for "a federal investigation of the hoodlums" controlling the ring. One of the most persistent of magazine campaigns has been that of *Argosy* to im-prove the administration of justice. Members of its Court of Last Resort, created in 1948, have included a former prison warden, a famous private detective, an expert on lie detection, and an authority on the medical aspects of crime. Co-chairman of the board has been Erle Stanley Gardner, mystery-story writer and lawyer. The board has thoroughly investigated the cases of persons thought wrongfully convicted of crimes; the magazine has given full publicity to the board's findings. In the first six years after its founding, the Court of Last Resort obtained the release from prison of twenty-one innocent people.

the muckrakers

Today articles seeking to reform, even by interpretation instead of advocacy, comprise a relatively small proportion of total magazine con-tent. The golden age of reform was the period of muckraking, which began in 1902. Rapid industrial expansion after the Civil War had created many evils and injustices. Trusts were a matter of public con-cern, and some observers saw an unhealthful alliance between business and politics. By coincidence *McClure's* for January, 1903, carried three articles similar in theme and treatment, all social criticism—Ida Tarbell's third article in her history of the Standard Oil Company, Lincoln Stef-fens' "The Shame of Minneapolis," and Ray Stannard Baker's "The Right to Work." That issue officially established the era of muckraking, al-though magazines had carried other articles about the trusts and corrup-tion in politics.

Magazine after magazine called public attention to conditions requiring correction. *American, Arena, Collier's, Cosmopolitan, Everybody's* and *Hampton's* joined the muckraking crew. Even the *Ladies' Home Journal* took time out from its efforts to improve the American woman's taste in art and architecture to give the muckrakers a hand in exposing the patent medicines. Its campaign included an article on phony testimonials, a full-page editorial demanding federal regulation of the manufacture and sale of patent medicines, and one especially telling feature—a repro-duction of an advertisement for Lydia Pinkham's Compound showing "Mrs. Pinkham in her laboratory" alongside a staff member's photograph of Mrs. Pinkham's tombstone in Lynn, Massachusetts. The slums, the overimportance attached to college athletics, the inequities and injustices of divorce laws, immorality in the theater, our interests in Mexico—these and others caught the muckrakers' interest.

Some subjects were treated with more rhetoric than fact, more sensationalism than sincerity. Sometimes the articles were not advocacy but probing reportage which drew on official documents and which was subjected to scrutiny by experts. C. C. Regier, a historian of muckraking, has concluded that the general reliability of the articles was high. Significantly, although the magazines and authors were often threatened with libel actions—Will Irwin at one time had six pending—few ever paid out any damages.

An important force by 1906, the muckraking movement ebbed two years later, hit another high point in 1911, then had spent itself by 1912. The public had tired of it, financial pressures had discouraged certain magazines from continuing it, and some of the evils it had assailed had been corrected. Regier credits muckraking with playing a part in a number of reforms, among them a federal pure-food law, child-labor laws, workmen's compensation acts, a tariff commission, and congressional investigations.

journals of opinion

Perhaps the most forthright attempts at persuasion in magazines have appeared in such journals of opinion, comment, and controversy as the Nation, National Review, New Leader, New Republic, and Progressive; their emphasis is on ideas rather than on reportage, and their positions are rarely neutral.

Most of the journals since the turn of the century have been organs of liberal thought, although a few, like the National Review, founded in 1955, have been spokesmen for conservatism. In their agitation for political reform and social justice, the magazines often have been far ahead of popular thinking. For that reason and others, their way has always been difficult; their circulations have been counted in the thousands instead of in the millions of the general-interest magazines, their advertising volume has been lean or non-existent, and their financial position has ever been precarious. Yet they seem to have wielded an influence all out of proportion to their circulations, for they have aimed at opinion leaders instead of the great mass audience. Frank P. Walsh once remarked that he had written an article about railroads for the Nation in the days when its circulation was about 27,000, and a series on the same subject for the Hearst newspapers when their total circulation was around 10 million. No one ever commented on the newspaper series, he said, but as soon as the Nation article appeared his phone jangled with calls from persons of importance. Charles Beard has credited the journals of opinion with contributing to such reforms as women's suffrage, old-age pensions, social-security legislation, wages-and-hours laws, public housing, and public ownership of hydroelectric sites.

Company Publications

A few years ago, the executives of a manufacturing company were honoring Joe Zipotas—the name is fictional but the incident is true —for twenty-five years of loyal service. A curious investigator decided to find out just how much Zipotas had learned about the company in his quarter-century with it. He discovered that Zipotas did *not* know the year in which the company was founded; the number of plants it had; more than two of the company's products, which exceeded 200; the name of the president, who had held that office for three years; the location of the company's headquarters; the source of a single raw material going into the company's products; the operation which preceded his or the one which followed it, except in a very general way; and what free enterprise means (he did not even recognize the expression).

On the other hand, Zipotas could give the name and number of his local union; the names of three of five union officers; four direct benefits which, he thought, the union had obtained for him, although it actually had obtained only two of them; and a reasonably accurate definition of collective bargaining.

terminology

It is in part to combat such ignorance that many companies publish magazines or newspapers for their employees. The term *company publications* is one of several used to describe the periodicals issued by big and little businesses to tell their stories to employees, salesmen, dealers, stockholders, customers, potential customers, and opinion leaders. For years the publications have been called *house organs,* a designation which company editors object to as having undeservedly shabby connotations. Some editors prefer the term *industrial publications;* indeed, the major organization of company editors is called the International Council of Industrial Editors. Some use the term "employee publications" when speaking of periodicals issued primarily for employees.

size and scope

By any name, company publications have become a permanent part of the publishing scene. Nor are they an inconsequential part. Whatever figures one reads, their number, circulation, and expenditures are impressive. In 1952, according to a writer for *The New York Times,* there were an estimated 8,000 company publications, with a total circulation of more than 150 million and representing an annual cost of more than $600 million. That same year *Reporting,* official publication of the

International Council of Industrial Editors, reported on a survey it had conducted. It found 6,500 company publications, a number about three and one-half times that of general-circulation daily newspapers. Their combined circulation was approximately 70,719,000—considerably larger than the combined circulation of all United States dailies. On those publications, industry spent more than $112 million a year. In the early sixties, *Printers' Ink* estimated their number at between 6,000 and 8,000, their combined circulation at more than 150 million. And a compiler of a mailing list has recently put the number of company publications at 10,000.

Company publications include magazines, newspapers, and newsletters. They range in size from two to sixty-four pages an issue. In quality they vary from crudely mimeographed collections of news notes to slick magazines which compare favorably in technical execution with the top commercial magazines. *Think* of the International Business Machines Corporation runs articles by well-known authorities on the arts, current affairs, education, and so forth for 100,000 leaders in business, the professions, and government around the world. It makes no references to I.B.M. in its editorial copy, carries no company advertising. *Ford Times,* with a circulation of more than a million, treats its readers to the works of Aldous Huxley, J. P. Marquand, and William Saroyan. In *What's News,* published by Abbott Laboratories, the reader encounters the work of Ogden Nash, Emily Kimbrough, Christopher Fry, and other popular authors.

Some of the publications have full-time staffs of six or more. However, the typical company publication is the work of a single editor, sometimes aided by a secretary and a part-time photographer. The editor gathers the material and writes the copy, supervises a crew of volunteer correspondents, prepares the copy for the printer, and lays out the issues.

types of publications

In general, company publications are of three types. The *internal* circulates within the company. It is exemplified by *Caterpillar Folks,* a biweekly tabloid "by and for the folks at Caterpillar Tractor Co., Peoria," and by *Hiltonitems,* a magazine for employees of the Hilton chain of hotels. The general aims of the internal publication are to bring about mutual understanding between management and employees as a means of effecting cooperation; to present management's policies, programs, and attitudes; and to help increase employee efficiency. The *external* circulates outside of the company. Examples include *Ford Times, Harvester · World* of the International Harvester Company, and *Steel Horizons* of the Allegheny Ludlum Steel Corporation. The aims of an external depend upon the specific reader group of the publication and the character of the issuing company. However, they often include improving business relations with customers and potential customers, telling the company's story to opinion leaders, or both. The *internal-external,* sometimes called the combination publication, goes to persons both within and without the company. Its aims combine those of the internal and external. A fourth type, the sales organ, is actually either an internal or an external. However, its specific aims may be so sharply different from theirs that it is sometimes put in a class by itself.

persuasive functions

Some company editors would argue heatedly that their publications are not organs of persuasion. They may admit to editing organs of information or even education, but they find persuasion too akin to propaganda to be palatable. A former newspaperman who edits an employees' magazine for a public-utilities company insists that his publication is strictly informational, since he covers the company as he used to cover his newspaper beat.

True, the best of the company publications are long on information, mercifully short on exhortation. The casual reader, for instance, might mistake *Friends,* a monthly distributed free by Chevrolet dealers, for a regular general-interest picture magazine. The magazine carefully avoids references to Chevrolet in its editorial matter, which covers gracious dining, hobbies of readers, scenic attractions across the land, and similar features; the few Chevrolet advertisements are carefully separated from the editorial features. Some internals seem edited on the assumption that employees will accept the policies and attitudes of management if they but have the facts. One company editor in Chicago admitted that he had looked sharply down his nose on industrial editing until he had become a part of it. "I considered the field narrow and extremely biased," he said. "It is conservative, admittedly. But its limits are being swept away so quickly one can hardly keep abreast of the advancement. And I am less certain each day that it is more conservative than the daily field."

Yet the aims of company publications require that they be persuasive organs, even if the persuasion is not always blatant. Company publications are not issued for philanthropic reasons. They are issued to build, modify, or change attitudes toward the company. The internal seeks to gain acceptance for company policies; the external seeks to increase sales, either by a direct bid for them or by building good will and prestige. One of the topics current in industrial editing shop talk is how editors can document the worth of their publications to management. This worth is inevitably measured by some change in reader behavior—by an improved safety record, by a reduction in waste, by an increase in sales. As the director of publicity and public relations for one major company put it, "The sooner managements and editors alike stop all the prattle about the philanthropic reasons behind their externals, and admit to themselves and to their readers their objectives . . . which, in plain words, are to sell merchandise, the better off everyone will be." True, the publications may seek to persuade by information, by fact, by figures, by entertainment. But they are persuasive in intent, for all of that.

causes of growth

Not long ago, a company editor—who should have known better—credited World War II with the swift proliferation of company publications in the United States. Certainly the war brought a rapid increase in their number. In 1940, there were perhaps 2,400, to judge from the shaky data available; today there are somewhere between 6,500 and 10,000. During the war, there were good reasons for their growth. They were useful in building and maintaining employee morale, in acquainting the flood of new employees with company jobs and routine, in keeping in touch with employees in the service. Tax policies, which in effect permitted employers to deduct the cost of company publications, also no doubt contributed to their growth. But to credit the war with being anything more than a stimulant to their development is to misread the history of the twentieth century.

Although one can trace the house organ back to the court circulars of the Han Dynasty, 200 B.C., the company publication in America seems to have had its birth in the nineteenth century. One of the first true employee publications was the *Triphammer* of the Massey Manufacturing Company, begun in 1885. Another early one was *Factory News,* started at the National Cash Register Company in 1891. Some of today's commercial magazines were in effect house organs in their early days in the nineteenth century. *McCall's* for instance, was begun to promote the sale of ladies' dress patterns, *Harper's Magazine* to promote the sale of books published by the four Harper brothers. *Printers' Ink* was originally a house organ for an advertising agency.

When cash came to business with relative ease during World War I, there was a blossoming of publications aimed at employees. Many of these war-born publications died with the peace, perhaps because their tasks were done, perhaps because of the recession of 1920–1921. Thereafter the development of the publications seems to have been slow until World War II. Of 6,500 publications surveyed by the I.C.I.E. in 1952, for instance, about 70 percent came into existence after 1938.

Five conditions seem to have fostered the development of company publications. One was the increased sense of public relations with which business became imbued after World War I but especially in the late 1930s. A second was the rise of the labor unions. In the 1920s, inertia characterized the labor movement generally, and membership dropped off abruptly and significantly. In the 1930s, encouraged by federal legislation, the unions began their climb to power. Between 1933 and the end of 1937, membership in the hotel and restaurant employees' union had quadrupled, that in the teamsters' union had tripled, and that in the electrical workers' union had doubled. A third influence on the development of the company publication, perhaps, was the labor press, which gained importance as the unions did. As organized labor strengthened its own press for reaching its members, management no doubt felt the need for some counter-voice.

Fourth, certainly the increased regulation of business and industry since the advent of the New Deal in the 1930s—a trend which some segments of management have seen as a threat to the free-enterprise system —has contributed to the growth of the company publication. Although editors disagree on the extent to which they should try to sell employees on the benefits of the free enterprise system, they are in strong agreement that one of their purposes is to give him an understanding of how the economic system operates.

Finally, the growth of the company publication no doubt was fostered by the emergence of the giant corporation. The large company developed mass-production techniques which often reduced individual jobs to almost incomprehensible specialties. The plants came to be scattered over wide geographic areas, and management became remote from employees. It became increasingly difficult for the individual employee to see his contribution to the finished product, to take any craftsman's pride in his work, to see his place in the company and the industry of which it is a part, to feel any bond with management and his fellow employees. The company publication became one tool for orienting the employee to company and industry, for acquainting him with his employers and fellow workers, for assuring him of his importance to the production scheme.

The Labor Press

In the 1930s, in the decade before the great surge in the growth of company publications, the labor press underwent a somewhat similar revitalization. Those lean years of widespread unemployment made workers feel keenly the economic struggle for existence, and the general climate under the New Deal was one favorable to unionism. In their great organizing drives after 1933, labor leaders saw the need for the mass dissemination of trade-union persuasion if they were to combat opposition to unionism and if they were to win and hold members. Between 1932 and 1938, more than 150 new labor and progressive periodicals joined those already in existence. Reliable figures on the scope of the labor press are hard to come by, for labor journalism, strangely, has rarely attracted scholars. In the early 1950s, according to one estimate, there were about 800 labor periodicals with a combined circulation of 30,000,000. The directory of the International Labor Press Association in 1957 mentioned 301 member periodicals with a total circulation of 20,000,000. The 1964 Ayer & Son's directory of periodicals listed 254 labor publications; the 180 reporting their circulations had an aggregate distribution of about 9,800,000.

Labor periodicals fall into several categories. They include organs of national and international trade unions, of state and national federations, of city and county federations, of locals, and of institutes and fraternal orders.

content and control

Just as company publications are the spokesmen for the interests of business and industry, so the labor periodicals are the voice of organized labor. They are the house organs of the trade-union movement. Both readers and editors evidently want them to concentrate on labor materials and to leave other types of information to the general-circulation media. What readers want in the labor press, according to a limited study made by Manny Schor in Toledo, is articles about their own trade or industry, shop columns, editorials and background articles about affairs affecting labor, letters from union members, and news stories about labor activities. Only a few of the editors surveyed thought that their periodicals should attempt to present the beliefs and objectives of labor to the community at large. Fewer still thought that their papers should run material not dealing with labor.

The several systems of control which are intended to keep the publications responsive to the wishes of union members probably help to perpetuate their house organ character. Many are controlled by boards of union members and elected officers whose primary responsibilities are in other areas. Some unions control their papers by electing the editors.

Despite such inhibiting factors, the labor press has changed in some ways over the years. Perhaps the greatest change has arisen from a transformation in the ideology of the labor movement. At one time, especially from about 1873 to 1886, labor sought to accomplish its objectives by modifying or scrapping the existing political and economic order. The radical labor press of that era, varying in tone from moderate to anarchistic, lacked a unity of purpose, since the periodicals often represented factions which had lost sight of a common goal.

Today, with few exceptions, the labor press tries to achieve its purposes within the framework of the free-enterprise system. While it tries to improve the lot of the individual worker and of organized labor, it does not advocate an end to the system itself. Consequently, the labor press now has a unanimity of purpose which it lacked in the nineteenth century.

Another change has been a technical improvement of the newspapers and magazines. On some publications, especially the national and international ones, experienced journalists have replaced amateur editors whose chief qualification was zeal. Facilities for news gathering have been expanded, and the physical appearance of the publications has been improved. Despite those improvements and despite considerable editorial enthusiasm, a good many labor papers, particularly local ones, still are below professional standards of technical competence.

Broadcasting

Until very recently, the overt persuasion of radio and television was largely in advertising. On specific issues, it may have modified attitudes as a result of its coverage of such events as the hearings of Senator Estes Kefauver's committee investigating crime and the hearings involving the late Senator Joseph McCarthy. But both radio and television were exceedingly slow to attempt to influence opinion by outright editorializing.

the Mayflower Decision

There were both legal and practical reasons for that reluctance. One inhibition was the Mayflower Decision. Radio station WAAB in Boston, owned by the Mayflower Broadcasting Corporation, had supported various causes and candidates for some years before 1941 without making its facilities available to those with opposing viewpoints. After investigating complaints about that practice, the Federal Communications Commission in 1941 issued what came to be known as the Mayflower Decision. In effect, the FCC ruled that "a licensee shall not be advocate" because the channel he holds is public property. Broadcasters were uncertain whether the FCC meant that a licensee could not advocate under any circumstances or only if he did not allow counter views to be heard. However, they interpreted it to mean that they were enjoined from editorializing altogether.

Although they never challenged it in the courts, broadcasters resented the Mayflower Decision. When a cross-section of AM station managers was surveyed in 1947, 85 percent said that they thought they should have the right to editorialize and 55 percent replied that they were sure they would do so if they had the right. The National Association of Broadcasters made the Mayflower Decision a part of a larger movement to abolish FCC concern with all program content.

Supporters of the decision contended that the station owner held his channel in the public interest. The right to editorialize would give him a preferred status over other members of the community, who did not have access to the airwaves. Editorializing, then, was quite a proper subject of regulation. They also contended that the editorials of broadcasters would likely have a sameness and conservatism not representative of the opinions of the public at large.

Broadcasters, on the other hand, used two major arguments against the decision. Regulation, they said, was originally justified on the grounds that the number of channels was limited. But the postwar expansion of AM channels and the advent of FM had ended the scarcity. Secondly, they argued that restrictions on editorializing infringed the First Amendment and even the Communications Act, which barred the FCC from censorship. Broadcasting could never achieve full stature, they said, unless it had the right to editorialize.

In June, 1949, after months of public hearings, the FCC redefined its position, ruling that a licensee could broadcast his own opinions on controversial subjects provided that he gave opportunity for the presentation of conflicting viewpoints. The FCC stated:

> Only insofar as it is exercised in conformity with the paramount right of the public to hear a reasonably balanced presentation of all responsible viewpoints on particular issues can such editorialization be considered to be consistent with the licensee's duty to operate in the public interest.

extent of editorializing

Despite that clarification, few broadcasters hurried to use the new privilege. Even those who most vigorously protested the Mayflower Decision did little editorializing. Some news directors of local stations explained that impartiality in news coverage was their greatest asset. They argued that listeners think local newspapers carry too heavy a load of opinion in their news columns and therefore trust the broadcast media because they do not dilute news with views. Taking almost an opposite line, others said that they do editorialize, inevitably, in selecting their news, in preparing it for the air, in broadcasting it, even if they do not devote time to editorials as such.

Sig Mickelson, former general manager of CBS News, gave four reasons for the small amount of network editorializing. One involves the difficulty of meeting the FCC's requirement of fairness and balance in issues involving controversy. Another is the undesirability of the network's setting an editorial policy for its affiliated stations, which are autonomous units. Third is that broadcasting historically has had little precedent for editorializing. Finally, there is the problem of how to editorialize. Should regular newsmen express opinions during regular newscasts, for instance, or should the network employ a number of commentators of differing opinions and permit each to speak his mind freely? Or should network management reserve for itself the right to editorialize? Nonetheless, Mickelson thought broadcasters should seriously consider using their right to comment.

CBS itself presented overt editorials three times in eight years after the FCC reinterpreted its Mayflower Decision: once in 1950 when President Frank Stanton spoke out for color television, again in 1954 when he asked for broadcast coverage of congressional hearings, and the third time early in 1958 when CBS News gave its own conclusions drawn from evidence in its program "Where We Stand." A survey of radio stations reported by Roy E. Carter, Jr., in the *Journalism Quarterly* in 1951 disclosed four "successful" local editorial campaigns. A southern station reported that rents of cabins at state parks had been reduced by from 10 to 25 percent after an editorial campaign against the high charges. Another station used one-minute spot editorials to influence local balloting on daylight saving time. A midwestern station devoted four editorials to ending favoritism by the city council in granting off-sale liquor licenses. A station in the Pacific Northwest devoted a program a week to such local issues as the desirability of parking meters and ordinances governing pinball machines. In March, 1958, a CBS-owned station in Hartford, Connecticut, started a weekly fifteen-minute program devoted to editorials on local issues. That same year some stations used their right to editorialize in "spots" opposing pay television.

But not until the Mayflower decision was a decade old was there a strong sign that broadcasters would firmly grasp their editorial privilege. Led by pioneers like WTVJ-TV in Miami, broadcasters began to break away from the straight news format. By 1963, *Broadcasting Yearbook* was reporting that 40 percent of radio and television stations were editorializing—1,231 of 3,780 AM radio stations, 212 of 561 television stations.

The power of broadcasting as a mass persuader under highly propitious circumstances had been twice demonstrated decades earlier.

Kate Smith, a well-known vocalist, made sixty-five separate sales talks for war bonds during an eighteen-hour rally over CBS on September 21, 1943. Speaking for just a minute or two at a time, she asked, begged, urged her listeners to buy war bonds. Her pleas resulted in pledges for $39 million for bonds. The wartime situation, the public image of Miss

Smith, and the appeals tailored to fit that image all contributed to the results of that performance.

On October 30, 1938, also over CBS, Orson Welles' Mercury Theater of the Air broadcast a dramatization of an invasion of this world by hostile forces from Mars. The show opened with an announcement that the play was based on H. G. Wells' *War of the Worlds,* then went into the dramatization with a heavy use of the techniques of on-the-spot broadcasting reporting. Across the United States, there was panic; many listeners accepted the invasion as fact. Some gathered in churches to pray; others crowded bus terminals to flee the disaster. Still others jammed the telephone switchboards of newspapers and police stations to ask for further information or advice. A man who helped stage the show suggested two reasons for its effect—its technical brilliance and its historical timing (in those tense days after the Munich crisis Americans stayed close to their radios for news presented by just such on-the-spot reporting). Social psychologists have explained, in brief, that highly susceptible listeners had no pre-existing standards of judgment adequate to cope with the event.

These broadcasts, however, were the exception, and the usual deliberate editorializing is not likely to match their effects. Radio and television remain media which usually avoid controversy, which primarily carry entertainment interspersed with some information and interpretation, and which are still exploring the effects of overt persuasion.

Motion Pictures

Motion pictures are regarded more as a medium of entertainment than as one of deliberate persuasion. Yet they are beyond dispute an influential force on customs, habits, manners, ways of thinking and doing. Indeed, the assumption of influence underlies the widespread legal censorship and public pressure.

Because the motion picture requires a mass audience, because the foreign market has been a major source of revenue, and because government control has hung over the industry as a perennial threat, producers have tried to oblige their complainants by offending no one. They have produced some films dealing with such social problems as juvenile delinquency, segregation, racketeering, and mental health. The House Committee on Un-American Activities in 1947 conducted a number of hearings to determine whether the movies had been used by the Communists for subversive purposes. Although several witnesses spoke of writers' attempts to inject pro-Communist material into several films, the hearings failed to point up any convincing evidence. The Hollywood movie with a message of any sort is relatively rare. When film producers have a message, they usually try to convey it through entertainment at worst or through art at best.

Powers of Persuasion

It is easy to overrate the efficacy of the mass media as persuaders. Many people see them as operating in simple terms of cause and effect, of communication stimulus and individual response. They think, for example, that if an editor runs a blistering editorial calling for some action, his readers scurry like puppets to perform his will. A growing body of research evidence shows, however, that the persuasive effects of the media are neither that direct nor that simple. A single communication usually has little direct impact on attitudes or behavior. It is only after constant exposure that the media, little by little, affect us. Then they are more likely to modify attitudes than to change them.

individual response

The reason is that much intervenes between the communication stimulus and individual response. Some uncertainty over the response to persuasion lies deep in human nature itself. How each of us reacts to a communication depends on our attitudes, values, needs, motivations, physiological set, the whole complex of our personalities.

People, as we have seen, tend to choose among and within the mass media. In general, they choose materials which do not challenge the opinions and values they already hold. They tend, in short, to select that which they agree with, to avoid that which they disagree with. That point became evident as early as 1940 when Paul Lazarsfeld of Columbia University and his co-workers made studies of voting behavior in Erie County, Ohio. The communications media, they found, had little effect on converting voters to candidates. By picking and choosing, people managed to block out the things they did not want to hear. Thus they managed by and large to retain the positions they already held.

Confronted with material they disagree with, people tend to interpret it in such a way that it will bolster their existing beliefs and attitudes. Consider what happened when an organization set out to diminish racial prejudice through a series of satirical cartoons featuring Mr. Biggott, a ridiculously prudish character with exaggerated feelings against minority groups. The organization thought that the cartoons might reduce prejudice in this way: Readers would see that Mr. Biggott's ideas were similar to their own, that Mr. Biggott was an absurd character, that it was absurd to share his ideas. What really happened was far from the intent. Strongly prejudiced readers tapped several mental devices for misunderstanding the point of the cartoons. They misread into the cartoons meanings which left their prejudices intact or strengthened.

Some people will remain uninformed and unpersuaded no matter what the level or nature of the material directed at them. They are probably quite numerous; in one study, they were estimated to comprise about one-third of the population being surveyed. People prefer the familiar to the unfamiliar. They often suspect the new, since it requires effort to comprehend it and because there are no established patterns to govern the response. After a large-scale campaign to inform the people of Cincinnati about the United Nations and to create favorable attitudes toward it, researchers discovered that the effort had been ineffective. Only those who already knew about the United Nations were interested. Others were uninterested or negative; they resisted the efforts to inform them.

personal influence

Personal influence also stands between a communication and the individual's response to it. Personal contacts with people "who know what they're talking about" have a strong influence. Each person has many authority points—acquaintances, friends, relatives—whose opinions he seeks or accepts on politics, movies, fashions, shopping, and so forth. One usually goes to opinion leaders on his own level in the social hierarchy, but he does not go to the same person for advice on all topics. For tips on fashion and movies, for instance, one is likely to turn to young women; for advice on shopping, to housewives with relatively large families; for advice on politics, to someone older than one's self.

These opinion leaders do not comprise a small élite; they are dispersed throughout the population. Their influence may be great with some individuals, non-existent with others. Likewise, they wield great influence in connection with some subjects, none with others. These opinion leaders, in turn, have their own authority points. Personal influence, then, runs a twisting, turning course throughout the population, and all the way it is important in shaping opinions and actions.

For personal contact has several advantages over the mass media. Our mental guard is down; we may be strongly affected by an offhand remark in casual conversation. We know our sources, and we trust them. They operate in the most intimate of circumstances. If they do encounter our resistance, they have the opportunity for conversational give-and-take, a two-way process of communication lacking in the media. Furthermore, they can reward or punish us by granting or withholding their approval.

The media, of course, exert influence through these opinion leaders. The leaders may get some of their information and ideas from the mass media and transmit them to others. For example, E. A. Wilkening ι. to find out what had influenced farmers in adopting certain farm practices. One of the mass media was cited as the chief influence by about one-fourth of the early adopters but by fewer than one-twentieth of the late adopters. Other farmers were the main influence mentioned by three-fifths of the late adopters. It seems apparent that some of the farmers who learned of the practice from the media influenced others who did not. There are indications that opinion leaders make greater than normal use of the media. In his study of Erie County, Lazarsfeld found that the opinion leader exposes himself to newspapers and radio about twice as much as the ordinary citizen, to magazines almost three times as much.

In attempting to persuade, the mass media also encounter a network of interpersonal relationships which may deflect or negate their messages. Each person is a member of small groups—families, circles of friends, work teams, clubs—which influence and support the opinions, attitudes, decisions, and actions of their members. Individuals conform to the opinions and attitudes shared by the group, the so-called group norms. When one reads or listens to the mass media, he checks what he learns against the norms of his group. If the message runs strongly counter to group norms, it rarely wins. However, a message from the media may make some headway in influencing the individual if no group norms exist, if the reader or listener thinks that the group has altered its norms, or if he is about to leave the group. It may also be effective if it helps one to meet the norms of his group. Suppose, for example, a person becomes a member of a group with taste in music more advanced than his own. The media may be influential if they help to raise his tastes to those of the group.

how the media influence

All this is not to say that the media cannot and do not influence opinions, values, and behavior. They can and do, within limits.

Research workers generally agree that the media are much more likely to modify attitudes than to change them. When a group opposing the Tennessee Valley Authority was subjected to propaganda favoring it, less intense opposition was far more frequent than conversion.

The media are not only powerful reinforcers, but they can also slightly redirect existing behavior patterns or attitudes into new areas. Some observers believe that the power of advertising lies in its almost exclusive concern with such "canalization," as this redirection is called. Most Americans, for instance, are accustomed to cleansing themselves with soap; but the particular brand they use concerns them little, and advertising can influence the choice of brand.

If the media can enjoy a monopoly, they may in time affect considerable changes in attitudes and behavior. The Soviet press, which from our viewpoint has a monopoly in Russia, is harnessed to serving the ends of the proletariat. In the United States, there can be a monopoly, or a situation approaching a monopoly, only of media messages which favor attitudes approved by the great bulk of the population.

In summary, then, what can we say about the influence of the mass media as persuaders? Wilbur Schramm has put it this way:

> Any given communication that comes to an adult enters into a situation where millions of communications have come before, where group norms are already ingrained, and where the mind is already made up and the knowledge structured on most subjects of importance. The new communication is therefore usually not an earthshaking event, but merely another drop in the long slow process that forms the stalactites of our personalities.

References

BENT, SILAS, *Ballyhoo: The Voice of the Press* (New York: Boni & Liveright, 1927).

BERELSON, BERNARD, AND GARY A. STEINER, "Mass Communication" and "Opinions, Attitudes and Beliefs," in *Human Behavior: An Inventory of Scientific Findings* (New York: Harcourt, Brace & World, Inc., 1964).

————, AND MORRIS JANOWITZ, eds., *Reader in Public Opinion and Communication*, enlarged ed. (Glencoe, Ill.: The Free Press of Glencoe, Inc., 1953).

HOVLAND, CARL IVER, IRVING L. JANIS, AND HAROLD H. KELLEY, *Communication and Persuasion: Psychological Studies of Opinion Change* (New Haven, Conn.: Yale University Press, 1953).

KATZ, ELIHU, AND PAUL F. LAZARSFELD, *Personal Influence: The Part Played by People in the Flow of Mass Communications* (New York: The Free Press of Glencoe, Inc., 1955).

KLAPPER, JOSEPH T., *The Effects of Mass Communication* (New York: The Free Press of Glencoe, Inc., 1960).

MERTON, ROBERT K., *Mass Persuasion: The Social Psychology of a War Bond Drive* (New York: Harper & Row, Publishers, 1946).

NEWCOMB, ROBERT, AND MARG SAMMONS, *Speak Up Management! How to Communicate with Employees and Public* (New York: Funk & Wagnalls Co., Inc., in association with *Modern Industry Magazine*, 1951).

REGIER, CORNELIUS C., *The Era of the Muckrakers* (Chapel Hill: University of North Carolina Press, 1932).

SCHRAMM, WILBUR, ed., *Mass Communications: A Book of Readings,* 2nd ed. (Urbana: University of Illinois Press, 1960).

————, ed., *The Process and Effects of Mass Communication* (Urbana: University of Illinois Press, 1954).

————, "The Effects of Mass Communications: A Review," *Journalism Quarterly* 26 (December 1949) 397–409.

WEINBERG, ARTHUR MYRON, ed., *The Muckrakers: The Era in Journalism that Moved America to Reform, the Most Significant Magazine Articles of 1902–1912* (New York: Simon and Schuster, Inc., 1961).

11

The

Professional

Persuaders

Since every major enterprise with a shred of sensitivity now engages experts to build a favorable image through public relations or advertising or both, it was probably inevitable that image building would become a large and sensitive enterprise and that the experts would set about constructing a favorable public image for themselves. So it is that most of the 100,000 or more public-relations men in the United States have been turning ever more assiduously to developing general respect for their craft, and most of the approximately 400,000 men and women in advertising are equally concerned with promoting their own calling.

A few advertising and PR men have confessed in their memoirs that they did work they detested for money they didn't earn to buy things they didn't need to impress people they didn't like. With most of them, however, to ask for a definition of public relations or advertising is tantamount to hearing a lofty response. When *Printers' Ink* asked a number of the leading public-relations firms to define their role the typical answer was: "Public relations is the skilled communication of ideas to the various publics with the object of producing a desired result." The most widely repeated definition, which was offered by Cyril W. Plattes, manager of the department of public services for General Mills, ran:

> Public Relations is that responsibility and function of management which (1) analyzes public interest and determines public attitudes, (2) identifies and interprets policies and programs of an organization, and (3) executes a program of action to merit acceptance and good will.

Perhaps the most widely accepted definition of the role of advertising was written by Frederick R. Gamble, former president of the American Association of Advertising Agencies:

> Advertising is the counterpart in distribution of the machine in production. By the use of machines, our production of goods and services has been multiplied. By the use of the mass media, advertising multiplies the selling effort. Advertising is the great accelerating force in distribution. Reaching many people rapidly at low cost, advertising speeds up sales, turns prospects into customers in large numbers and at high speed. Hence, in a mass-production and high-consumption economy, advertising has the greatest opportunity and the greatest responsibility for finding customers.

Gamble's insight is valuable, but it fails to point up the essential similarity of public relations and advertising. Although advertising certainly does accelerate distribution, and it is most obviously at work in pushing particular brands, like public relations it is centrally concerned with winning acceptance and good will—for products, for people, for companies, for ideas. The only real difference between advertising and public relations is in method, and this difference dictates a different use of the mass media. Martin Mayer, author of *Madison Avenue, U.S.A.*, points up the distinction:

> Advertising, whatever its faults, is a relatively open business; its messages appear in paid space or on bought time, and everybody can recognize it as special pleading. Public relations works behind the scenes; occasionally the hand of the p.r. man can be seen shifting some bulky fact out of sight, but usually the public relations practitioner stands at the other end of a long rope which winds around several pulleys before it reaches the object of his invisible tugging. . . . The advertising man must know how many people he can reach *with* the media, the public relations man must know how many people he can reach *within* the media.

Essentially, public relations and advertising are selling devices. Their basic aims are so much alike that they are linked in fact—some advertising agencies have public-relations departments, some public-relations firms have advertising departments, many corporations place advertising and public relations in a single department—and they are linked in public consciousness: *The Man in the Grey Flannel Suit* is a novel about a public-relations man, but the title is almost universally applied to the advertising world.

Public Relations

To increase the sale of garbage cans for a client, one public-relations firm drew up a model ordinance ostensibly designed to protect public health by preventing or controlling the spread of diseases carried by rats. Among other things, the ordinance provided that all garbage must be deposited in containers of galvanized steel or other nonrusting material. After the ordinance had been approved by the United States Public Health Service, the public-relations firm sent copies of it, along with promotional kits, to every city and county health officer in the United States. Within a year, more than 300 cities had adopted the ordinance.

Edward L. Bernays, noted public-relations expert, used a different approach to stimulate the sale of bacon for a client: he got physicians to advocate hearty breakfasts. To promote the sale of luggage, he arranged for society leaders to come forth with the statement that a woman should take at least three dresses along on even the most informal weekend visit. The public-relations department of the Pan-American Coffee Bureau once set out to make the employees' coffee break, which had become common during World War II, an American institution. It surveyed top management on the benefits and drawbacks of the coffee break, then publicized the findings. It sent forth a flood of publicity about companies which had found that the coffee break improved morale, increased efficiency, and reduced employee fatigue.

The difference between those approaches and a national advertising campaign to promote sales is obvious.

But the public-relations practitioner is concerned with much more than the sale of products. His objective may be to change the public image of an individual or corporation, or to alter public attitudes toward company policies. The Illinois Central Railroad, slicing north to south across mid-America, at one time was stigmatized as being controlled by Wall Street. In 1938 the company made three changes to remove conditions which contributed to that impression. It moved its financial offices from New York to Chicago, replaced its directors from the East with businessmen from along its route, and began to hold its monthly directors' meetings in Chicago instead of New York.

objectives

Our public relations are those aspects of our behavior that have social consequences. As Harwood L. Childs puts it:

> Our problem in each corporation or industry is to find out what these activities are, what social effects they have, and, if they are contrary to the public interest, to find ways and means of modifying them so that they will serve the public interest.

What is the public interest? In effect, says Childs, what the public says it is.

But in practice only a few corporations subscribe to those objectives of public relations. Nugent Wedding of the University of Illinois studied eighty-five representative business firms to learn how they carried out their public relations. Only about 35 percent of them regarded public relations as consisting of forming proper policies and then interpreting those policies to the public. Almost 11 percent regarded public relations as solely a publicity activity.

Because American business persists in emphasizing words rather than deeds, it is wasting enormous sums of money on ineffective efforts to convert the public, according to Bernays. Public relations, he believes, must emerge as a form of social statesmanship. Its practitioner, with the full cooperation of his clients, must attempt, as his four objectives:

> To define the social objectives of his client or to help him define them.
>
> To find out what maladjustments there are between these objectives and the elements in our society on which his client is dependent. These maladjustments may be distortions in the mind of the public due to misinformation, ignorance, or apathy, or they may be distortions due to unsound action by the client.
>
> To attempt to adjust the client's policies and actions to society so that the maladjustments may be resolved.
>
> To advise the client on ways and means by which his new policies and actions, or old policies and actions, if it is deemed advisable to retain them, may be understood by the public.

Apart from the 35 percent which had a concept roughly equivalent to Bernays', the firms surveyed by Wedding had narrow views of the objectives of public relations: to create favorable public opinion and good will, 29.4 percent; to perform one aspect of the selling job, 10.6; to interpret business to the public and the public to business management, 8.2; and to whitewash business when business is under fire, 1.2.

history

The term *public relations* seems first to have been used in its modern sense in the closing years of the nineteenth century. One of the first to use it was Dorman Eaton of the Yale Law School in 1882 in an address, "The Public Relations and Duties of the Legal Profession." In 1906 and again in 1913 it turned up in talks by executives of the Baltimore and Ohio Railroad about railroads and their problems of "public relations." By the 1920s, when Bernays coined the expression "public relations counsel," it was fairly common, although it was ridiculed as an absurdly pompous synonym for the use of press agents.

Shortly before World War II, the term became imbedded in the vocabulary of American business. In its issue of March 1939, *Fortune* observed:

> The year 1938 may go down in the annals of industry as the season in which the concept of public relations suddenly struck home to the hearts of a whole generation of businessmen, much as first love comes mistily and overpoweringly to the adolescent. Indeed, during 1938 there was scarcely a convention that did not feature an address on public relations, scarcely a trade magazine that did not devote some space to the subject, scarcely a board of directors that did not deliberate weightily on the powers of the new goddess. And they found that the sphere of this Mona Lisa was all of industry and that she presided over its most bewildering and least tangible aspects.

But if the term is fairly recent, the practice is certainly not new in this country. Some historians say that public relations in America expanded after the Civil War; gained ground as a result of the onslaughts on big business at the turn of the century; emerged as a new profession in the 1920s when it began to tap the techniques of the social sciences; and came of age in the 1930s when the depression convinced management of its need.

In fact, if not in name, practitioners of public relations have existed for centuries, and they have used several of the techniques employed by today's specialists. In the eleventh century, for instance, William the Conqueror used what were essentially public-relations methods to consolidate his gains in conquered Britain: Among other things, he sought to learn the native tongue so that he could dispense justice in it. In the eighteenth century, Samuel Adams and others used manipulated events and the shrill voice of publicity to help engineer consent for the American Revolution.

The modern forerunners of the public-relations man emerged after the Civil War. They were the press agents for politicians, stage shows, and circuses, later for hotels, railroads, and shipping interests. They tricked, cajoled, and bribed newspapers into giving them space in the news columns. Some of them used techniques and tools employed by present-day public-relations counselors. P. T. Barnum, that master promoter, had a fine talent for creating events which became legitimate news. Thus he arranged for one of his major attractions, General Tom Thumb, to have an audience with Queen Victoria. Here is an example of creating news on the one hand and of obtaining the testimonial of a prominent figure on the other. But Barnum's public relations went beyond mere words. To build good will for himself, he gave lectures for charity and contributed to welfare societies. To overcome church opposition to his shows, he emphasized their Christian character and admitted clergymen and wives free.

Business and industry seem to have begun showing a conscious—one might almost say a self-conscious—regard for the effects of their policies on the public in the last years of the nineteenth century. The acknowledged pioneer was The Bell Telephone Company under Theodore Vail, who saw that sound policies were as important as pious words as early as 1883. That year, requesting a report from an affiliate in Iowa, he asked, "Where there has been any conflict between the local Exchange and the public, what has been the cause of the difficulties, and what has been the result?" When Vail saw that male telephone operators lacked the necessary tact and patience, he replaced them with women. In 1908 the company launched a campaign, which has continued down to the present in its basic approach, to give the public facts about the telephone system, to tell how calls should be made, and to urge subscribers to answer their telephones promptly. The company schooled its employees in dealing politely and sympathetically with the public. The company was sensitive to charges of monopoly, and it recognized that the impressions people got about it were from contacts with its employees. As one vice-president of the company said in 1909, "They know us as a monopoly, and that creates hostility at once because the public does not like monopolies. They have no opportunity to see us or know us. . . ." It is probably significant that the telephone companies, leaders in public relations, have emerged virtually unscathed from governmental investigations.

The concept of public relations spread to other businesses and industries. By 1949, according to *Fortune*, 4,000 corporations had public-relations departments or programs; in addition, there were 500 commercial public-relations firms, supported mainly by business. Today churches, schools, colleges, medical associations, philanthropic organizations, social-welfare agencies, and government bodies all have public-relations departments. Many of them, perhaps most, put greater emphasis on the dissemination of information than on Bernays' ideal twofold task of forming sound policies and interpreting them to the public. In 1957, according to a vice-president of Carl Byoir and Associates, there were about 100,000 persons working in all aspects of public relations in America and annual expenditures on it were approximately two billion dollars. He predicted that by 1968 the number of persons in the field would grow to 200,000, and expenditures would swell to between four and five billion dollars annually.

growing need for public relations

Several historical developments may have sharpened the interest of business and industry in public relations. One may have been the reaction to the robber barons who dominated the period of headlong industrial expansion after the Civil War. As they felled their forests, took their oil and ore from the earth, and built their railroads and factories, they held labor in close check, squeezed out their competitors, manipulated corporations and stocks, and bought legislation for their own benefit. They took the view that what they did and how they did it were their own concerns. Their attitude was exemplified in the public mind by Vanderbilt's phrase, "The public be damned!"

As abuses mounted, so did public criticism. Critics and reformers shouted against corruption in business and politics. Muckraking magazines, in the first dozen years of the twentieth century, exposed the evils perpetrated by the railroads, packing companies, oil companies, insurance firms, patent-medicine manufacturers, and political bosses. The government investigated anti-labor practices and passed legislation regulating lobbies, monopolies and the food and drug trade. For a time, the individualistic entrepreneur passed from public hero to public villain.

A second cause of the interest in public relations no doubt was World War I. The vast outpouring of war propaganda on an unprecedented scale demonstrated the efficacy of words in shaping public attitudes. This intensified a general concern with the whole broad subject of public opinion on the part of scholars and laymen alike. And it gave experience in opinion manipulation on a large scale to some men who, with the peace, were to use their skills on behalf of business.

A third factor affecting the course of public relations was probably the depression of the 1930s. Public faith in the free-enterprise system declined, and thousands of Americans listened attentively to new prophets with their share-the-wealth plans and other cures for economic ills. Besides selling products, American business had to re-sell itself to the public. Its task was complicated by labor troubles and unrest. Words might still be an indispensable tool of public relations, but policies in accord with the public interest took on an increased importance.

criticisms

Public-relations men—who have transformed robber barons into benign philanthropists in the public image—ironically have never enjoyed good public relations themselves. Today newspapermen, from whose ranks many public-relations specialists are recruited, tend to look down on them —perhaps a little in envy of their higher salaries, perhaps much more in disdain of their "selling out to the special interests." Intellectuals scorn them as insincere hired manipulators, sometimes sinister, sometimes no more than offensive. The very term "public relations counsel" seems to have been adopted in a quest for status similar to that which led undertakers to call themselves morticians, janitors to call themselves maintenance engineers, and garbage collectors to call themselves sanitary haulers. The fact is that today's public-relations worker has inherited a legacy of criticism. The criticism goes back to the press agents of the nineteenth century whose tactics aroused the enmity of editors, publishers, and just plain casual observers. From 1908 through the 1920s, the American Newspaper Publishers Association conducted a campaign against free publicity and free advertising. The trade press repeatedly denounced press agents, with which public-relations men were regarded as synonymous. In 1913 there were even attempts to make the use of press agents a legal offense.

the modern publicists

P. T. Barnum set the tone for publicity in the entertainment world, and especially for circus promotion. The press agent for Barnum's own circus, Richard F. "Tody" Hamilton, was said to be incapable of writing a sentence with fewer than five adjectives. "To state a fact in ordinary language is to permit a doubt concerning the statement," Hamilton held. The famous writers of circus bills at the end of the nineteenth century, Charles A. Davis and Charles Stow, contributed hugely to the image of a publicist as one who treats the truth casually. Davis promoted exotic circus attractions with a book titled *Progress and Civilization* that was used in several rural schools—and as a result there may yet be aged southerners who believe that Ohio was purchased from Siam and that Napoleon was a Cherokee scout. Stow's favorite circus bills announced that rival shows playing the same area had been quarantined with smallpox.

From the 1930s through the 1950s, the king of the circus publicists was Roland Butler, who was so fond of exaggeration that a reporter once asked, "Have you ever told the cold, unequivocal truth, devoid of embellishment, stripped of polysyllabic garnishments, unadorned and unembroidered, reduced to unstained fact?" Butler pulled forth a pencil and notebook and asked, "How do you spell those middle words? I can use them." This was probably flattery, for Butler had carefully worked out patterns of rhythm and alliteration using only polysyllabic words, some of which he coined. Newspapermen became so fascinated with Butler's prose style that they sometimes offered his rich verbalisms straight, with explanations in brackets. One *New York Times* story quoted him:

> "Twenty-six displays, boy, with scores of acts. Funambulists [wire-walkers] with unparalleled terpsichorean gyrations that beggar description; probiscibean mammals [Mr. Butler means elephants] directed by Baptiste Schreiber in the most amazing display of pachydermic skill the world has ever known."

Butler once captured an entire column on the editorial page of the *Times* by making a shrewdly simple announcement that the circus band was thinking of doing away with "that noisy old piece of plumbing, the tuba." Soon after, "Topics of the Times" was given over to a light essay that included this passage: "Lovers of the tuba are of the quiet, brooding sort, slow to anger and slow to forgive. They are sensitive, and it is safe to say that Mr. Butler has permanently alienated them." He was similarly inventive when a reporter asked whether he could prove that the circus was actually more thrilling than ever before. "Why, of course," Butler answered, "it's reflected in the peanut-eating. When the acts are dangerous people eat peanuts out of nervousness. They've been eating them by the ton." The wire services spread the story that peanut eating was held to be an accurate gauge of circus acts. Butler released statistics along the circus route, at one time reporting that after sixty-five performances the public had consumed 27,741,000 peanuts.

With the advent of television and the resulting decline of the circus, other entertainment publicists became better known. New York *Daily News* columnist Robert Sylvester found his mail continuously heavy with the bright sayings of Arthur Murray and set out to determine how the dancing master's feet and sense of humor could remain so agile for so long. He found that they were housed separately. In fact, Murray had been buying his reputation for wit for twenty-five years and was paying six press agents, one of whom said that he was averaging $1,000 a week supplying Murray's jokes. One made its way into a book:

> Arthur Murray's favorite story is about the gambler's funeral, attended by dozens of his dice-rolling and poker-playing friends. During the eulogy the speaker declaimed: "Spike Morrison is not dead—he only sleeps."
> Whereupon Butch Blackburn, in the rear, got up and yelled: "I got a hundred dollars says he's dead."

Murray is credited, however, with at least one original *mot*. At a time when he was employing only a single wit, Murray discovered that he had not made the papers for a long period. Walking in on the press agent, he demanded, "What ever happened to my sense of humor?"

New York press agents usually give Hollywood publicists credit for only one quality, that of going about their business as though they were crating oranges, but Russell Birdwell of Hollywood is an exception. He boosted Zsa Zsa Gabor into public consciousness, in part by advising her to wear a black patch while announcing that Porfirio Rubirosa had slugged her. Birdwell's special talent is the long-range promotion, which became clear when he conducted a widely heralded two-year search for an actress to play Scarlett O'Hara in *Gone With the Wind* even though Vivien Leigh had already signed a contract for the role. He made a national celebrity of Jane Russell before she ever appeared on the screen. And he was paid $50,000 plus expenses for publicizing the movie version of the controversial novel *Lolita*. One part of his promotion became apparent when a church elder in a congregation in the midget municipality of Lolita, Texas, demanded ringingly that the town change its name because of "that nasty, sex-filled book." The wire services carried the story.

Many varieties of publicists specialize in getting their clients mentioned in newspapers, from the sophisticated Richard Maney to Eddie Jaffee, whose specialty is the unbelievable item that is published as a curiosity. Jaffee put over Rosita Royce, a dove dancer, by announcing that her birds had collapsed with a nervous breakdown. Zorita the Snake Dancer was the beneficiary of a bulletin holding that she was undergoing analysis because she had fallen in love with her snake.

modern public relations

Public relations is a large umbrella that covers many specialists, and the great majority protest that they should not be equated with the press agents who follow in the Barnum tradition. Indeed, they contend that publicity is only one facet of modern public relations—one among many tools used in many media. A news story, a speech, a film, a photograph—each is a tool of public relations. The channels that carry the tools—a newspaper, a club meeting at which a film is shown, a magazine—are media.

There is much more to the modern concept of public relations than the simple creation of publicity. Bernays and a few others began bringing respectability to a much-maligned craft by promoting the Total Program. They argued that public relations must run much deeper than mere publicity. In *The Engineering of Consent* Bernays pointed out:

> The [company] president's acceptance of membership on advisory boards of national importance—indicates corporate inter-

est in the national welfare. Speaking engagements of plant managers before local service groups highlight management's civic
mindedness. . . . All of these symbol-projected themes—civic
mindedness, interest in education and youth and the like—
gradually form a composite and favorable picture in the public
mind.

How the Total Program works and how it has been developed over the
years is illustrated by the experiences of Paul Garrett, who was the only
public-relations employee of General Motors when he joined the company in 1931. Garrett was asked when he arrived at company headquarters in Detroit, "How do you make a billion dollars look small?"
Acutely sensitive about the company's size and visibility in troubled
times, the management's chief aim was to grow inconspicuously. Garrett
said not only that he could not answer the question; he did not think
providing an answer was part of his job. Public relations is the practice
of winning confidence, he argued, not putting on an act. As a consequence of his prodding, over the years General Motors has engaged in a
wide-ranging permanent program calculated to win acceptance and good
will. Eventually, that resulted in the company's setting up related departments known as Plant City and Field Relations, Educational Relations,
Speakers Bureau, and Institutional Advertising—all designed to persuade
everyone that General Motors is a desirable, if huge, concern. When
Garrett retired as a vice-president after twenty-five years, General Motors
was spending more than one million dollars a year on a public-relations
program that involved more than two hundred employees.

It is a measure of the importance of PR in the modern economy that
public-relations specialists are holding scores of corporate vice-presi-
dencies, and many are serving as company directors. The atmosphere
has proved so heady that PR men speak increasingly of their "profession"
and its fast-developing "prestige." One leading counselor, E. Edward
Pendray, even holds that "To public-relations men must go the most important social engineering role of them all—the gradual reorganization
of human society piece by piece and structure by structure."

There is reason to doubt this sweeping role, and even more reason to
question some of the methods of modern PR. This became especially
clear when the firm of Carl Byoir & Associates undertook to defeat a bill
that would have allowed increased size and weight limits for trucks on
Pennsylvania roads. Byoir was paid $150,000 by the Eastern Railroads
Presidents Conference. The firm earned the money in devious ways,
primarily by setting up front organizations—the New Jersey Citizens Tax
Study Foundation, the Empire State Transport League—to feed publicity
unfavorable to truckers into Pennsylvania. The governor vetoed the bill,

but the truckers brought a suit that eventually disclosed methods the presiding judge summed up as "the big lie." He commented, "This technique, as it appears from the evidence in this case, has been virtually adopted *in toto* by certain public-relations firms under the less insidious and more palatable name of the third-party technique."

Leading spokesmen for public relations argue that only a small percentage of the practitioners use devious methods and that the entire profession should not be tarred with the same brush. It is nonetheless significant that the standard-setting association, the Public Relations Society of America, did not ask Byoir to withdraw. *Tide* surveyed one hundred "top counselors" for their opinions on the use of front organizations. Some simply responded with the suggestion that "front" is a loaded word; "allied interest group" would be better. Others seemed to miss the ethical point entirely, replying that fronts are ill-advised because the opposition can blow up a campaign by exposing the deception. Only a small minority would approve legislation requiring the public disclosure of fronts.

In a candid speech to the Society of Magazine Writers, one spokesman described the problem of the wide assortment of "problem people" in public relations:

> We're struggling to find a way to protect ourselves. We haven't found it yet. We have no mechanics for licensing. We have no firm code on malpractice for weeding out these people. But gradually we'll find some way of establishing standards of ethics so that you can tell us apart.

Advertising

In 1923, Claude Hopkins wrote a book titled *Scientific Advertising* which began, "The time has come when advertising in some hands has reached the status of a science." Hopkins, who was reputed to be the best of the copywriters, was referring only to mail-order advertising, which involved printing coupons in ads that consumers could clip and send in with a dollar or so to receive a product. It was possible to gauge roughly the effectiveness of mail-order advertising by the number of returns, as Hopkins demonstrated in his 20,000-word book and in hundreds of mail-order campaigns.

Mail-order advertising is still an important facet of advertising, but, as the mass media show every day, there are many other kinds, and it is seldom possible to measure the effect of each with any real precision. Nonetheless, the methods of the behavioral sciences are so evident throughout the structure of the advertising world that it is clear that modern merchandising is attempting to make Hopkins' prescription apply to all advertising. Nearly every major agency spends a large share of its annual budget on research and on continuous efforts to take some of the guesswork out of appealing to masses of consumers.

Research in advertising is far too complicated to discuss in detail, but some understanding of the broad aims is available through considering the four major kinds of appeals, which have been described by Albert Frey in his book *Advertising:*

> Primary: those aimed at inducing the purchase of one *type* of product.
>
> Selective: those aimed at inducing the purchase of a brand.
>
> Emotional (sometimes termed *short-circuit* and *human-interest* appeals): those aimed at the emotions rather than the intellect.
>
> Rational (sometimes termed *long-circuit* and *reason-why* appeals): those directed at the intellect.

Research studies in the application of these appeals have revealed these five rules of thumb for copywriters:

> News techniques in advertising copy are likely to attract readers in much the same way readers are attracted to non-advertising news.
>
> Advertising related to the problems of consumers is more effective than boasting.
>
> Believable testimonials are effective, but readers are likely to be offended by the obviously spurious testimonial, no matter how famous the celebrity.
>
> Overimaginative, tricky advertising is ineffective. Making a single point imaginatively is positive, but elaborate appeals are negative.
>
> People are more interested in people than in things; each sex is more interested in seeing its own sex in an ad; repetition, up to a point, is effective.

There is, of course, a distinct limit to the value of analyzing appeals, in part because selling by advertising depends on so many other influences. Garrit Lydecker of J. Walter Thompson Company has pointed out: "I once made a list of all the factors that can influence sales. I had forty-five of them written down before I got bored with it. I'm sure there are more. Advertising was one of the factors."

General analysis is limited, too, by the fact that leading figures have some highly individual notions as to how advertising should be presented.

One example is Rosser Reeves, chairman of the board of Ted Bates & Company, a sometimes frenetic and always enthusiastic proponent of technical authority. Reeves describes the doctor who advises the Bates agency on drugs as "the man we believe to be the world's greatest pharmacologist." Another doctor, who offered advice on a soap campaign, Reeves says is "conceded to be one of the three leading experts in the United States on dermatology."

Reeves' chief contribution to advertising theory is known as USP, outlined in detail in his book *Reality in Advertising,* which was briefly a best-seller. Reeves describes his agency's method:

> We can't sell a product unless it's a good product, and even then we can't sell it unless we can find the Unique Selling Proposition. There are three rules for a USP. First, you need a definite proposition: buy this product and you get this specific benefit. Pick up any textbook on advertising and that's on page one—but everybody ignores it. Then, second, it must offer a unique proposition, one which the opposition *cannot* or *does not* offer. Third, the proposition must sell. Colgate was advertising "ribbon dental cream . . . it comes out like a ribbon and lies flat on your brush." Well, that was a proposition and it was unique, but it didn't sell. Bates gave them "cleans your breath while it cleans your teeth." Now every dentifrice cleans your breath while it cleans your teeth—*but nobody had ever put a breath claim on toothpaste before.*

Nearly every advertising man agrees with Reeves about the necessity for keeping everlastingly at it, for continuing the repetition. One agency man holds, "When the client begins to tire of an ad, you know it's beginning to catch on with the public." But there is considerable difference of opinion about Reeves' basic philosophy. This is emphasized by David Ogilvy of Ogilvy, Benson & Mather, who acknowledges the value of USP for advertising some products but holds that it is limited. Ogilvy is the high priest of brand-image advertising, specializing in building an aura of sophistication. A booklet he gives new employees points out: "It pays to give your brand a *first-class ticket* through life. People don't like to be seen consuming products which their friends regard as third-class."

Oglivy is noted for choosing models who reflect elegance. He hired Baron George Wrangell of the Russian nobility to pose, black eye-patch prominently shown, as "the man in the Hathaway shirt." Commander Edward Whitehead became the symbol of Schweppes. In a speech at a meeting of the American Association of Advertising Agencies, Ogilvy pronounced his major theme: "Let us remember that it is almost always the total *personality* of a brand rather than any *trivial product difference* which decides its ultimate position in the market."

Still another approach is promoted by Norman B. Norman of Norman, Craig & Kummel. Although most agencies rely to some degree on the power of unconscious suggestion, Norman was trained as a social psychologist and has a distinctively Freudian orientation. His agency aims at empathy, seeking to involve consumers at deep levels, and motivational research is basic. Some of the ads are highly suggestive—notably those for Maidenform bras and Veto deodorant—but the key is often subtlety. An ad campaign for Ronson lighters was built on research showing that flame is a sexual symbol.

One of the most admired agencies, Doyle Dane Bernbach, shuns all rules, relying instead on originality. In effect, William Bernbach simply hires the most creative copywriters and artists he can find, then encourages them to work together. He is one of the few agency presidents who think little of market research, holding that advertising is not a science but an art. Speaking to other advertising specialists, he has said:

> Why should anyone look at your ad? The reader doesn't buy his magazine or tune in his radio and TV to see and hear what you have to say. . . . What is the use of saying all the right things in the world if nobody is going to read them? And, believe me, nobody is going to read them if they are not said with freshness, originality, and imagination.

Few of the other large agencies promote anything that can be properly described as a philosophy, but there is general agreement on the goal: to reach the maximum number of users or potential users of a product at a minimum of cost. One authority, Otto Kleppner, has outlined three basic plans for using the mass media: the zone campaign, the cream campaign, and the national campaign. With the zone plan, the advertiser puts his maximum effort into a definite and restricted geographic area—a city, state, or recognized trading territory—gets what business he can there, then passes on to another. With the cream plan, he goes after the best prospects first, no matter how widely scattered, then goes after the next best, and so on down the scale. The national campaign combines the others on an enormous scale to get maximum sales from all possible prospects.

Whichever sales strategy the advertiser selects, he chooses media carefully. Long books have been written about media selection, but it is possible to set forth here the general guidelines.

geographic selectivity

Selecting prospects geographically involves several choices of media for reaching them. Newspapers can carry a message to the cities the advertiser is most interested in reaching. He can limit advertising to the cities where his product has adequate distribution, where he thinks it has the greatest sales potential, where weather or seasonal conditions promise demand for it, where employment is high and the economic picture bright. Furthermore, the speed with which newspapers are produced allows flexibility.

Radio and television, through their spot commercials and through programs which the advertiser can sponsor in cooperation with local dealers, also enable him to reach prospects on a geographical basis. Even with network facilities, he need buy only a part of the entire national market.

Magazines also enable an advertiser to seek out customers and potential customers in definite regions. Some magazines concentrate their circulations in specific areas. *Sunset* circulates primarily in the western states, for instance, and *New Hampshire Profiles* has chosen a single state for its major concentration. *Successful Farming* draws the bulk of its audience from the rich agricultural heart of the midwest.

Some magazines circulate nationally and offer the advertiser a widely scattered but homogeneous body of readers sharing common tastes, interests, or even occupations. They are ill-suited for geographical selectivity. In recent years especially, however, a number of large-circulation national magazines have given advertisers the option of buying either their entire circulation or just a part of it. In 1959 *Look,* with a total circulation of nearly six million, inaugurated a Magazone Plan under which advertisers could use any one or any combination of editions reaching seven standard marketing areas. About the same time, the *Saturday Evening Post* also offered advertisers who did not want to contact its entire circulation of six million the opportunity of buying space in regional editions under what it called its Select-A-Market Plan. Now magazines as diverse as *Sports Illustrated* and *Farm Journal* also are published in several editions.

prospect selectivity

But what of the advertiser who wants to reach only the most likely prospects for his product or service?

If his products are found in most households—as, for example, soaps, detergents, cigarettes—and especially if they are comparatively inexpensive, he may feel that he is reaching his market without undue waste if he gets his sales message before as many persons as possible. Sheer numbers may suit his purpose, then, and he can use the big-circulation national magazines, network television shows, Sunday supplements and a combination of dailies. But if his product appeals to some distinct body of purchasers or if it is relatively expensive, then he must carefully screen the audience for his sales pitch.

Magazines, because of their high selectivity of readers, are an excellent medium for such an advertiser. There are magazines for people with similar concerns, such as rearing children, protecting health, or home-making; with similar hobbies, such as stamp collecting, skin diving, hunting, fishing, yachting, or driving a hot rod; with similar interests, such as music, literature, science, fashions, or foreign affairs; and with similar occupations. There is scarcely a vocation, an interest, a facet of the personality that is not appealed to by some magazine.

The screened audience attracted by editorial content is the magazine publisher's stock in trade. Condé Nast once likened the magazine publisher to a name-broker: The publisher baits his pages with reading matter intended to attract either a large number of readers or a special class of readers, sells those pages at less than cost, and makes a profit by charging advertisers for the privilege of addressing the distinctive audience he has assembled. Nast's own magazines reached a wealthy, sophisticated few, and Ilka Chase in her *Always in Vogue* repeats the allegory he used to explain his publishing rationale:

> If you had a tray with two million needles on it and only one hundred and fifty thousand of these had gold tips which you wanted, it would be an endless and costly process to weed them out. Moreover the one million, eight hundred and fifty thousand which were not gold-tipped would be of no use to you, they couldn't help you, but if you could get a magnet that would draw out only the gold ones what a saving!

Obviously, Nast regarded his magazines as just such a magnet.

Network broadcasting and newspapers, attracting large, heterogeneous followings, do not permit the degree of audience selectivity that magazines do. Nevertheless, they can give the advertiser a coarsely screened audience. By the type of television program he sponsors and the time at which he schedules it, the advertiser can engage an audience with some of the characteristics he is looking for. He should know that about twice as many men as women watch televised boxing matches, for instance; that about seven times as many women as men tune in one daytime serial; that men constitute only 7 percent of the total television audience in mid-morning but nearly one-third between eight and nine in the evening. By his choice of newspapers, he can reach populations which are predominantly rural or predominantly suburban. One metropolitan newspaper may give him an audience different from that of another.

The New York Times is addressed to quite a different segment of the population than the New York *Daily News,* although each offers a good market for a specific purpose.

Defending the Persuader

Selling has always carried a stigma. Anarchus said, "The market is the place set aside where men may deceive each other," and there have been echoes of that statement ever since. It is a curious fact, however, that two authorities who have conducted searching examinations of professional persuasion through public relations and advertising have fashioned meaningful defenses.

Robert L. Heilbroner, a respected writer on economics, wrote an exhaustive study of public relations for *Harper's Magazine* that did not overlook the chicanery that is characteristic of some PR. However, he summed up by quoting a public-relations specialist who holds that the large corporation gets nervous unless people say what wonderful public relations it has: "So it has to *have* wonderful public relations. It has to *act* lovable. It has to *be* progressive." Heilbroner concluded: "Hence, by an unexpected twist, public relations has become a weapon whose recoil is greater than its muzzle blast. Good Public Relations has come to be something very much like the corporate conscience—a commercial conscience, no doubt, but a conscience nonetheless."

Martin Mayer, author of *Madison Avenue, U.S.A.,* is also unstinting in criticism of advertising, but he, too, finds a value not generally recognized:

> Any realistic approach . . . ought to start with the premise that successful advertising *adds a new value to the product.* . . . A lipstick may be sold at Woolworth's under one name, and in a department store under another, nationally advertised name. Almost any teen-age girl will prefer the latter, if she can afford to pay the difference. Wearing the Woolworth's brand, she feels her ordinary self, wearing the other, which has been successfully advertised as a magic recipe for glamour, she feels a beauty—and perhaps she is.

These defenses do not, of course, render valuable garish and false PR and advertising. No defense is possible, but an explanation is in order. It is, clearly, that like the mass media themselves, public relations and advertising are shaped largely by the American milieu. In the end, it is fruitless to ask that they be much better than the industrial economy to which they owe their existence.

References

BENDINER, ROBERT, "The 'Engineering of Consent'—A Case Study," *The Reporter*, 13 (August 11, 1955) 14–23.

BERNAYS, EDWARD L., "American Public Relations: A Short History," *Gazette* (International Journal of the Science of the Press), 2 (November 2, 1956) 69–77.

CATER, DOUGLASS, *Power in Washington* (New York: Random House, 1964).

HEILBRONER, ROBERT L., "Public Relations: The Invisible Sell," *Harper's Magazine* 214 (June 1957) 23–31.

HILL, JOHN W., *The Making of a Public Relations Man* (New York: David McKay Co., Inc., 1964).

MAYER, MARTIN, *Madison Avenue, U.S.A.* (New York: Harper & Row, Publishers, 1958).

PIMLOTT, JOHN ALFRED RALPH, *Public Relations and American Democracy* (Princeton, N.J.: Princeton University Press, 1951).

PRESBRY, FRANK S., *The History and Development of Advertising* (Garden City, N.Y.: Doubleday & Company, Inc., 1929).

"The Public Is Not Damned," *Fortune*, 19 (March 1939) 83–88, 109, 110, 112, 114.

SANDAGE, CHARLES H., "The Role of Advertising in Modern Society," *Journalism Quarterly*, 28 (Winter 1951) 31–8.

SANDAGE, CHARLES H., AND VERNON FRYBURGER, eds., *The Role of Advertising: A Book of Readings* (Homewood, Ill.: Richard D. Irwin, Inc., 1960).

WOOD, JAMES PLAYSTED, *The Story of Advertising* (New York: The Ronald Press Company, 1958).

12

The

Media

as Entertainers

In February, 1933, over station WXYZ in Detroit, George
Trendle began broadcasting a half-hour radio program in
which a masked avenger called the Lone Ranger galloped
about the West correcting injustices. Listeners were so
pleased that Trendle started looking around for other
stations to help bear program costs. After a good deal of
work, he signed up WGN in Chicago and WOR in New
York. Then a number of New England stations wanted the
program and later so did the Don Lee broadcasting system
in California. In 1934 the stations which had cooperated
in broadcasting the show banded together into the Mutual
Broadcasting System. The Lone Ranger, among countless
other noble deeds, could take credit for helping to create
a major broadcasting network.

The Lone Ranger was responsible for a multitude of
other accomplishments in the next quarter-century. He became a big business, the Lone Ranger Enterprises, for which
a Texas industrialist paid $3 million in 1956. By then, the
Lone Ranger had brought the Whitman Publishing Company some $20 million from the sale of books about his
exploits. He performed his missions in a comic strip carried by 144 daily and 89 Sunday newspapers. He was the
inspiration for a series of phonograph records issued by
Decca. He was a busy endorser of guns, holsters, masks, and

other paraphernalia for youngsters. He undoubtedly encouraged boys and girls to stow away millions of bowls of breakfast cereal for his sponsors, and the passage from Rossini's "William Tell Overture" that was his theme became perhaps the most widely heard bit of operatic music of all time.

One can draw a number of conclusions about the entertainment content of the mass media from this story, and there is considerable additional evidence to support each of them. One is that through entertainment the media are capable of creating folk heroes. Matt Dillon, Superman, and Dick Tracy, like the Lone Ranger, all are endowed with virtues larger than life, making certain that good triumphs over evil.

Another conclusion is that the media are parasitic. Whatever succeeds in one medium is often taken over by the others. Characters who have first appeared in books—Perry Mason, for example—later turn up in films or on television. Magazine short stories and serials often form the basis for subsequent movies or television programs. One successful author of humorous short stories a few years ago deliberately set out to write a quantity of them for a women's magazine so that he could resell them as a television series starring his central character. He succeeded in getting his television series—and a book for good measure. Hollywood has long looked to best-selling novels for movie plots, and in recent years some book publishers have reversed the process by bringing out novels based on film scripts. Book publishers and movie-makers recognize that they can mutually profit from the public interest generated when one of them has a success. When M-G-M released a new screen version of Lew Wallace's classic *Ben Hur*, book publishers issued eleven new editions of the work in addition to those already in print. On the other hand, Otto Preminger rushed production of the film version of *Anatomy of a Murder* so that theaters could show it while the book was still on the best-seller lists.

Appeal of Entertainment

Perhaps the most obvious conclusion of all, however, is that entertainment has a powerful appeal. Many newspapers have changed from organs devoted chiefly to enlightenment to those of entertainment, according to some observers. It is beyond dispute that much newspaper content is intended simply to divert its readers. Studies of newspaper readership show that adults give greater attention to human-interest articles, comics, and illustrations than to information about public affairs or advertisements. About half the readers of a daily read the banner story on page one, according to one research report, yet about two-thirds read the comics, and more look at the picture page than at anything else in the paper. Consider the readership of an issue of one California daily. Researchers found that 30 percent of the men and 18 percent of the women read the major news story from Shanghai in the top right-hand corner of the front page. But 60 percent of the men and 66 percent of the women read a feature on page 21 about how the heroes who had rescued a little girl were still unemployed.

Indeed, the entertainment features apparently give newspapers their strongest hold on readers. The liberal Washington *Post* bought and absorbed the conservative *Times-Herald* in 1954. Readers of the *Times-Herald* were dismayed at first. But, as it turned out, they were oriented to the comics and sports section of the paper rather than to the editorials; and when the *Post* took over their favorite comic strips, their favorite sports writers, and their favorite columnists, they were scarcely aware of any change, according to Stanley K. Bigman, who reported their reactions in the *Journalism Quarterly*. Several readers remarked, "So far as I'm concerned, it's still the *Times-Herald*."

Even before 1895—that being the year when the records of best-sellers became somewhat systematized—entertainment items bulked large among the books which had the widest sales in America: the novels of Sir Walter Scott, James Fenimore Cooper, Charles Dickens, Alexandre Dumas, Nathaniel Hawthorne, and a number of other authors now almost completely forgotten. Since then books of entertainment—along with self-help volumes—have captured high and frequent positions on the best-seller lists. According to a study by Alice Payne Hackett, the authors who have most consistently appeared on the best-seller lists over the years since 1895 have been purveyors of entertainment—Mary Roberts Rinehart with eleven titles, Sinclair Lewis with ten, Zane Grey and Booth Tarkington with nine each.

Magazines are heavily weighted with stories and articles calculated to beguile the reader. People put entertainment at the top of their list of reasons for reading magazines, slightly higher than the desire to increase their knowledge, according to research by the Curtis Publishing Company. Serving the wish for entertainment, magazines carried a high proportion of light fiction in the 1920s and 1930s. Although they began giving increased space to nonfiction in the 1940s, a good share of the space still has sheer entertainment as its goal. The magazines with the largest circulations include *Reader's Digest, Life, Look,* and the *Saturday Evening Post,* all of which devote a generous measure of space to their readers' amusement.

Movie-making and broadcasting are commonly referred to as entertainment industries, and amusing the public is their acknowledged primary function. The magnet that pulls people into theater seats and drive-ins may be a particular star or the promise of the story. Yet at bottom the appeal is entertainment; people go to the movies to enjoy escape from care and routine, to feed their daydreams. An occasional movie may grapple with social issues, but its message is usually secondary to keeping the audience entranced. The greatest movies of all time so far as box-office gross is concerned—among them *Gone with the Wind, The Robe, The Greatest Show on Earth, White Christmas, This is Cinerama,* and *Quo Vadis*—have made no pretensions beyond giving large numbers of persons wholesome stories, lavish spectacles, or both. Entertainment is so universally accepted as the objective of movies that debate is seldom over whether or not they should be anything else but rather over whether or not they should be artistic entertainment or mass diversion geared to the box office.

Commercial television and radio have a potential for education, true, and both have devoted a little time to edifying their audiences. NBC-TV has proudly announced that the number of persons Dr. Harvey E. White was able to reach with his physics lessons on "Continental Classroom" would have taken him 1,300 years to teach in the conventional classroom. Yet the great majority of the broadcast audience expects television and radio to entertain. The television set is an electronic door to the land of enchantment. (People value it more highly than such household items as refrigerators, stoves, or even beds, according to the improbable results of one network survey.)

difficulty of definition

Few would deny that the mass media carry an enormous amount of sheer diversion. Perhaps half of all media content is avowedly entertainment of some sort. Actually, however, the proportion seems immeasurable. For no one is quite certain what constitutes entertainment. The newspaper editor might argue that his column of advice on readers' personal problems is instructional; many of his subscribers would contend that it is entertainment. A television producer might hold that his quiz show is educational; a good many viewers would argue that the show simply amuses the audience and that any education is the most accidental of by-products.

Some media content is obviously intended as entertainment and no more—the newspaper human-interest story, the magazine tale of young romance, the television variety show, the Hollywood spectacle. Despite the intention, some readers and viewers may use that content for instruction. On the other hand, some content ostensibly intended to inform or instruct at times verges on entertainment. For example, some network television shows aimed at educating mass audiences in the wonders of science have invoked formats of disarming informality, using cartoon inserts, animated gadgets, and benign moderators with patronizing questions and answers, all on the dubious assumption that the most complex of ideas can be made clear to the meanest intelligence. Showmanship befogs the lesson. Some observers have remarked that the weekly news magazines often package entertainment in the guise of news, that a few of the large-circulation religious magazines do much the same thing with religion.

One way of deciding what is and what is not entertainment is to by-pass the content itself and to consider its effect, which a number of social researchers have done. Some of them think that content is escapist if it relieves tensions by affording the media user respite from his personal problems. Joseph T. Klapper in *The Effects of the Mass Media* has reviewed the different meanings which social scientists have given to the term "escapist," and fashioned a common-denominator definition: "that communication which provides emotional release by diverting the reader from his own problems or anxieties."

What is escapist for one person, then, is not necessarily so for another. If one uses media content primarily for pleasure, it is escapist no matter what else it is. Thus a businessman who relaxes with a magazine article about science or a scientist who takes refuge in the sports page of his newspaper is using the mass media for diversion. Under that concept, all media fare is potentially entertainment. Whether it is or not depends upon the use to which the reader, viewer, or listener puts it.

historical origins

Entertainment, to some extent, has been a product of the press since shortly after William Caxton introduced printing to England in 1476. Long before the first newspaper emerged, Englishmen were diverted by the broadside, a medium which continued to delight the wellborn as well as the masses down to the opening of the present century. For more than 300 years, broadsides were the chroniclers of the sensations and the scandals of their times—the murders, hangings, accidents, battles, deaths of famous persons—and they told their stories in moralizing prose, grace-less ballad, or both. They were single sheets, usually printed on one side, and issued as occasion warranted. Their vendors, who as often as not sang their verses, hawked the broadsides on the streets of provincial towns, on the corners of London and even, when they dealt with murder and the execution of criminals, at the foot of the gallows itself. In the American Colonies, too, broadsides found a ready market. For the masses who could neither afford nor comprehend the newspapers of their time, broadsides were an exciting source of topical entertainment. The Clown in Shakespeare's *Winter's Tale* spoke for a host of broadside fanciers when he said, "I love a ballad but even too well, if it be a doleful matter merrily set down, or a very pleasant thing indeed and sung lamentably."

Other media within the pocketbook range and attuned to mass inter-ests drove the broadside into oblivion. In England in the eighteenth century, as literacy spread through the middle classes and penetrated down-ward, presses were kept busy supplying the demand for entertaining reading matter. At least one new magazine a year appeared in London during the fifty years after 1730, most of them with at least some divert-ing content. Novelists came from the ranks of country parsons, house-wives, and clerical workers, and they convinced readers that they were being uplifted while being entertained. Popular dailies and weekend newspapers sprang up with a heavy load of amusement for the laboring class. So it was in America. By the middle of the eighteenth century, Colonial newspaper editors were lightening their pages with essays and poetry, albeit as fillers. With the emergence of the penny press in the 1830s, the newspaper was off to conquer a mass audience with human interest and other entertainment as its come-on. A half-century later magazines were beamed at the mass market they had been neglecting.

difficulties of presenting quality entertainment

The entertainment function of the media was intensified and in other ways affected as the media changed from a comparatively restricted audi-ence to a broad-based popular one. In the nature of the communications system, one can find an explanation for critics' complaints that the mass media at best have made small contributions to art and at worst have debased popular culture on the one hand and have blurred the line between enlightenment and entertainment on the other. Both art and education are predicated upon a critical and discriminating reception; the conditions under which the mass media operate make such a reception difficult.

Intended for mass consumption, the media usually strive for mass appeal. Few find it economically feasible to consider the tastes of the individual members of their audiences, and must play to the average tastes of large numbers. Nor, usually, can the owner of a medium indulge in the luxury of satisfying his individual tastes. He must produce what-ever it is profitable to give great numbers of other people.

The media have not set out to corrupt public taste. But ordinarily they cannot serve persons with discriminating tastes unless such persons exist in sufficient numbers to constitute a profitable market. Seeking the ap-proval of large followings, their production hastened and tempered by budgetary concerns, the media in general are obliged to eschew the subtlety, the ambiguity, the experimentation, and the iconoclasm which are among the characteristics of art. Their products for the most part are the work of skilled technicians, most of whom prefabricate for the market, few of whom seek self-expression. The audiences of the media usually attend them passively and with little participation in the formula-tion of critical standards. Neither condition is conducive to the creation of art.

With the object of momentarily engaging the busy masses, the transient products of the media issue forth in an endless torrent, the significant cheek by jowl with the trivial, the good and substantive emphasized little more than the bad and the shallow. The media must compete with themselves, with other claims on the individual's time and attention, with the individual's own lethargy. Somehow they must get through to their readers, listeners, and viewers. The nature of their task dictates their approach to content, and the approach to content contributes to their blending of entertainment with enlightenment. To capture and captivate their audiences, the media generally try to enliven and simplify their messages.

Newspapers have done so since the days of the penny press. According to the sociologist Robert E. Park, newspapers exist in their modern format only because a few publishers discovered in 1835 that people prefer news to editorial opinion and that they prefer being entertained to being edified. "This, in its way, had the character and importance of a real discovery," he says. "It was like the discovery, made later in Hollywood, that gentlemen prefer blondes. At any rate, it is to the consistent application of the principle involved that the modern newspaper owes not merely its present character but its survival as a species." In short, the newspaper came to emphasize the interesting rather than the important, to use William Randolph Hearst's distinction.

This is not to say that newspapers ignore serious content seriously presented. They are probably doing a better job on that score than they were when Park made his comment in 1940. It is true, however, that in undertaking serious discussion or in presenting information newspapers must always reckon with their reception. Because of the heterogeneous nature of the readers, reporters must not only translate complex issues and complex subjects into terms intelligible to the masses but must do so interestingly. The chief aim of the reporter, after all, is to get his stories read. The aim of the deskman is to arrest attention with a headline. If the handling of a story and the headline which surmounts it attract readers to serious fare, that in itself is justification. But sometimes there is a narrow line between interesting the reader and merely entertaining him.

Especially among the magazines leading in circulation, the pressures to find and keep a large audience have sometimes contributed to a fusion of the functions of entertainment and enlightenment. Since World War II, magazines have shortened nonfiction articles on the assumption that readers no longer have the patience for long ones. But it is difficult to treat some subjects more than superficially in the allotted space. To catch and hold the attention of readers, many magazine writers develop their articles not by straight exposition but by presenting a few generalities, each illuminated by numerous anecdotes and dramatized examples. Quite often the net result is a little information surrounded by a copious gilt-wrapping of entertainment. Having discovered that readers are more interested in people than in ideas, a number of magazines use personalities as a peg on which to hang treatments of general topics. A news magazine may review current problems of organized labor in a cover story centering around a well-known union official or may discuss the economic health of Great Britain in a personality sketch of its chancellor of the exchequer. The technique, while a perfectly legitimate one to sustain reader interest, is often in danger of subordinating information to entertainment.

Network broadcasters feel obliged to offer something for everybody. As Robert S. Salant, a CBS executive, expressed it:

> For the fact is that broadcasting is a truly mass medium; it has to be. Unless it can enlist and hold the interest of most of the people, a good part of the time, it is just too expensive to survive. It must, in its spectrum of programming, have something—even the great majority of its material—that will appeal not just to the thousands or hundreds of thousands but to millions and tens of millions.

A medium which is compelled to interest the tens of millions, one which counts most first-graders among its regular users, usually finds its common denominator in entertainment. It is television's preoccupation with providing mass escapism which lay behind a remark by Edward R. Murrow: "If television and radio are to be used to entertain all of the people all of the time, then we have come perilously close to discovering the real opiate of the people."

In its entertainment fare, broadcasting must make certain compromises in subject matter and treatment as a result of the demands of the market. Paddy Chayefsky, who earned a reputation as a television playwright before he concentrated on writing for the movies, once said that he had never encountered sponsor or network interference with his television dramas, thanks to a producer who took a firm position. But he added:

> On the other hand, every one of us, before we sit down and write a television show, makes that initial compromise of what we're going to write. We don't sit down and write for television or conceive a television idea that we know is going to be thrown out the window. That's the compromise. I have never, never written down in television in my life, but I never aimed very high. . . . You make that same compromise in the movies, and you make it on the stage too, but in a relatively less degree.

What Chayefsky recognized was that the television playwright must accommodate himself to a mass audience and to an advertiser who regards any controversy in the shows he sponsors as bad business. For most of the television programs they are concerned with, advertising agencies approve all scripts in advance, study the story lines and dialogue, and have program representatives present to keep an eye on the daily production work. In all of this, the agency is guardian of the sponsor's interest.

Limitations on dramatic subject matter arise partly because the advertiser does not wish to offend anyone. Several advertising-agency executives who testified at hearings conducted by the Federal Communications Commission agreed that programs which displease a substantial number of viewers represent a misuse of the advertising dollar. Because the sponsor wants to leave his audience with a favorable impression, he usually avoids dramas which treat socially taboo subjects, portray extremes of misery or desolation, leave the viewer sad and depressed, or deal with politics—politics being controversial and capable of alienating customers.

Other limitations arise because of the interests of the sponsor. A program must not contain anything which will reflect unfavorably on the sponsor or his products. Evidently at the request of the American Gas Association, one of the sponsors, a reference to the gas chambers of Hitler's concentration camps was cut out of the script when "Playhouse 90" dramatized the Nuremberg trials over CBS television. An aspirin manufacturer would never permit a drama in which a person committed suicide by an overdose of aspirin, an advertising executive told the FCC. He also said that the manufacturer of filter cigarettes wanted the villains in a television drama to be shown as preferring nonfilter cigarettes, whereas the maker of nonfilter cigarettes wanted the villains in his shows to smoke filter cigarettes.

Effects of Entertainment

When a sponsor is concerned about what the characters in his television drama say and do, he is recognizing that entertainment may have effects beyond mere diversion. One effect is persuasion, but social scientists have hypothesized several others. While these by-products of entertainment are still largely surmise, they deserve some attention.

persuasive powers

As other chapters show, entertainment is probably capable of affecting the way people think and act. Indeed, the assumption that entertainment can influence the minds of men underlies a good deal of censorship. Fear of the persuasive and corruptive possibilities of entertainment lies behind much of the public concern over comic books, paperback novels, crime on television, and sensation in newspapers.

Convinced that entertainment is subtly forceful in propaganda, men have been using it for centuries. During the Revolutionary War, newspapers, almanacs, and broadsides sought to lighten the burden of battle with anecdotes, jests, parodies, satires, and songs which were also designed to promote the cause of freedom. The popular novel has been a widely used form of social protest, and cartoons have been a frequent weapon of crusaders at least since *Harper's Weekly* ran pictures by Thomas Nast to break the political power of the Tweed Ring in New York in 1870–1871. Today in West Germany, Heinrich Baer in his magazine *Tarantel* has used cartoons, jokes, and skits to combat the Communist regime in East Germany.

Empirical research involving the persuasive powers of entertainment is not scanty, but some of the findings are contradictory. Studies do show, however, that certain types of entertainment—the radio soap opera, for example, and magazine stories—are effective. It is reasonable to suppose that entertainment has some effects similar to those of informational and avowedly persuasive content. That is, entertainment works outright conversion only rarely; more often it slightly modifies existing attitudes. Little by little, over a long period, it probably contributes to the attitudinal prism through which people perceive their environment and with which they interpret the multitudinous messages reaching them.

Entertainment probably gains its greatest effect through strengthening existing attitudes. It is generally accepted that a communication is most likely to be effective if it harmonizes with the predispositions of its audience. Entertainment, by stressing commonly accepted values and attitudes, does just that, as numerous studies have shown. Hence, there seems some basis for the frequent observation that media entertainment contributes to a perpetuation of the status quo.

Magazine fiction from the 1930s onward has emphasized the conventional virtues and has idolized the little man, according to a study by Patrick Johns-Heine and Hans H. Gerth. While ostensibly preaching racial equality, it subtly perpetuates discrimination against minority groups and glorifies the white Protestant American of Anglo-Saxon stock, according to another study by Bernard Berelson and Patricia Salter. Even the "Orphan Annie" comic strip helps to reaffirm the accepted values of the broad middle class. Lyle Shannon, who analyzed it, summarized his conclusions in this fashion: "The strip emphasizes reliance on 'providence,' faith, hope, and charity—but not too much charity. . . . Orphan Annie is for the church, truth, hard work, and pressure when necessary to get what she wants. She opposes crooks, politicians, slowness in government, and foreigners who would like U.S. military secrets."

emotional release

In a comprehensive study of the effects of the mass media, Joseph T. Klapper reported that people sometimes use entertainment to escape from feelings of inferiority and insecurity by identifying themselves with successful characters in stories, articles, films, and broadcasts. By enabling them to share vicariously in the good life and triumphs of others, identification provides a sense of prestige. At worst this is harmless, Klapper concluded; at best, helpful.

Some observers think that media entertainment offers a safety valve for pent-up aggressions and aberrant impulses and consequently performs a useful social function. While many people have become agitated about comic books, for example, some authorities contend that they may serve the emotional needs of children. Dr. Lauretta Bender, associate professor of psychiatry at New York University Medical School, has written:

> When the aggressive threat to society, or the immediate family, is so overwhelming as to be unbearable, the comics can present the problem symbolically and repetitively so as to allay anxiety. During the war when Superman and Wonder Woman could protect our ships at sea from Nazi submarines through their quick seeing eyes and lightning feet and magic strength—they were a great help to children whose fathers were in the service.

Material heavy in sex may serve a similarly useful purpose. One authority has concluded that "contrary to popular misconception, people who read salacious literature are less likely to become sexual offenders than those who do not, for the reason that such reading often neutralizes what aberrant sexual interests they may have."

By enabling people to work off their impulses and hostilities vicariously, then, the media may help to quiet disruptive forces in society. This basic argument is at least as old as John Milton's *Areopagitica*, in which, to be sure, it took a somewhat different cast. While Milton no doubt would be appalled at being cited to justify comic books, he nevertheless argued that reading is the best way to learn of evil. No man can be virtuous without a knowledge of evil, he said, and it is far better to learn vicariously through reading than through experience.

The relatively scanty available research evidence does, in fact, suggest that well-adjusted children take violence in the media in their stride—indeed, use it as an emotional outlet. Katherine M. Wolfe and Marjorie Fisk discovered that comics contribute to the development of the normal child who reads them moderately by amusing him and strengthening his ego. They may satisfy the emotional needs of the maladjusted child as well. The great danger is that they may postpone correction of the maladjusted child's basic troubles by allaying the symptoms. Television programs of crime and violence help children who are well adjusted and secure in their peer groups to vent their aggressions, according to a study conducted by John and Matilda Riley. For secure children, the programs probably do no harm. But for maladjusted, insecure children, they build up rather than release tensions and create a world of unhealthful fantasy.

possible dangers of escapism

Some perceptive students of mass communication, albeit with little research evidence to back them up, have expressed concern over the misuse or excessive use of entertainment. They fear that overexposure to escapist material, by diverting people from the problems of daily living and by encouraging their retreat into a dream world, may promote individual and group apathy and thus inhibit social progress.

Klapper has argued against that viewpoint. He sees little reason for believing that escapist material diverts people from serious media fare. True, some people overindulge, he concedes, but they might be more dangerously preoccupied if the media were not so readily available. He grants that those who make heavy use of the media for escape probably have little interest in serious social problems, but he submits that their lack of interest is more likely the cause rather than the result of their tastes.

Other observers are concerned because some users of the mass media depend upon entertainment for information and advice. This can work harm in any of several ways. For one thing, the advice is usually so superficial or impractical that it is certain to be futile. For another, it can lead people to a passive acceptance of whatever ills and misfortunes befall them in the confident hope that everything will work out all right sooner or later.

Still other authorities believe that certain types of media entertainment can seduce the weak-willed and the immature into lives of crime or immorality. The codes of performance for the comic-book, motion-picture, and broadcasting industries all recognize this danger by urging that criminals never be glorified, crime never be portrayed attractively and sin never be glamorized. Stated simply, the fear is that some people, especially children, may imitate the worst of what they are exposed to in the media.

Herbert W. Case, former police inspector in Detroit, has been quoted as saying, "There hasn't been a sex murder in the history of our department in which the killer wasn't an avid reader of lewd magazines and books."

Yet equally competent authorities are as quick to discount imitative effect. As early as the 1930s, psychologists were showing that delinquents and criminals were prone to blame the movies for the crimes they committed. In evaluating those studies, Klapper has concluded, "The evidence they adduced, however, cannot substantiate any cause-and-effect relationship, and can be easily accounted for by the more established thesis that mass media material tend to further the development of already existing personality traits." Authorities sharing Klapper's view contend that the media do not teach the transgressor his bad impulses, which arise from a complexity of causes; at worst, they may teach him the methods of carrying out those impulses.

Despite this distinction, leading researchers are now convinced that entertainment directly affects behavior, especially with children. Eleanor Maccoby summarized several studies: "The nature of the effects depends upon many limiting conditions. . . . But the impact of the media is real. What the child absorbs while he is being 'entertained' he uses in the interpretation of his real-life experiences, and in preparing himself for roles that he will play in the future, as well as for immediate action. And the media may influence moods (e.g., produce moods of pessimism) or transmit persuasive beliefs (e.g., that the world is a threatening place), as well as present bits of information or bits of action for imitation."

Entertainment and Libertarian Theory

Traditional libertarian theory has taken little cognizance of the entertainment function of the mass media. True, entertainment is one of the six social functions ascribed to the press, but it has no rationale, as does servicing the political system or making a profit; it seems to have been included as a function merely because the press has virtually always entertained. In neither England nor America, where libertarian theory evolved, has entertainment ever been considered important to the successful functioning of political institutions, as it has been under certain modern totalitarian regimes. Quite the contrary, it has often been suspected of threatening allegiance to the state, corrupting morals, and debasing the natural good taste of the public.

Therefore, entertainment has never been allowed the freedom accorded to informational content. As Fred Siebert has pointed out, the entertainment media have been subject to strict government control and supervision, in theory if not in practice, from the earliest period of modern times. The theater in England fell under government control centuries ago when it turned from religious to secular drama; even today all public theaters in England must be licensed and their offerings submitted for censorship before they are performed. Only in recent years have there been indications that the courts in this country are at last willing to free the motion picture from the legacy of state control which it inherited from the stage.

However, there is another reason for stricter control over the movies—and over radio and television, as well—than over the printed media. It lies in their very nature.

motion pictures

The motion picture has been presumed to have a power over its audience that the other media do not possess. Although research on the effects of movies is scanty, numerous critics have speculated on the power of film to gain its viewers' uncritical acceptance of what it portrays. Some observers ascribe the supposedly unique power of the film over its audience to two things: the conditions of film showings, and the techniques and content of the films themselves.

The conditions of mass film showings, some authors contend, are similar to those for inducing hypnosis. Hugh Mauerhofer, in *Penguin Film Review No. 8,* has described what he calls the "cinema situation." Reactions of the viewer include a change in the sense of time ("the course of ordinary happenings appears to be retarded") and a change in the sense of space, which may endow the unconscious with a larger than normal role. Results of the cinema situation are "continually imminent boredom, intensified power of imagination and voluntary passivity." Thus the spectator gives himself voluntarily and passively to the action on the screen, according to Mauerhofer, and to an uncritical interpretation supplied by the unconscious mind. Further, he writes, the anonymity of the film experience prevents a "community" from being formed in the theater, so the individual is thrown back on his most private associations. His personal participation is intensified; he identifies himself uncritically with the figures on the screen.

broadcasting

Just as tradition and the nature of the medium have worked to give movies a narrower scope of freedom than the printed media, those same forces have helped to restrict the freedom permitted to the broadcaster.

Despite their perceptive excursions into the treatment of public affairs, both radio and television have been identified in the public mind as primarily entertainment media. Moreover, they transmit programs directly into the living room, where they are attended by both adults and the very young. As the television code of the National Association of Broadcasters holds, "It is the responsibility of television to bear constantly in mind that the audience is primarily a home audience, and consequently that television's relationship to the viewers is that between guest and host." And yet radio and television are more than mere entertainment. They combine aspects of the theater and motion picture with those of the magazine and newspaper. They focus on events with authenticity and an almost terrifying immediacy. By their very nature they raise a host of moral and legal problems which the printed media do not.

That point became apparent when the Columbia Broadcasting System televised an hour-long interview with Nikita Khrushchev, First Secretary of the Communist party of the Soviet Union, over 105 affiliated stations. Herbert Mitgang, who analyzed the aftermath for the Fund for the Republic, wrote:

> If a newspaper had published an interview with Khrushchev, no responsible person in any communications field would have thought of questioning the propriety of the publication. But when a television network, after great precautions to protect the integrity of the performance and after making its intention known to the highest level of government, telecast an interview with the Kremlin leader, the propriety was seriously questioned. The President of the United States made a statement which at least implied criticism. Important members of Congress openly challenged the wisdom of the presentation. The press was ambivalent.

This reaction to a serious broadcast intended to enlighten the public clearly indicates that television is seen as deserving far less than full freedom. Given the common view that television is an electronic amusement device, it is not surprising that even such a traditionally liberal journal as the *New Republic* can discuss censoring it without raising an outcry from its readers.

use of entertainment in totalitarian states

In sharp contrast with libertarian theory, which does not see entertainment as contributing to the functioning of political institutions, the theories of totalitarian states have assumed that entertainment can and should be harnessed to serve the political and economic order.

In Germany, the Nazis believed that all art forms should contribute to the propagation and maintenance of the ideals of the Third Reich. Closely controlled by the state, broadcasting was regarded as a prime tool for disseminating propaganda. Joseph Goebbels, the propaganda minister, ticked off its strengths: It rallied the population on short notice; it gave the listener a sense of participation in events; it depended on the spoken word, which could reach the literate and illiterate alike and which fostered an emotional rather than a critical response; it permitted the creation of personalities whose very voices attracted followings. No doubt he had those points in mind when he said that, if used to its fullest potential, "radio is the most important and far-reaching instrument in leading the people." From the time they came to power, the Nazis also held the motion picture in high esteem as a means of influencing people at home and abroad. By a number of measures, the state controlled the allegiance of movie-makers to the racist and political principles of the Third Reich.

Benito Mussolini's Fascists in prewar Italy also used the theater, music, art, broadcasting, and film to further the interests of the state. The Ministry of Popular Culture included a division responsible for the "direction and coordination" of radio and the development of television; a substantial amount of program time was devoted to political talks. The state maintained control over motion pictures, working through a film section in the Ministry of Popular Culture and through another in the state banking house, which financed undertakings that the government wished to encourage. All incoming foreign movies were kept consistent with Fascist ideology by the forbidding of original or subtitled versions and the requirement that all movies be dubbed into Italian.

In Soviet Russia today not only broadcasting and the film but literature, music, painting, and sculpture have been brought under control to promote and maintain the dictatorship of the proletariat. Because the Communist party is responsible for the cultural education of the people, Soviet radio serves greater helpings of serious music and literature than it would if its programming were left to popular choice, according to Alex Inkeles. The emphasis given to the listeners' political education results from the Soviet view that radio is chiefly an instrument of government policy, not primarily a source of entertainment.

The revolutionary potential of the motion picture was recognized by Lenin as early as 1907, when he remarked that "when the masses take possession of the film and it comes into the hands of true supporters of socialist culture, it will become one of the most powerful means of educating the masses." Arnold Hauser, in *The Social History of Art*, has singled out the film as the only art form in which Soviet Russia has made important achievements. One reason, he suggests, is that a close affinity existed between the young Communist state and the new form of cinematic expression.

> Both are revolutionary phenomena, moving along new paths, without a historical past, without binding and crippling traditions, without presuppositions of a cultural or routine nature of any kind. The film is an elastic, extremely malleable, unexhausted form which offers no inner resistance to the expression of new ideas. It is an unsophisticated, popular means of communication, making a direct appeal to the broad masses, an ideal instrument of propaganda. . . .

promoting America's interests

The entertainment media in the United States are left relatively free to promote whatever interests they will, but they usually tend to perform a similar function. Catering to the great majority, they play on its aspirations, beliefs, and values; accommodating themselves to the commercial interests which support them, they tacitly accept and subtly reaffirm the major assumptions of those interests. The net result is that, by the overwhelming weight of their output and by the absence of much real questioning of fundamental propositions, they generally support the existing social, economic, and political order.

References

GRIFFITH, RICHARD, AND ARTHUR MAYER, *The Movies* (New York: Simon and Schuster, Inc., 1957).

ROSENBERG, BERNARD, AND DAVID MANNING WHITE, eds. *Mass Culture: The Popular Arts in America* (New York: The Free Press of Glencoe, Inc., 1957).

SCHRAMM, WILBUR, JACK LYLE, AND EDWIN B. PARKER, *Television in the Lives of Our Children* (Stanford, Calif.: Stanford University Press, 1961).

SCHUMACH, MURRAY, *The Face on the Cutting Room Floor* (New York: William Morrow & Co., Inc., 1964).

WERTHAM, FREDERIC, *Seduction of the Innocent* (New York: Holt, Rinehart and Winston, Inc., 1954).

WHITE, DAVID MANNING, AND ROBERT H. ABEL, eds., *The Funnies, An American Idiom* (New York: The Free Press of Glencoe, Inc., 1963).

13

Criticism

of the Media:

The Major Themes

Even before the newspaper had come into being, critics were shooting barbs at the authors of ballads, the newsmen of sixteenth-century England. In 1591 one critic peevishly noted that "scarce a cat can look out of a gutter, but starts a half-penny Chronicler." The following year another critic lamented:

> A company of idle youthes, loathing honest labour and dispising lawful trades, betake themselves to a vagabond and vicious life, in every corner of Cities and market Townes of the Realme, singing and selling ballads and pamphlets full of ribaudrie, and all scurrilous vanity, to the prophanation of God's name, and withdrawing people from Christian exercises, especially at faires, markets, and such public meetings.

When the American press was being used as an instrument of political warfare in the early 1800s, Thomas Jefferson, a man with far more than usual tolerance for the frailties of editors, wrote to a friend: "The newspapers of our country, by their abandoned spirit of falsehood, have more effectively destroyed the utility of the press than all of the shackles devised by Bonaparte."

In 1859 Lambert A. Wilmer wrote the first book entirely devoted to criticism of the American press, *Our Press Gang;*

or, a Complete Exposition of the Corruption and Crimes of the American Newspapers. Thereafter the attacks gradually increased in force and intensity.

In the twentieth century, as the press became a ubiquitous and pervasive institution, criticizing it became a popular indoor pastime. For the most part, the early critics adopted what we might call a conspiratorial theory of press malfunction. The press is guilty of the grave charges they tick off, the critics said, because publishers have conspired with big business to promote and to protect their mutual interests. Some publishers themselves are a part of big business; others are in league with it. In exchange for suppressing and distorting media content so as to keep big business powerful, publishers can share in such rewards as handsome advertising contracts, social position, and political prominence.

Over the years, critics have played variations on these seven general themes:

> The media have used their great power to promote the interests of their owners. The owners have propagated their own views, especially in politics and economics. They have ignored or played down contrary views.
>
> The media have been the tool of big business generally. At times advertisers have controlled policies and content.
>
> The media have resisted social change; they have perpetuated the status quo.
>
> The media, in reporting current happenings, have generally been more concerned with the superficial and the sensational than with the significant. In providing entertainment, they have been heavily weighted with fare lacking substance or artistic merit.
>
> The media have endangered public morals.
>
> The media without good cause have violated the privacy and debased the dignity of individuals.
>
> The media have been controlled by individuals of a single socio-economic class, the business class, and newcomers have had a hard time starting up new communications enterprises. As a result, the free and open market of information and ideas has been endangered.

Newspaper Critics

In 1911, in a series in *Collier's* magazine, Will Irwin set the pattern for much of the later criticism of the newspaper. Although a rash of articles praising or condemning the press had broken out in other periodicals in the preceding four or five years, he wrote, his series and other articles springing from it would be among the first attempts in the United States to assess journalism fully and candidly.

In exchange for its financial support of the newspaper, Irwin wrote, advertising demanded and often got suppression of certain types of news, biased news accounts, and similar concessions:

> Slowly at first, then with increasing momentum, advertisers learned their power. Indeed, in certain quarters, advertising solicitors helped to teach them. For the less conscientious and solidly run newspapers began offering comforts and immunities as a bonus to attract customers. Advertisers got into the way of asking for these special privileges; often, in communities where the newspapers were timid and mushy, for every privilege, even to dictating policies. The extent of their demands varied with the local custom of their communities. But finally . . . the system had grown so set that [the publisher] must make concessions or fail.

The concessions that advertisers asked for were sometimes a whole change of editorial policy, Irwin said, but most often the concession concerned insertion of publicity for and the suppression of news harmful to the advertiser, his family, or his business associates.

With more perception than most early critics, Irwin made a point which social scientists were to return to decades later: That many of the shortcomings of the press arise not just from the baneful influence of advertising but from the commercial nature of publishing.

> The advertiser pays most of the revenue, but he is paying for circulation. The greater the circulation, the greater the advertising rate, and the more eagerly advertisers will buy. This is a kind of double product. You must have circulation first, last, and all the time, though circulation pays you no profit, except as you turn it into advertising—as a stockfeeder gets his profits not from his hay and corn, but from his fattened steers.

Unlike some later students of the press, however, Irwin believed that over the long haul only a good product, a truthful product, could attract and hold a large circulation. Commercial and conscienceless, publishers persistently ignored that point, he said, and for a short-term advantage colored their product to the taste of the advertisers.

But Irwin also saw that the advertiser was not the only influence working on a publisher. He observed that newspaper publishers are businessmen and the newspapers they control will necessarily reflect the viewpoint of the businessman.

The newspaper field had become increasingly difficult for the new-comer to enter, Irwin noted, an observation which seems rather percep-tive since daily newspapers then were only two years past their peak numerically. He noted also that the influence of newspapers had shifted from their editorial columns to their news columns.

later critics

Irwin was followed by a line of critics who reiterated his themes, although often without his acuteness of observation, and who in essence charged, "You can't believe what you read in the papers because the press is controlled by advertisers and big business."

One of the early critics was Upton Sinclair, who in 1919 published *The Brass Check*, a title emphasizing the analogy he saw between journalism and prostitution. Sinclair already had a national reputation as a reformer. In 1904, two years after he had aligned himself with the socialists, he had written *The Jungle*, a novel exposing conditions in the Chicago stockyards. Written for a socialist paper and then published in book form, *The Jungle* was a best-seller in America and England and was translated into seventeen languages. Public indignation aroused by the book led to the Pure Food and Drug Act of 1906. Thereafter books streamed from Sinclair's pen, most of them with some sort of message, and on his eightieth birthday, in 1958, he could point to a book for each year of his life.

The Brass Check, like its author, proved durable. By 1926 it had gone into its ninth edition, and in 1936 it was reprinted in a revised edition. Half of the book deals with Sinclair's personal experiences with the press; the remainder calls on other witnesses to the prostitution of a free press.

"The Empire of Business," Sinclair wrote, controls journalism by four devices. First and most direct is ownership of many of the nation's periodicals. A second and most important means has been to achieve ownership of the owners. By playing on the ambitions of publishers, by applying pressure on their families, by club associations and gentlemen's agreements, big business has strengthened its hold on the press. A pub-lisher is a member of the ruling class in his community, Sinclair noted, and by accommodating the right people he may become a senator, a cabinet minister, even an ambassador. Advertising subsidies are the third means by which business controls the press. They make publishers prone to suppress ideas inimical to advertising interests, news embarrassing or detrimental to advertisers. Finally, Sinclair said, business at times resorts to outright bribery to promote its views and censor antagonistic ideas.

Sinclair's belief that conspirators manipulate the press to their own ends was shared by George Seldes, a former head of the Berlin and Rome bureaus of the Chicago *Tribune* and war correspondent in Spain for the New York *Post*. One of the most diligent critics of American journalism, Seldes set the theme for much of his subsequent criticism in his book *Freedom of the Press* in 1935: "Unfortunately, there are powerful forces which do not want the facts, from a millionaire's divorce to a war scare, presented truthfully. There are corrupting influences."

The corrupting influences he saw and tried to document are the influences of the financial, political, social, and advertising worlds. These have been responsible for such suppressions as that of news of an epidemic of amebic dysentery in Chicago during the Chicago World's Fair of 1933 and for such propaganda as that used by the utilities against publicly owned power.

The arch conspirators are the members of the American Newspaper Publishers Association, the house of lords of the press, Seldes argued in his *Lords of the Press* in 1938. The publishers gather behind closed doors at their annual meetings, he said, because their conspiracies against the public welfare cannot bear the light of publicity:

> . . . in the closed sessions they defend the employment of child labor, they take united action against a Congressional measure which would keep drugmakers from poisoning or cheating the American people, and they gloat over their own strikebreaking department which offers scabs not only to members but to anyone who wants to fight the unions.

Both professional and amateur critics have complained that newspapers have reflected the biases of their owners and the viewpoints of big business in their coverage of major election campaigns since the 1930s. Newspapers were accused of giving unfair treatment to the Democratic candidate, Adlai Stevenson, in both the 1952 and 1956 Presidential campaigns. They did not confine their support of the Republican candidate, Dwight Eisenhower, to their editorial columns, critics charged; instead, many newspapers of the overwhelming majority which supported Eisenhower played down Stevenson's speeches and played up his opponent's.

Second thoughts began to grow in 1960. Most political reporters were clearly for Democrat John Kennedy in his Presidential race against Republican Richard Nixon, although publishers generally supported Nixon. Some Democrats admitted privately that the reporters had helped elect Kennedy. Researchers then began to reassess the easy and traditional assumption that reporters had to slant their stories in the direction of the publishers' leanings. Some thoughtful observers now hold that some of the power of the late thunderers of the publishing world—the William

Randolph Hearsts and the Robert R. McCormicks—has passed to the reporters.

Many of the comfortable assumptions of decades were upset in 1964. Most political reporters were clearly for Democrat Lyndon B. Johnson in his race with Republican Barry Goldwater—but so were most of the committed newspapers. Johnson was supported by 445 dailies with an aggregate circulation of nearly thirty million; Goldwater was supported by 368 dailies with an aggregate circulation of less than ten million. Even more striking was the lack of newspaper commitment; 60 percent of United States dailies either declared themselves neutral or failed to support either candidate. This was, of course, an unusual election. But one should not ignore the fact that newspaper independence-neutrality has long been tracing a steep curve. Only one daily in twenty failed to take a stand in 1932. In the 1960 election, one in three took no stand.

critics of news values and techniques

A conspiracy to bias and censor is not the only charge against newspapers. A number of critics, including some newspapermen, have found fault with current standards of news evaluation and with some techniques of news presentation. A familiar criticism, repeated over the years, has been that newspapers play up the sensational, the superficial, the silly, at the expense of the significant. Thus they give more space and attention to a torso murder in Cleveland, a marital entanglement in Hollywood, a nudists' convention in New Jersey, or a rape in Delaware than to an important session of the United Nations. Another familiar charge is that the technical presentation of the news—the headlines, the inverted pyramid structure of the stories, the fetish of objectivity—prevent the reader from seeing a coherent picture of current events.

To a large extent, the citizen is deprived of necessary information and discussion because the press is preoccupied with reporting trivia and conflict, the Commission on Freedom of the Press charged in 1947. The compulsion to attract a large audience has led the press to emphasize "the exceptional rather than the representative, the sensational rather than the significant."

> Many activities of the utmost social consequence lie below the surface of what are conventionally regarded as reportable incidents: more power machinery; fewer men tending machines; more hours of leisure; more schooling per child; decrease of intolerance; successful negotiations of labor contracts; increase in participation in music through the schools; increase of sale of books of biography and history.

Instead of adequately reporting such developments, the commission said, the press gives disproportionate attention to riots, strikes, and murders.

Much earlier, Walter Lippmann had questioned the technical ability of the newspaper to report the social conditions underlying news of consequence. Newspapers, he said in his *Public Opinion,* do little more than station reporters at points of record—at the police station, say, and the courthouse. Here they catch only what he called the obtrusions of social conditions. A reporter might note a businessman filing for bankruptcy, for instance, but he is not equipped to explore the conditions leading up to that situation until it actually happens. Thus, said Lippmann, what the reader gets is a somewhat distorted picture of social conditions, a picture much like a halftone made with an exceedingly coarse screen.

Newspapers have failed to give the reader a coherent picture of the news, several critics have charged. In 1939 Sidney Kobre called on newspapers to increase their amount of depth reporting. Their coverage of spot news needs little further development, he said; what is needed is an attempt to weld the findings of the rapidly developing social sciences to the newspaper so that the reader could understand not only the surface event but also what lay beneath. He quoted with approval a remark by Irwin Edman, a philosopher at Columbia University, who described the newspaper as "the worst possible way of getting a coherent picture of the life of our time. It is a crazy quilt, a jazz symphony, a madness shouting in large type. . . . The mind of the newspaper reader, if it could be photographed after ten minutes of reading, would not be a map, but an explosion."

To give the reader an orderly and understandable picture of the life of our time, Herbert Brucker proposed a number of reforms in *The Changing American Newspaper* in 1937. In the old days, before the world had become complex and the reader harried, he wrote, it was enough for a newspaper to run separate stories on the day's happenings and to scatter them helter-skelter throughout its pages. Today that practice often bewilders the reader. Like Kobre, Brucker suggested that newspapers give more attention to background and interpretation, that their staffs rewrite wire stories for coherence and round them out with additional facts supplied by their own research departments. Moreover, he recommended that newspapers take greater care in organizing the news to make it comprehensible. The entire front page might be devoted to concise but adequate summaries of all major happenings, classified by subject matter, he said. Within the paper, fuller accounts, sometimes combining several individual stories, might be departmentalized by subject matter, somewhat as the news magazines group stories.

Contributing to the chaotic portrayal of the day's events are misleading headlines, written to catch the lethargic reader and to fit a given space with little regard for meaning, according to some critics. "As now em-

ployed by most dailies, the headline is a convenient device gone wrong,"
wrote nine Nieman Fellows in their blueprint for a better press. "Newspapers have converted its limitations—brevity and emphasis on the cate-
gorical imperative—into a commercial asset, a shabby trick to sell papers."
Most readers shun the full account and read only the headline. Too often
the headline is not warranted by the facts of the story. The reader then
gets a distorted view of events, the charge runs. Even the reader who
moves into the story may be misled. For, according to the Nieman Fellows, the impact of a bold, black headline may be greater than that of the
story itself.

A number of newsmen, foreign and domestic, have complained that the
five-W lead and the inverted pyramid form of newswriting, despite their
practicality, make for dull, repetitious stories. "Perhaps this formula has
become more important than the end originally sought," Herbert Brucker
wrote. "At least one wonders whether its advantages in practice justify its
strange results in newswriting." When the reader is hit in the face with
the most important facts in the first sentence or paragraph, the logical
sequence of events is destroyed, according to critics. The story is told
piecemeal, with repetition, and all tension and interest vanish. That
point was reiterated by Urs Schwarz, foreign editor of *Neue Zürcher
Zeitung*. He noted that the Grimm brothers opened their story of Rum-
pelstiltskin in this fashion: "Once upon a time there was a miller; he was
a poor man, but he had a beautiful daughter." In the hands of an American reporter, he said, the opening would have come out something like
this: "A queen's success in pronouncing his name led a dwarf to tear
himself to pieces, and saved a child's life."

Yet another criticism of newspapers is the fetish of objectivity. Newsmen are so afraid of editorializing in the news columns, so this charge
runs, that they cheat the reader. By giving only the objective facts instead
of interpreting those facts, they often turn out stories which are distorted,
incomplete, even incomprehensible. By striving to present all sides in a
controversial situation, they often give the same credence to a known liar
and a known truth-teller. Hence the objectivity they cherish is far too
often not objectivity at all but a form of distortion. Critics acknowledge
that the reporter who interprets the news must walk a narrow line between fact and opinion, yet walk it he must if he is to put the facts into
a context that gives them meaning.

Magazines

Magazines have shared in the criticisms directed against the mass
media generally, but they have come in for remarkably little criticism on
their own.

True, critics like Upton Sinclair have lumped magazine publishers with newspaper publishers as parties to the conspiracy with big business to keep the public uninformed or misinformed on certain issues. Advertising pressure has killed off the magazines which dared to tell the truth, Sinclair charged, and has made the survivors spineless. It has even corrupted the authors of magazine fiction, who tend to treat themes favorable to big business and the status quo, he said.

True, too, even some friends of magazines have remarked on their bland editorial diet. Robert Heilbroner, a free-lance magazine writer and a former president of the Society of Magazine Writers, put that criticism this way in the *Saturday Review* of January 14, 1956:

> We are all too familiar with the bland stew of ingredients that have been in the icebox too long: the meat is the weary expose ("The Russians Are Tunneling Under Alaska"); the vegetables are moldy ("Is There Sex After Death?"); the stock watery ("Can Animals Read?"); and the spice tired ("I Lived and *Loved*—among the Aborigines"). But if some magazines court inanity (if you can call a long-standing marriage courtship), not all magazines are so disposed, and even the blandest of the bland will come up, from time to time, with articles that are forceful, courageous, and controversial.

Another magazine writer, Morton Sontheimer, has cited the observer who noted that the bulk of all magazine articles would fit into three categories:

> Oh, the glory of it!
> Oh, the shame of it!
> Oh!

True, too, individual publications have stirred the critic's pen. A number of authors, most of them seemingly disenchanted former employees, have found fault with Time Inc. and its magazines. The *Reader's Digest* has been the subject of a book-length dissection.

For the most part, however, the charges against magazines have been those leveled against the media as a whole. Magazines have been accused of a general conservatism, inhospitality to significant new ideas, reluctance to change the status quo. They have been accused of overemphasizing the material side of life, and they have been charged with catering to a low common denominator of taste in their eagerness to give the public what it wants.

Most of the criticisms directed specifically against magazines seem to have been aimed at periodicals lurking in the dark shadows along the fringes of the industry—at the scandal magazines, the pornographic magazines, the comic books. Perhaps the shrillest criticism has been of the comic book, which some authorities consider a factor in juvenile crime, delinquency, and maladjustment. In his *Seduction of the Innocent,* Dr. Fredric Wertham, a psychiatrist and one of the most persistent critics, has summed up the eight specifications in indicting comic books:

> They invite illiteracy with their format.
> They create an atmosphere of cruelty and deceit with their heavy load of material about crime.
> They make readers susceptible to temptation.
> They encourage unwholesome fantasies.
> They suggest ideas which may lead to crime or sexual perversion.
> They provide a rationalization for the execution of those ideas.
> They give detailed information on criminal techniques and other undesirable practices.
> They may weight the scales in favor of delinquency or maladjustment.

Motion Pictures

Ever since 1896, when an indignant public protested a shocking kiss in *The Widow Jones,* the motion picture has been attacked and ridiculed. Intellectuals have scorned the Hollywood product as entertainment fit only for a twelve-year-old mentality. The morally righteous have exerted pressure to stop portrayals of what they have regarded to be flagrant immorality on the screen. Minority groups of various kinds have protested against the way in which the movies have depicted their members and treated their interests.

In the revolution of manners and morals after World War I, there was an erosion of the old taboos against public discussion of sex, a development which affected the various media. The confession magazine was born of this changing attitude and perhaps even contributed to it. Some movie-makers took advantage of this new freedom to film stories recognizing sex as a motivating force in human affairs. Some went too far. Theater marquees carried such titles as *Passion* and *Forbidden Fruit,* and movie advertising attracted customers with purple prose and suggestive illustrations. Off screen, a few movie stars became involved in widely publicized scandals. Hangers-on of the industry became involved in still more and contributed to a popular image of movie-making as a business characterized by loose living and shoddy morals.

acceptance of pressure

Religious, civic, and women's organizations spoke out in protest during the early years, as did many magazines, both secular and religious. After studying film content, the General Federation of Women's Clubs demanded state legislation. A precedent existed, since Chicago had set up a censorship board in 1909; between then and 1922, eight states passed laws providing for movie censorship.

Anxious to protect its investments in stars and studios, the movie industry in 1922 began to experiment with self-regulation. From those early attempts there came, in 1930, a production code which outlined standards of performance. Four years later, under pressure from the National Legion of Decency, a Catholic organization, the industry set up machinery for enforcing the code.

The movie industry adopted its code in self-defense against the widespread charge that the movies endanger public morals. In exchange for its attempt to still that criticism, the industry acquired a new one—the criticism that the movies traffic in inanity. The real curse is conformity, according to Robert Ardrey, a film writer who analyzed the state of American movies in *The Reporter*. And conformity came about when Hollywood gave in to the "puritan uproar" which culminated in the production code. "It was a mistake that the theater never made," he wrote. "Down the drain went the best and the worst, the fine and the wicked, the baby with the bath water. Public relations replaced private instinct; brains replaced glands: the cautious the courageous: the package the substance."

In decrying the inanity of the movies, Ardrey is by no means alone. Time and again the movies have been attacked for creating a dream world of unrestrained fantasy. For the most part, the critics concede that a certain proportion of purely escapist films—the sentimental romance, the action-packed western, the slapstick comedy, the star-studded musical—works no great harm. What they object to is that these films constitute the overwhelming bulk of Hollywood's offerings. They deplore Hollywood's reluctance to attempt serious drama, to base movies on themes with relevance to twentieth-century life. Allan A. Hunter, pastor of Mount Hollywood Congregationalist Church in Los Angeles, made the point in this way in a symposium:

> Too rarely does Hollywood tackle an issue involving such relationships as cartels, monopoly, lynching, segregation, imperialism, or the urgency of international cooperation with regard to raw materials, waterways, and markets.

the American image abroad

A corollary criticism is that Hollywood gives a false picture of American life, culture, and institutions to the rest of the world. American movies are immensely popular throughout the world, and the foreign market is important to movie-makers. In the ideological conflicts of the twentieth century, some authorities contend, it is especially important that the movies give a fair representation of American life.

Yet, these same critics assert, the picture which the movies convey abroad is distorted, showing Americans as wasteful, extravagant, and insensitive; inordinately concerned with material gain and comfort; indifferent to social injustice; preoccupied with physical beauty, sex, and amorous intrigue; given to lawlessness and violence. As a member of the British Parliament once remarked, "Anyone who suggests that the American films portray the American way of living is an enemy of the United States."

It is quite easy to demand that American films give a balanced portrayal of American life, of course, but quite a different thing to define just what that balance should be.

the image of minorities

In their failure to portray things as they really are, according to another common complaint, the movies have often given stereotyped and even harmful pictures of members of racial, professional, and occupational groups. The typical reaction has not been criticism alone but pressure on the industry by groups believing themselves harmed by their treatment on the screen.

Movie-makers have been exceedingly sensitive about their portrayals of racial groups ever since D. W. Griffith's *The Birth of a Nation* was denounced by the National Association for the Advancement of Colored People in 1915. Negro and white leaders alike have been quick to object to movies showing Negroes in servile positions, as villains, in parts thought detrimental to the interests of their race. When Walt Disney adapted Joel Chandler Harris' Uncle Remus stories in *Song of the South*, certain Negro groups picketed theaters in protest against what they believed to be an unflattering picture. Others have complained that the movies usually show Negroes as servants, singers, and dancers, not in the representative positions they hold in their communities.

Physicians, lawyers, teachers, and others have objected when the movies have shown members of their professions as villains or have otherwise portrayed them unfavorably.

Sensitive to pressure, anxious to please, Hollywood has had difficulty in presenting an accurate picture of the many racial, religious, professional, and avocational groups which make up American society. Moreover, there seems validity to the charge that the movies have tended to depict some as stereotypes instead of individuals. In general, for instance, they have shown Negroes in subordinate positions, college professors as amiable, forgetful eccentrics, and newspaper reporters as offensively brash, hyperactive extroverts.

Broadcasting

Although the charges against radio and television have varied, most of them have fallen into perhaps a half-dozen broad categories.

A basic criticism of radio made during the 1930s and 1940s was that the advertiser had taken programming out of the hands of the broadcaster. The broadcaster sold the advertiser not merely the time for his commercials; he sold the program time surrounding it as well. The advertiser to a large degree decided just what would be broadcast in the quarter-hour, half-hour, or full hour he had purchased. More than that, he and his agency packaged the show, hired the performers, supervised the entire production. The situation was far different from that of newspapers and magazines, which merely sell the advertiser space for his sales message and themselves decide on the editorial content.

This criticism has seldom been made of television. By the time television came along in the mid-1940s, the networks were keeping a much firmer hold on programming. Whereas advertising agencies had either produced or controlled the majority of shows when radio was at its peak, they have done comparatively little producing and supervising of today's television programs. Only about 1.5 percent of commercial network shows are produced by agencies, according to one estimate, and a small additional percentage is selected and authoritatively supervised by them.

The networks are damned if they do and damned if they don't. One television columnist has contended that programming would be more responsive to viewers' likes and dislikes if it were returned to control by the advertising agencies. "Under agency program determination and control, the viewer has a voice in guiding the programming aimed specifically at him," wrote Janet Kern of the Chicago's *American* in *Advertising Age*. "The viewer's voice is heeded by those to whom he is not an infinitesimal fraction of a statistic but a cash-on-the-barrelhead customer! . . . Today's system of giving the public whatever shows the Hollywood filmsters and New York networkers have rightly or wrongly invested in, can't hold an electronic candle, in my book, to the old system of building shows on the basis of what the client's customers most enjoy."

A second complaint is that the airwaves are filled with sales talk—obtrusive sales talk, much of it in questionable taste. The correct time is brought to the listener by courtesy of a watch manufacturer, the weather outlook by a feed dealer, an important news bulletin by a manufacturer of headache remedies. Programs are interrupted by pleas that the viewer or listener buy this soap or that automobile. In all this, critics complain, the broadcaster has lost sight of the important point that the airwaves belong to the public and not to the pitchman. But the pitchman dominates them, say the critics, and a medium with extraordinary potential for educating the public has become a vehicle for vending cigarettes, laxatives, beer, and dog food.

Because radio and television broadcasters have become interested primarily in building huge audiences for advertisers, another charge runs, they have skimped on unprofitable serious educational programs but have dished out lavish helpings of entertainment. Addressing a convention of radio and television news directors, Edward R. Murrow lamented the reluctance of networks to undertake serious programs of news and public affairs which are expensive to produce and which do not add to profits: "I am frightened by the imbalance, the constant striving to reach the largest possible audience for everything; by the absence of a sustained study of the state of the nation." He added:

> Our history will be what we make it. And if there are any historians about fifty or a hundred years from now, and there should be preserved the kinescopes for one week of all three networks, they will find there recorded in black and white, or color, evidence of decadence, escapism, and insulation from the realities of the world in which we live. I invite your attention to the television schedules of all networks between the hours of eight and eleven P.M. eastern time. Here you will find only fleeting and spasmodic reference to the fact that this nation is in mortal danger. There are, it is true, occasional informative programs presented in that intellectual ghetto on Sunday afternoons. But during the daily peak viewing periods, television in the main insulates us from the realities of the world in which we live.

Not only does entertainment comprise an inordinate proportion of broadcast fare; much of it is of low caliber, at that, critics say. On television especially, they deplore the preponderance of programs involving murder, mayhem, violence of all sorts, and the inanities exemplified by the quiz show.

A fourth charge is that the viewer or listener gets a fictitious choice even in cities with competing radio or television stations. This springs from the imitativeness of broadcasters. Once the appeal of a western or a domestic comedy has been demonstrated, other broadcasters hasten to put similar programs on the air. Consequently the viewer or listener does not have a real choice between the cultural and the commercial at a given hour; he has a choice between two westerns or two domestic comedies or two variety shows, both pretty much alike.

Local stations have been accused of being scarcely more than mouthpieces for the large national networks. They generally have failed to develop local talent, critics say, and they have been sadly inadequate in providing an effective platform for the discussion of local issues.

Advertising

No less than the media which carry it, advertising has felt the sharp stab of the critic's pen. The cries of the critics, the threatening cloud of government regulation, the organized movements of consumers, the increased awareness of advertising leaders to their social responsibilities—all have influenced advertisers toward higher standards of performance, according to Willard L. Thompson of the University of Minnesota in a study of self-regulation in advertising.

Advertising which gulled the unwary consumer was perhaps what most frequently stirred critics down to the end of the nineteenth century and in the first years of the twentieth. Jurists, essayists, reformers, some editors, and even some advertisers from time to time decried the fraudulent and deceptive advertising which turned up in the press. As the nineteenth century closed, such critics were heard more and more frequently, perhaps in part because of the rapidly increasing volume of advertising, largely because of the blatantly misleading patent medicine advertising, which roused a number of magazines to attack.

In the years just prior to World War I, some critics found a new cause for anxiety—the social and economic effects of advertising. The high cost of living no doubt helped to focus attention on those aspects, for soaring prices were a subject of widespread concern. Congress heard proposals for investigating the high cost of living, and government agencies planned studies of distribution costs. Quite naturally, some wondered whether advertising added an extra and unnecessary burden to those costs.

Many critics thought it did. They contended that most advertising simply tries to persuade the consumer to buy a particular brand at a price inflated by advertising instead of an equally good product not so extensively extolled.

criticisms summarized

The range of criticism broadened as the century grew older. Most of the charges which have been made against advertising were summarized in a ten-point indictment issued in a talk before the Advertising Club of Grand Rapids, Michigan, by Colston E. Warne, president of Consumers Union and professor of economics at Amherst College. As reported in *Printers' Ink,* Warne complained that advertising:

> Stressed inconsequential values.
> Brought a false perspective as to merit of products, often bewildering rather than informing.

Lowered our ethical standards by the all-too-frequent insincerity of its appeals.

Corrupted and distorted the news.

Wasted much good timber and chemicals, and spoiled much of the landscape and radio enjoyment.

Blocked the speedy use of correct medication.

Created many parental problems by "abominable" radio programs.

Turned our society into one dominated by style, fashion, and "keeping up with the Joneses."

Retarded the growth of thrift by emphasizing immediate expenditures.

Fostered monopoly through its large-scale use by only a few financially favored companies.

fosters wastefulness

In *The Tragedy of Waste,* which appeared in 1928, Stuart Chase wrote that advertising is not only nonproductive; it is counter-productive, cutting into the economy by sidetracking a part of the working force. Other critics have lined up with Chase. What advertising does, they say, is to harness a good deal of potentially productive effort to the unproductive task of diverting consumers from one company or product to another, both usually of equal merit.

Moreover, critics hold, advertising creates an artificial obsolescence by making consumers dissatisfied with goods long before they have ceased being useful. A man is urged to buy a new automobile even though the present one has years of potential service; a woman discards last year's dress, still worth months of wear, because advertising tells her it is outmoded. Such artificial obsolescence results in a tremendous waste of America's resources and productive effort, critics say.

fosters materialistic attitudes

The loud voice of advertising, trumpeting the wonders of worldly possessions, has forced Americans to place undue emphasis on material values to the detriment of more enduring values, some critics have charged.

In their own land, Americans tend to measure their fellow man by the size of his income and automobile, by the elegance of his home, and by the number of possessions in it. Abroad, they tend to judge foreign lands by the extent of such material comforts as modern plumbing and electrical refrigeration. They put the dollar above principle, the material above the spiritual. So say the critics; and while they do not put the sole burden on advertising, they insist that it must share a substantial part of the blame.

fosters monopoly

Advertising also has been condemned because it creates monopolies. The manufacturer has the power to raise the possibility of monopoly, according to a few critics, for, by an incessant barrage of advertising, he is able to convince consumers that his product serves them better than any similar product. Take aspirin, for a hypothetical example. Although all aspirin tablets are nearly alike, since they must meet certain minimum specifications set by the government, one manufacturer might so dominate the advertising picture that he convinces consumers that there is no really effective aspirin but his own. As his sales increase, so does his economic power. It becomes increasingly difficult for competitors to get a share of the market.

On the other hand, C. H. Sandage has pointed out that such a monopoly rests on control of human attitudes, not of supply, and that it is highly uncertain because of consumers' shifts from brand to brand. Moreover, he adds, the chief aim of such control is increasing sales rather than prices, since any significant price increase might send customers flocking to competitors' products.

Criticism at Mid-Century

One can detect a change in the nature of criticisms of the media since the early 1940s. In the twenties and thirties what we have called the conspiratorial theory of press malfunction was especially prevalent. Its theme was that business and advertising interests directly influence what the media carry and do not carry. Its assumption was that publishers and broadcasters are in covert league with big business to suppress or distort much information and opinion of social consequence. In short, the critics blamed men, not the system.

In his *America's House of Lords,* which appeared in 1939, for instance, Secretary of the Interior Harold L. Ickes argued that newspapers would be all right if their editorial direction were left to editors and reporters; unfortunately, however, owners of even small newspapers are dominated by a big-business psychology which causes them to require a considerable amount of suppression, fabrication, and distortion. Criticism of that sort was quite common in the 1930s when faith in business and businessmen was at low ebb. Publishers sat for a number of unflattering individual and group portraits. In 1936 Ferdinand Lundberg's *Imperial Hearst* painted William Randolph Hearst as a sinister press lord who had played a "great and ghastly part in shaping the American mind" and who had been able to make America accept "his deceptions and debaucheries of its political institutions" in regard to such issues as war with Spain, military preparedness, and sales and income taxes.

Some defenders of the press tried to show that what the critics called instances of suppression often simply represented differences in news judgment. Putting a story on page 32 instead of on page 1 was not necessarily burying it, as the critics charged; it appeared on page 32 because that was where it belonged under any standard of news values. Some news which did not appear in newspapers at all simply did not warrant space, they contended. And certainly, some charges of bias sprang from critics who had clearly identifiable biases of their own.

From the early 1940s onward, critics seem to have shifted the blame for many of the shortcomings of the media from the individual publisher or broadcaster to the system. A common viewpoint today is that mass communications are influenced by social processes. Social and economic forces, our system of values, indeed the whole of our culture, have been at least as important as men in shaping our media and in affecting their performance. If we wish to alter the performance of our media, then, we may well have to make some rather fundamental changes in the order in which they operate.

There seems to be a growing awareness that many of the criticisms of the media are, at bottom, really criticisms of our society and its system of values. The critics dislike the materialism which is ingrained in our entire culture, not just in the mass media. Their protests represent their frustration that Americans, despite their system of free, universal education, prefer Popeye to Plato and the Beatles to Beethoven.

There seems to be a growing recognition that publishers, broadcasters, and movie producers are not necessarily evil men, conspiring to propagandize the public in their own interests. They are becoming accepted as men of honest conviction whose attitudes toward business are usually conditioned by the simple fact that they are businessmen. Their dilemma is becoming generally recognized: On the one hand, they are expected to perform an important public service; on the other, they are required to make a profit.

Nor do the barons of business plot and scheme to control the media for their own selfish ends, critics are now coming to realize. Joseph T. Klapper, a perspicacious student of the media, wrote in *The American Scholar:*

> The influence of big business on the content of mass media is probably not exerted in any large conscious Gestalt designed to perpetuate a social system. The conscious and manifest purpose

of a radio program sponsor is primarily, and almost wholly, to sell his soap. Although the maintenance of the existing social and economic system may be a precondition of the sale, such social guardianship is, for the usual sponsor, at most a secondary and latent purpose—except in the face of direct attack.

There is a growing awareness, furthermore, that advertising is not the prime evil it was once thought to be. It is no longer blamed for every ill. After all, some of the shortcomings which have stirred critics are also found in media which do not carry advertising. What is now seen to be at fault is the commercial basis of the press, which exerts pressure for building large audiences. Seeking large audiences—in order to hold down their unit costs and to attract advertising—they must necessarily aim at a low common denominator, must avoid offending any sizeable portion of their market, must traffic in what the majority wants and believes.

This does not mean that criticism of the mass media has abated since the 1940s. If anything, it is more prevalent today. But contemporary criticisms, for the most part, take into account the changes which industrialization and other forces have wrought in the communication system.

Serious students such as Paul Lazarsfeld, Robert K. Merton, and Joseph T. Klapper have commented on the tendency of the media to reaffirm existing attitudes. "Since the mass media are supported by great business concerns geared into the current social and economic system, the media contribute to the maintenance of that system," Lazarsfeld and Merton remarked in *The Communication of Ideas.*

> This contribution is not found merely in the effective advertisement of the sponsor's product. It arises, rather, from the typical presence in magazine stories, radio programs, and newspaper columns of some element of confirmation, some element of approval of the present structure of society. And this continuing reaffirmation underscores the duty to accept.

The barrage of media content favoring the status quo has two advantages, according to Klapper. One is its static position. There is little counter-argument, little challenging of the sanctioned attitudes, few attempts to present the unaccepted view. Any effort to depart from the majority taste or attitude, he observed, would jeopardize the media's chances of amassing their essential large audiences. Thus big business goes unopposed in its direct bids and in its reaffirmation of existing attitudes. "Two cigarette manufacturers may compete with each other," Klapper remarked, "but neither will ever directly criticize the other's product, and never will either allow some other advertiser to inveigh against smoking." The second advantage is that the media implement existing drives, do not create new ones. With little resistance, they channel behavior one way or another after the basic behavior pattern or basic attitude has been established; they rarely try to instill significantly new behavior patterns or new attitudes. "For Americans who have been socialized in the use of a toothbrush, it makes relatively little difference which brand of toothbrush they use," Lazarsfeld and Merton noted; it is quite another thing, they remarked, to persuade them to overcome deep-seated prejudices against a racial or ethnic group. The media have been far more successful in rechanneling the existing system of values, they concluded, than in reshaping it.

If present-day critics are right in putting the bulk of the blame for the shortcomings of the media upon the system instead of on the men who run them, the task of improving media performance is large and complex. No longer can one assume that performance can be improved simply by wheedling, exhorting, or educating media personnel into a more serious acceptance of their responsibilities. No longer can one assume that the happy free trade in ideas of yesterday can be recaptured simply by breaking large communication units into a multiplicity of small ones. Before advancing any realistic solution, one must clearly understand the communication system in the context of its historical and contemporary setting. Only from that beginning can there emerge any solution which will not be anachronistic, ineffective, or both.

References

COMMISSION ON FREEDOM OF THE PRESS, *A Free and Responsible Press* (Chicago: University of Chicago Press, 1947).

ERNST, MORRIS L., *The First Freedom* (New York: The Macmillan Company, 1946).

JENSEN, JAY W., "A Method and a Perspective for Criticism of the Mass Media," *Journalism Quarterly* 37 (Spring 1960) 261–66.

LIEBLING, A. J., *Mink and Red Herring: The Wayward Pressman's Casebook* (Garden City, N.Y.: Doubleday & Company, Inc., 1949).

———, *The Press* (New York: Ballantine Books, Inc., 1961).

———, *The Wayward Pressman* (Garden City, N.Y.: Doubleday & Company, Inc., 1947).

MACDONALD, DWIGHT, *Against the American Grain* (New York: Random House, Inc., 1962).

MEHLING, HAROLD, *The Great Time-Killer* (Cleveland: The World Publishing Company, 1962).

PACKARD, VANCE, *The Hidden Persuaders* (New York: David McKay Co., Inc., 1957).

PETERSON, THEODORE, "Why the Mass Media Are that Way," *Antioch Review* 23 (Winter 1963–64) 405–24.

ROWSE, ARTHUR, *Slanted News* (Boston: Beacon Press, 1957).

SELDES, GEORGE, *Freedom of the Press* (Garden City, N.Y.: Garden City Publishing Company, Inc., 1937).

————, *Lords of the Press* (New York: Julian Messner, Inc., 1939).

SELDES, GILBERT, *The Seven Lively Arts* (New York: Sagamore Press, Inc., 1957).

SIEPMANN, CHARLES A., *Radio, Television and Society* (New York: Oxford University Press, Inc., 1950).

SINCLAIR, UPTON, *The Brass Check: A Study of American Journalism* (Pasadena, Calif.: The Author, 1931).

SVIRSKY, LEON, ed., *Your Newspaper: Blueprint for a Better Press, by Nine Nieman Fellows 1945–1946* (New York: The Macmillan Company, 1947).

INDEX OF NAMES
AND
INDEX OF SUBJECTS

Index

of Names

Index

of Subjects